COLLECTED WHEEL PUBLICATIONS

VOLUME 24

NUMBERS 362 – 376

BPE

BPS Pariyatti Editions

BPS Pariyatti Editions
An imprint of Pariyatti Publishing
www.pariyatti.org

First BPS Pariyatti Edition, 2026
ISBN: 978-1-68172-216-0 (Print)
ISBN: 978-1-68172-217-7 (PDF)
ISBN: 978-1-68172-218-4 (ePub)
ISBN: 978-1-68172-219-1 (Mobi)
LCCN: 2018940050

Contents

WH 362 Lives of the Disciples: Anuruddha
Hellmuth Hecker ... 1

WH 363 & 364 Two Dialogues on Dhamma
Bhikkhu Nyanasobhano ... 25

WH 365 & 366 Mettā: The Philosophy and Practice of Universal Love
Ācariya Buddharakkhita ... 71

WH 367 to 369 Dāna: The Practice of Giving
Bhikkhu Bodhi, Susan Elbaum Jootla, Lily de Silva, M.O' C. Walshe, Nina van Gorkom, Ācariya Dhammapāla ... 103

WH 370 & 371 Satipaṭṭhāna Vipassanā: Insight through Mindfulness
Ven. Mahasi Sayadaw ... 153

WH 372 The Message of the Velāma Sutta
Susan Elbaum Jootla ... 193

WH 373 & 374 Looking Inward
Tan Acharn Kor Khao-suan-luang ... 217

WH 375 & 376 The Essential Practice, Part I
Ven. Webu Sayadaw ... 255

Key to Abbreviations

A	Aṅguttara Nikāya	Paṭis	Paṭisambhidamagga
Ap	Apadāna	Peṭ	Peṭakopadesa
Bv	Buddhavaṃsa	S	Saṃyutta Nikāya
Cp	Cariyāpiṭaka	Sn	Suttanipāta
D	Dīgha Nikāya	Th	Theragāthā
Dhp	Dhammapada	Thī	Therigāthā
Dhs	Dhammasaṅgaṇī	Ud	Udāna
It	Itivuttaka	Vibh	Vibhaṅga
Ja	Jātaka verses and commentary	Vin	Vinayapiṭaka
Khp	Khuddakapāṭha	Vism	Visuddhimagga
M	Majjhima Nikāya	Vism-mhṭ	Visuddhimagga Sub-commentary
Mil	Milindapañha	Vv	Vimānavatthu
Nett	Nettipakaraṇa	Nidd	Niddesa

The above is the abbreviation scheme of the Pali Text Society (PTS) as given in the *Dictionary of Pali* by Margaret Cone.

The commentaries, *aṭṭhakathā*, are abbreviated by using a hyphen and an "a" ("-a") following the abbreviation of the text, e.g., *Dīgha Nikāya Aṭṭhakathā* = D-a. Likewise the sub-commentaries are abbreviated by a "ṭ" ("-ṭ") following the abbreviation of the text.

The sutta reference abbreviation system for the four Nikāyas, as is used in Bhikkhu Bodhi's translations is:

AN	Aṅguttara Nikāya	DN	Dīgha Nikāya
MN	Majjhima Nikāya	Sn	Saṃyutta Nikāya
J	Jātaka story	Mv	Mahāvagga (Vinaya Piṭaka)
Cv	Cullavagga (Vinaya Piṭaka)	SVibh	Suttavibhaṅga (Vinaya Piṭaka)

Lives of the Disciples: Anuruddha

Master of the Divine Eye

by

Hellmuth Hecker

Translated from the German by

Nyanaponika Thera

WHEEL PUBLICATION NO. 362

Anuruddha
Master of the Divine Eye

1. Early Life and Ordination

The Buddha's father, King Suddhodana, had a brother, the prince Amitodana, who had five children. Among them was Ānanda, who was later to be the Buddha's faithful attendant, and Mahānāma, heir to the Sakyan throne. A third brother was Anuruddha. Anuruddha briefly tells of his youth:

> Then was I born within the Sakyan clan,
> As Anuruddha known; by dance and song
> Attended and by clang of cymbals waked. (Th 911)

From this we gather that during his youth in the Sakyan capital of Kapilavatthu, in the foothills of the Himalayas, he lived amidst the luxuries of an Indian prince, in the company of dancers, actors and artists. Thus he passed his time in joyful pursuit of fleeting pleasures. Enchanted with life, he gave little thought to the meaning and purpose of existence, though the ancient hymns and myths which he must have heard did moot these questions. There came, however, a day that was to be the turning-point of his life.

His brother Mahānāma had been thinking about the fact that many members of the Sakyan clan had joined the Sangha, the Buddha's Order of Monks, while so far none had done so from his own family, though there were four vigorous young brothers. Mahānāma, however, did not have a strong enough urge and initiative to take that step himself and thus set an example for the others. Rather, he went to his brother Anuruddha and told him about his thoughts. He ended by saying that either he or Anuruddha should leave home and join the Buddha and his Sangha. At first Anuruddha was not at all ready to have his brother's decision thrust upon him. He replied that he felt himself to be too delicate physically to withstand the rigours of an ascetic life.

Mahānāma then vividly described to him the burdens of a householder's life that he would have to shoulder. There was ploughing to be done, and planting, watering, digging, taking care of crops, harvesting and managing, and all that year in and year out. Anuruddha said that this was all right since all that hard work served a purpose, namely, to enable one to enjoy the pleasures of the five senses. Yet, he admitted, all this work left one with hardly any time for enjoyment. Mahānāma agreed: many are the fetters that bind one to duty endlessly. Their father and their grandfather had done the same, and they themselves would have to lead the same kind of life.

This thought of the endless cycles of rebirth into a life of never-ending toil took hold of Anuruddha's mind. Again and again he saw himself bound to live and struggle and die in an endless round. When he saw this, his present life appeared to him stale and devoid of meaning. So he decided to follow the Buddha and try to break through the cycle of continuous becoming. Immediately he went to his mother and asked her for permission to become a monk, but she refused, as she was not willing to be separated from even one of her sons. But when Anuruddha repeatedly entreated her, she told him that if his friend, Prince Bhaddiya, viceroy and successor to the Sakyan throne, would be willing to enter the Order, then she would give him her permission. She may have thought that Bhaddiya would not wish to give up his chance to be the next king, and that Anuruddha would then not choose to part from his friend.

Anuruddha next went to Bhaddiya and told him that his ordination depended on Bhaddiya's joining him. Bhaddiya said: "Whether it depends on me or not, there should be ordination. I with you ..." Here he stopped in the middle of the sentence. He had wanted to say, "I shall come with you," but he then felt regret. His wish for worldly power and enjoyment overtook him and he said: "Go and be ordained, according to your wish." But Anuruddha asked him again and again: "Come, friend, let both of us go forth into the homeless life of a monk." When Bhaddiya saw the sadness in his friend's face, he softened and said that seven years from now he would be ready. Anuruddha replied that this was too long to wait, and by his repeated entreaties Bhaddiya reduced the time, step by step, to seven days. He would need at least this time to settle his worldly affairs and instal his successor. He was true to his word, and so Anuruddha was free to go with him. This decision naturally caused much disturbance in the royal family, for Anuruddha's example led other princes, too, to follow the great son of the Sakyas and join the Buddha's fraternity of monks.

So one day six Sakyan princes together with Upāli, the court barber, and an armed escort, set out from their homes intending to enter the Sangha. They were the Sakyans Bhaddiya, Anuruddha, Ānanda, Bhagu (Th 271–274), Kimbila (Th 118, 155–156) and Devadatta. To avoid arousing suspicion over the purpose of their departure, they left as if on their usual outing to the pleasure gardens. Having gone a long distance, they then sent the escort back and entered the neighbouring principality. There they took off their ornaments, tied them into a bundle and gave it to Upāli, saying, "This will be enough for your livelihood. Now return home!" But the barber Upāli, while already on his way back, stopped and thought: "The Sakyans are a fierce people. They will think that I have murdered the princes, and they might kill me." He hung the bundle on a tree and hurried back to join the princes. He told them of his fears and said, "If you, O princes, are going forth into the homeless life of monkhood, why should I not do the same?"

The young Sakyans, too, thought Upāli was right in not going back and allowed him to join them on their way to see the Blessed One. Having arrived where the Master dwelt, they asked him for ordination and added: "We Sakyans are a proud people, O Lord. Here, this is Upāli, the barber, who had attended on us for a long time. Please, Lord, give him ordination first. Since he will then be our senior, we shall have to salute him and do the duties proper to his seniority. Thus will the Sakyan pride be humbled in us." The Buddha did as requested and thus these seven received ordination, with Upāli, as the first. (Vinaya, Cullavagga, Ch.VII)

Within one year most of them had achieved some spiritual attainment. Bhaddiya was the first to attain Arahantship (*arahatta*), as one liberated by wisdom (*paññā-vimutta*) and endowed with the three knowledges.[1] Anuruddha attained to the divine eye, Ānanda, to the fruit of Stream-entry, and Devadatta to ordinary

1. The three knowledges (*tevijjā*) are: remembrance of former rebirths, the divine eye, and extinction of the cankers (*āsavakkhaya*, i.e. Arahantship).

(i.e. mundane) supernormal powers. Bhagu, Kimbila and Upāli became Arahants later, as did Ānanda, and Anuruddha. But Devadatta's reckless ambition and misdeeds led him to hell.

2. The Divine Eye

Among those who were pre-eminent in a particular skill was the venerable Anuruddha, who was praised by the Buddha as being foremost in developing the divine eye (AN 1, Ch. 19). Once, when a number of eminent monks were living together in the Gosiṅga Forest, the question arose among them as to which kind of monk could lend brilliance to that forest. Anuruddha replied that it was one who, with the divine eye, could survey a thousand world systems, just as a man standing on a high tower could see a thousand farmsteads (MN 32). On another occasion Anuruddha said that it was through his cultivating the four foundations of mindfulness (*satipaṭṭhāna*) that he obtained the divine eye (SN 52:23). He also helped his own pupils to attain the opening of the divine eye (SN 14:15). His verses relate his experience:

> In fivefold concentration rapt,
> The mind in peace and unified,
> Inner tranquillity I gained
> And thus was purified my eye divine.
> In fivefold jhāna standing firm,
> I knew the passing and rebirth of beings,
> Their coming and their going I perceived,
> Their life in this world and beyond. (Th 916–917)

The divine eye (*dibba-cakkhu*) is the ability to see beyond the range of the physical eye, extending in Anuruddha's case to a thousandfold world system, which may perhaps be identified with a galaxy in modern astronomy. This faculty can be obtained by one who has reached the fourth meditative absorption *jhāna* and takes this meditation as the basis for further development as described in *The Path of Purification* (*Visuddhimagga*).[2] The divine eye is of a mundane (*lokiya*) character. It can be obtained by an

2. Translated by Ñāṇamoli (Kandy, Buddhist Publication Society, 1979). Ch. XIII, §§ 95-l01, pp. 469-471.

unliberated worldling (*puthujjana*) as well as by those on the four stages of emancipation. Anuruddha attained it before he became an Arahant.

The Buddha himself used this faculty during his daily routine, when, in the early morning, he would survey the world for beings who could be helped by the Dhamma. Through his divine eye he also saw when one of his disciples experienced difficulties in his progress on the path. Seeing this, he often went to that disciple to give him advice and encouragement. As one of the three higher knowledges (*tevijjā*) the divine eye has the name and the function of "the knowledge of the passing away and re-appearing" of beings (*cutūpapātañāṇa*).

3. Anuruddha's Road to Arahantship

Having acquired the faculty of the divine eye, the venerable Anuruddha made use of his meditative skill to further his progress towards Arahantship. But before reaching that height, he had to face many a battle within his mind. Three reports tell of it.

Once the venerable Anuruddha lived in the Eastern Bamboo Park together with his cousin Nandiya (Th 25) and the Sakyan noble Kimbila (Th 118; AN 5:201, 6:40, 7:56; SN 54:10). These three monks were so mature in the practice of the teaching that each of them could live alone for himself, devoted to his spiritual practice. Only every fifth night would they meet to discuss the Dhamma, undisturbed by things or people. The harmony existing between these three forest hermits has become legendary and stands in sharp contrast with the quarrelsome monks of Kosambi.

When the Buddha visited the three monks, he asked Anuruddha how it was that he lived in peace and harmony with his two companions. Anuruddha replied: "In deeds, words and thoughts I maintain loving kindness towards these venerable ones, in public and in private, thinking: 'Why should I not set aside what I am minded to do and do only what they are minded to do?' And I act accordingly. We are different in body, venerable sir, but only one in mind."

After the Buddha had inquired about their life in concord, he asked Anuruddha whether they had gained any spiritual attainment transcending average human capacity. Then Anuruddha told of a difficulty they had experienced in a very sublime meditation they had practised. They had perceived an inner light and radiance[3] and had a vision of sublime forms.[4] But that light and vision of forms disappeared very soon, and they could not understand the reason.

The Buddha explained that one who wanted to experience these subtle states of mind in full and have a steady perception of them should free himself from eleven imperfections (*upakkilesa*). The first is *uncertainty* about the reality of these phenomena and the significance of the inner light, which might easily be taken for a sensory illusion. The second imperfection is *inattention:* one no longer directs one's full attention to the inner light, but regards it as something unremarkable or inessential, and thus dismisses it as unimportant. The third imperfection is *lethargy and drowsiness:* the fourth, *anxiety and fright,* which occurs when threatening images or thoughts arise from the subconscious regions of the mind.[5] When these imperfections have been mastered, *elation* may arise, which excites body and mind. Such exultation is often a habitual reaction to any kind of success. When that elation has exhausted itself, one may feel drained of that happy emotion and fall into *inertia,* a heavy passivity of mind. To overcome it, one makes a very strong effort, which may result in an *excess of energy.* On becoming aware of this excess, one relaxes and, in a repeated alternation of extremes, falls again into *sluggish energy.* In such a condition, when mindfulness is weak, *strong longing* may arise for desirable objects of the celestial or the human world, according to the focusing of the inner light which had been widened in its range. This longing will reach out to a great variety of objects and thus lead to another imperfection, a large *diversity of perceptions,* be it on the celestial or the human plane. Having become dissatisfied with that great diversity of forms, one chooses to contemplate one of them, be it of a desirable or undesirable nature. Concentrating intensely on the chosen object will lead to the eleventh imperfection, the *excessive meditating* on these forms.

3. *Obhāsa-saññā*; this is the inner vision of light preparatory to fully absorbed concentration (Comy.: *parikammobhāsa*).

4. *Rūpānaṃ dassana.* Comy.: seeing them with the divine eye.

5. The Commentary says that this may occur when the range of the inner light is widened excessively.

Addressing Anuruddha and his two companions, the Buddha thus described vividly, from his own experience, the eleven imperfections that may arise in the meditative perception of pure forms, and he explained how to overcome them (MN 128).

When Anuruddha had perfected himself more and more in the *jhānas* and in those refined meditative perceptions, he one day went to see the venerable Sāriputta and said: "Brother Sāriputta with the divine eye, which is clarified and supernormal, I am able to perceive a thousandfold world system. My energy is strong and inflexible; my mindfulness is alert and unconfused; my body is calmed and unexcited; my mind is collected and unified. Yet my mind is still not freed, without clinging, from the defiling taints (*āsava*)."

Thereupon Sāriputta replied: "When you think, brother Anuruddha, that with your divine eye you can perceive a thousandfold world system, that is self-conceit in you. When you think of your strenuous energy, your alert mindfulness, your calmed body and your concentrated mind, that is agitation in you. When you think that your mind is still not liberated from the cankers, that makes for scruples in you. It will be good if the revered Anuruddha would discard these three things, would not pay attention to them and would instead direct his mind towards the Deathless-element (*Nibbāna*)."

Having heard Sāriputta's advice, Anuruddha again resorted to solitude and earnestly applied himself to the removal of those three obstructions within his mind (AN 3:128).

On another occasion, Anuruddha lived in the country of the Cetiya people, in the Eastern Bamboo Grove. There it occurred to him in his contemplations that there were seven thoughts that should be cherished by a truly great man (*mahāpurisavitakka*), namely: that the Buddha's Teaching will suit only one who is frugal, contented, bent on seclusion, energetic, mindful, concentrated and wise, and that it will not suit one who lacks these qualities. When the Buddha perceived in his mind the thoughts of his cousin and pupil, he appeared before Anuruddha and approved of his thoughts thus: "Good, Anuruddha, good. You have well considered seven thoughts of a great man. You may now also consider this eighth thought of a great man: 'This teaching is only for one who inclines to the Non-diffused; this teaching is not for one who inclines to worldly diffuseness and delights in it.'"[6]

The Buddha said that when Anuruddha contemplates these eight thoughts, he will be able to attain at will the four meditative absorptions. He would then no longer be affected by worldly things, but would regard the four simple requisites of a monk[7] in the same way as a lay person would enjoy his luxuries. These requisites would make his mind joyous and unperturbed, and thus be helpful to his attainment of Nibbāna. In parting, the Buddha advised Anuruddha to stay on at the Eastern Bamboo Grove. The venerable Anuruddha did so, spending the rainy season there. It was during this time that he attained the consummation of his striving: he gained Arahantship (*arahatta*), which is the state of Nibbāna during life (AN 8:30).

At the hour of his attainment he uttered the following verses:

He knew my heart's intent, the Master, he
Whose peer the world has not, he came to me
By mystic power with body wrought by mind.
To me, when further truths I wished to learn,
The Buddha (the last truth) revealed;
He who delights in freedom from diffuseness,
That freedom from diffuseness taught to me.
And I who heard the blessed Dhamma dwelt
Constantly intent to keep his Rule;
The Threefold Wisdom have I made my own,
And all the Buddha's ordinance is done.

(AN 8:30; Th 901–03)

4. Anuruddha's Cultivation of Mindfulness

The venerable Anuruddha's spiritual path is marked by two prominent features: first, his mastery of the divine eye and other supernormal faculties, and second, his cultivation of the four

6. "The Non-diffused" (*nippapañca*) is the final freedom from the vast multiplicity and complexity of phenomenal existence, i.e. Nibbāna. "Diffuseness" (*papañca*) accordingly means existence in its aspect of enormous variety.

7. The four requisites are robes, almsfood, shelter and medicine.

foundations of mindfulness (*satipaṭṭhāna*). He often stressed the wide-ranging potency of an arduous practice of mindfulness.

Frequently, the venerable Anuruddha was asked how he gained proficiency in the "great direct knowledges" (*mahābhiññatā*), which includes the five mundane supernormal types of knowledge and, as sixth, Arahantship. He always replied that it was through the constant practice of the four foundations of mindfulness (SN 47:28; SN 2:3,6,11), mentioning in particular the supernormal powers (*iddhividha;* SN 52:12) and his recollection of former lives extending to a thousand aeons (SN 52:10). He also said that the four foundations of mindfulness (*satipaṭṭhāna*) enabled him to gain that perfect control of emotive reactions called the "power of the Noble Ones" (*ariya-iddhi*), by which one can regard the repulsive as non-repulsive, and the non-repulsive as repulsive, or view both with equanimity (SN 52:1).[8] He further stresses the importance of that practice by saying that whoever neglects it is also neglecting the Noble Eightfold Path (SN 52:2), and that this fourfold mindfulness leads to the end of craving (*taṇhakkhaya;* SN 52:7). Just as the river Ganges would not deviate from its course to the ocean, in the same manner a monk who practises the four foundations of mindfulness could not be deflected from his life as a monk and made to return to the worldly life (SN 52:8).

Once, when Anuruddha was ill, he surprised the monks by his equanimity in bearing pain. They asked him how he was able to bear up as he did, and he replied that his composure was due to his practice of the fourfold mindfulness (SN 52:10). Another time the venerable Sāriputta came to see Anuruddha in the evening and asked him what he now regularly practised so that his facial expression was always one of happiness and serenity. Anuruddha again said that he spent the time in the regular practice of the four foundations of mindfulness, and that this was the way in which Arahants live and practise. The venerable Sāriputta thereupon expressed his joy at having heard Anuruddha declare his attainment in such a way (SN 52:9). Once, when questioned by Sāriputta and Mahā Moggallāna about the difference between those who are still

8. See Nyanaponika, *The Heart of Buddhist Meditation* (London, Rider & Co. 1962), p.181 and note 45.

"in training" toward Arahatship (*sekha*)[9] and an Arahant who is "beyond training" (*asekha*), he said that they differ in the practice of the fourfold mindfulness: while the former accomplishes it only partly, the latter does so completely and perfectly (SN 52:4–5). Anuruddha also professed to possess those lofty qualities called the "ten powers of a Tathāgata" (*dasa tathāgatabala*), though as the Commentary remarks, he possessed them only in part and to a lesser degree than a Buddha (SN 52:15–24).

5. Anuruddha and Women

While most of Anuruddha's talks cited so far dealt with topics of meditation, there are also quite a number of texts concerning women whom Anuruddha had met: There is, for instance, a text in which the following incident is told.

Once, when Anuruddha lived alone in a forest, a female deity from the realm of the Thirty-three Gods, Jālinī by name, appeared before him. In Anuruddha's previous existence, when he was Sakka, the ruler of that celestial realm of the Thirty-three Gods where she still lived, she had been his wife and chief queen. Out of her old attachment to him, she longed to be reunited with him in that heavenly world where they had lived together. So she urged him now to aspire for rebirth into that world. But Anuruddha replied:

> "On bad course, truly, are those celestial maidens
> Who, in attachment, cling to selfhood and desire.
> On bad course likewise are those beings
> Who would be husbands of these celestial maidens."

But that deity had no understanding for words and ideas such as these and thus she replied:

> "They do not know of happiness
> Who have not seen the 'Joyous Pleasance',
> Which is the mighty gods' abode,
> The glorious gods of Thirty-three."

9. These are the stream-enterer, the once-returner and the non-returner.

Anuruddha:

> "You do not understand, O fool,
> The words declared by Arahants:
> 'Impermanent are all conditioned things,
> Subject to rising and decay.
> Having arisen, they will disappear,
> Their ceasing is happiness.'
> No longer shall I dwell, O Jālinī,
> In deities' realms. For me
> Rebirth has come to end." (SN 9:6)

On another occasion, many female deities called "the Graceful Ones" appeared before him, and having saluted him, they told him all the marvellous things they could do. They could instantly assume any colour they wanted; they could produce any sound or voice at will; and third, they could obtain instantly any pleasurable feeling they wanted. To test them, Anuruddha mentally wished that they would become blue; and so they became blue, as they could read his thoughts. When he wished them to change into other colours, they did that too. Now these female deities thought that Anuruddha was pleased with their presence and they started to sing and dance very beautifully. But the venerable Anuruddha turned his senses away from them. When the deities noticed that Anuruddha did not find pleasure in their performance, they instantly left (SN 9:6).

If we remember how Anuruddha had spent his youth as a prince, enchanted by the arts and music, we may understand better how this scene could still belong to him. Had he not listened to the Buddha's words, he might quite possibly have taken rebirth among these deities who were superior in rank to the Thirty-three Gods.

Anuruddha must have thought this experience worth telling, for when he saw the Buddha in the evening he recounted it to him. He then raised the question: What attributes should a woman have to be reborn in the realm of those graceful spirits? His thirst for knowledge made him wish to know the moral level of these deities. The Buddha replied willingly and said that eight qualities were needed in order to be reborn in that realm. First, the wife has to show willingness and friendliness towards her husband.

Second, she should be courteous and hospitable towards people her husband holds dear, such as his parents and certain ascetics and priests. Third, she should do her housework carefully and with diligence. Fourth, she was to care for and guide the employees in a purposeful manner. Fifth, she should not squander her husband's possessions, but should guard them well. Sixth, she should not be given to alcoholic drinks and should not be a cause for her husband's ruin. Seventh, as a lay follower, she should take refuge in the Triple Gem and should observe the five moral precepts. And last, she should find joy in sharing and be generous in giving, showing concern for those in need (AN 8:46).

While on both these occasions female deities materialised before Anuruddha, there are other reports in which Anuruddha directs the power of his divine eye to understand how women are born in heaven or in hell. He also once asked the Buddha which qualities led a woman to hellish worlds and he was told that there were primarily five: lack of spiritual faith, lack of shame and moral scruples, anger, and lack of wisdom; further, such qualities as revengefulness, jealousy, avarice, committing adultery, immorality, sloth and lack of mindfulness would also lead to rebirth in hell. Only those with the opposite qualities would be reborn in a heavenly world (SN 37:5–24). Another time Anuruddha reported to the Buddha that he had often seen how a woman after her death was reborn in a lower world, even in hell. The Buddha replied that there are three harmful qualities which will lead a woman to hell: if in the morning she is full of avarice, at noon full of envy, and in the evening full of sensual desire (AN 3:127).

Reports of Anuruddha's past lives also refer to his relation to women. There is only one instance that mentions his rebirth as an animal. Once, when he was reborn as a wood pigeon, his mate was seized by a hawk. Tormented by passion and grief, he decided to fast until he had overcome his love for her and the grief of separation.

> Once full of greediness my mate and I
> Sported like lovers both about this spot.
> Her a hawk pounced on, and away did fly.
> So, torn from me, she whom I loved was not!
> In various ways my cruel loss I know;

I feel a pang in everything I see;
Therefore to fasting vows for help I go,
That passion never may come back to me.

(J 490; trans. R. A. Neil)

Other rebirth stories tell us the following: Once when Anuruddha was born as a king he saw a lovely fairy woman in the forest, fell in love with her and shot at her husband in order to possess her. Full of the pain of sorrow, she cried out and denounced the king's cruelty. Hearing her accusations, the king sobered up and went his way. At that time Anuruddha was the king, Yasodharā was the fairy woman, and her husband was the Bodhisatta, who was now Anuruddha's Master and whom in that past life he had almost killed out of lust for a woman (J 485).

In a divine form of existence, as Sakka, king of the gods, he helped the Bodhisatta to regain his reputation when he was the famous musician Guttila. As a test three times he made appear on earth three hundred celestial maidens who danced when Guttila played on his lute. Then Sakka invited Guttila into his heavenly world at the request of the heavenly nymphs who wanted to hear his music. After he had played to them, he asked them to tell him which good deeds had brought them to this heavenly world. They told him that in the past they had given small gifts to monks, heard their discourses, shared what they had with others, and were without anger and pride. Hearing this, the Bodhisatta rejoiced in the benefit he had thus gained in his visit to Sakka's heaven (J 243).

In Anuruddha's life as a monk, there was one incident which led to the promulgation of a disciplinary rule by the Buddha. Anuruddha and his brother Ānanda were the only ones among the close circle of the Buddha's disciples who occasioned the setting forth of a Vinaya rule. In both cases it concerned women.[10]

Once the venerable Anuruddha was wandering through the kingdom of Kosala towards Sāvatthī. In the evening he reached a village and found that there was no place in it where wandering ascetics and monks could stay. At the village inn, which was managed by a woman, he asked for a night's lodging and this was

10. In the case of Ānanda it was Pācittiya Rule 83 that was proclaimed.

granted. Meanwhile more travellers began to arrive at the inn to stay for the night, and the dormitory where Anuruddha was to stay became crowded. The inn hostess, seeing this, told the venerable Anuruddha that she could prepare his bedding in an inside room where he could spend the night peacefully. Silently Anuruddha agreed. She, however, had made this suggestion only because she had fallen in love with him. She now perfumed herself, put on her jewellery and thus approached Anuruddha, saying: "You, respected sir, are handsome, you are graceful and good looking. And so am I. It will be good if the respected sir will take me as his wife."

Anuruddha, however, remained silent. Then the inn hostess offered him all her riches. Anuruddha still remained silent. Then the woman took off her upper garment and danced in front of him, sat down, lay down in front of him. But Anuruddha had his senses well under control and paid no attention to her. Seeing that none of her allurements moved him, she exclaimed: "Astonishing it is, dear sir, extraordinary! So many men have offered me hundreds and thousands to win me. But this ascetic whom I myself have asked does not desire my wealth or me!"

The woman then put on her upper garment again, fell at Anuruddha's feet and asked for forgiveness for having tried to seduce a venerable ascetic. He now opened his mouth for the first time to pardon her, exhorting her to guard herself in the future. She then left. On the next morning she brought him his breakfast as if nothing had happened. Anuruddha then proceeded to give her a talk on Dhamma which so touched her that she became a devout lay follower of the Buddha.

Anuruddha, however, continued his journey and when he reached the monastery at Sāvatthī he told the monks about his adventure. The Buddha called him and reproached him for having spent the night in a woman's quarters. He then proclaimed a rule which prohibited this (Vinaya, Sutta Vibhaṅga, Pācittiya 6).

This story shows well the venerable Anuruddha's self-restraint which had saved him from becoming a slave to sense-impressions. His strength of character had made such a deep impression on that woman that she repented, listened to him and took refuge in the Buddha. Thus Anuruddha's self-control was not only for his own good, but also brought benefit to the woman. But when the Buddha yet reprimanded him, he did so because weaker characters could well succumb to temptation in such situations. Hence, out of compassion for them, the Buddha prescribed the rule that a monk should not expose himself to such dangers. Frequently we can observe that the Buddha wanted to prevent weaker characters from over-rating their strength and trying to emulate an ideal too high for them.

This story closely parallels a similar experience which befell St. Bernard of Clairvaux, who resembles Anuruddha in his strength of will. One day, as a young monk, Bernard came to an inn and asked for lodgings for the night. He was offered a bench in the public room, as there was no other place available. The innkeeper's daughter had fallen in love with that handsome young Cistercian monk and went to him during the night. He, however, turned to the wall, drew his cape up and said to her, "If you are looking for a place to sleep, there is room enough!" This total disinterest in her person sobered her and she slinked away ashamed. Like Anuruddha, he too had mastered the situation, not through arguments, but simply through the strength of his purity.

6. Various Experiences

Once the court carpenter, Pañcakaṅga by name, invited venerable Anuruddha for an alms meal. From other texts we know that Pañcakaṅga was a person well versed in the Dhamma and devoted to its practice. So, after the meal, he asked a rather subtle question from the venerable Anuruddha. He said that some monks had advised him to practise the "measureless liberation of mind," and others recommended the "exalted liberation of mind." He wanted to know whether these two are different or the same.

Anuruddha replied that these two meditations are different. The "measureless liberation of mind"[11] is the cultivation of loving kindness, compassion, altruistic joy and equanimity. But the "exalted liberation of mind"[12] is the meditative practice of

11. *Appamāṇā cetovimutti.* This is another name for the four sublime states (*brahmavihāra*) on the level of *jhāna.*

12. *Mahaggatā cetovimutti.* This meditation proceeds by widening the inner perception and is obtained by expanding the reflex image (*paṭibhāga-nimitta*) of the *kasiṇa* which arises by concentration on a limited surface of earth, water, colour disks, etc.

widening the inner perception from a limited extent to a vast ocean-like extent.

After giving this instruction to Pañcakaṅga, Anuruddha spoke of a class of deities, the Radiant Gods,[13] and said that although they all belong to the same order of celestial beings, there are differences among them in their radiance, which may be limited or measureless, pure or not quite pure. He explained that these divergences are due to the different quality of the meditation that had caused their rebirth in that world. On being questioned by a monk, Anuruddha confirmed that his intimate knowledge about these deities derived from his own experience, saying that he had previously lived with them and conversed with them (MN 127).

There is yet another scene in which Anuruddha figures. Once the Buddha was sitting in the open, surrounded by many monks whom he was teaching. On the occasion he asked the venerable Anuruddha whether they all were contented in leading the ascetic life. When Anuruddha confirmed this, the Buddha praised such contentment and said:

> Those who have left the home life while still young, becoming monks in the prime of their life, did not do so fearing punishment by kings, nor being motivated by loss of property, by debts, worries or poverty. Rather, they took to the ascetic life out of their faith in the Dhamma and inspired by the goal of liberation. What should such a one do? If he has not yet gained the peace and happiness of the meditative absorptions or something higher, then he should strive to get rid of the five mental hindrances and other defilements of the mind so that he may achieve the bliss of meditation or a peace that is still higher.

In concluding his discourse, the Buddha said that when he declares the attainment and future destiny of disciples who have died, he does so to inspire others to emulate their example. These words of the Blessed One gave much contentment and joy to the venerable Anuruddha (MN 68).

---

13. *Ābhassarā devā.* Their realm within the fine-material sphere (*rūpāvacara*) corresponds to the level of the second *jhāna.*

Once one of the Brahma gods conceived the idea that no ascetic would be able to penetrate to the heights of the Brahma-world. When the Buddha perceived in his mind the thoughts of that deity, he appeared before him in a blaze of light. Four of his great disciples—the venerables Mahā Moggallāna, Mahā Kassapa, Mahā Kappina and Anuruddha—considered at that time where the Blessed One might then be dwelling, and with their divine eyes they saw him seated in the Brahma-world. Then, by their supernormal power, they too appeared in that heavenly world and sat down at a respectful distance from the Buddha. Seeing this, the deity was cured of his pride and acknowledged the superior power of the Buddha and his disciples (SN 6:5).

Another time the venerable Anuruddha had woken up in the middle of the night and recited verses of the Dhamma until dawn broke. A female spirit with her small son was listening devoutly to the recitation and she told her son he should be very quiet: "It may be, if we understand the holy words and live accordingly, that it will be a great blessing for us and may free us from rebirth in the lower spirit worlds" (SN 10:6).

At the time when there was a quarrel between two groups of monks at Kosambī, the venerable Ānanda went to see the Buddha, who asked him whether that quarrel had been settled. Ānanda had to tell him that the quarrel still continued: a pupil of his brother Anuruddha insisted on creating disharmony in the Sangha, and to this the venerable Anuruddha did not say a word. This happened at a time when Anuruddha, together with Nandiya and Kimbila, had gone to the Gosiṅga Forest to devote themselves to a strictly meditative life. Ānanda's criticism was that Anuruddha had taken on pupils and then did nothing to guide them when there was discord among them.

The Buddha, however, came to Anuruddha's defence, saying that there was no need for Anuruddha to concern himself with that. There are others like Ānanda himself, Sāriputta or Mahā Moggallāna who are quite capable of dealing with such disputes. Besides, there are incorrigible monks who are quite pleased when others quarrel as this would divert attention from their own bad conduct and thus they could avoid being sent away (AN 4:241).

An example of this is the story of two conceited monks who tried to outdo each other in disputations. One of them was a pupil of Ānanda, of whom we know how carefully he concerned himself with all affairs of the Sangha; the other monk was a pupil of Anuruddha who, as we saw above, had a more detached attitude. Those two vainglorious monks just acted according to their character though they had different teachers to guide them (SN 16:6).

7. Anuruddha's Earlier Lives

Of Anuruddha's earlier lives, we have several stories handed down to us, especially in the Jātakas, the Birth Stories. Once when he was a poor man, he made a gift to an ascetic (Th 910) and at the time of the Buddha Kassapa he had honoured his grave by lighting oil lamps.

Anuruddha said of himself:

I know my former lives, and where and how
I lived in years gone by; among the gods
Thirty and Three I stood of Sakka's rank.
Seven times a king of men I held my sway,
Lord of the earth from end to end foursquare,
A conqueror, of Jambudīpa chief,
Using no force or arms I ruled by right.
Thence seven, and other seven spans of life,
Even fourteen former births I recognise,
Even then when in the world of gods reborn. (Th 913–15)

In the Jātaka tales, there are no less than twenty-three accounts telling us of Anuruddha's earlier lives. In most cases he was Sakka, king of the gods (J 194, 243, 347, 429, 430, 480, 494, 499, 537, 540, 541, 545, 547). Once he was Sakka's messenger, a deity called Pañcasikha, who was a celestial musician. In the seven earthly lives that are mentioned, he was most often an ascetic (J 423, 488, 509, 522), and he was twice a brother of the Bodhisatta. In three other lives of his human rebirth he was a king (J 485), a court priest (J 515) and a court charioteer (J 276). Only once his rebirth as an animal is reported, namely, as that amorous wood pigeon mentioned above (J 490). As far as is recorded in the Jātakas, he was fifteen times a deity, seven times a human being, and once an animal.

The fact that he was so often a king, celestial or human, indicates the power and strength in his nature. But he was quite a different god-king than Zeus with his amorous liaisons, and different also from Jehovah, who often inflicted harsh punishment on people. As Sakka, king of the Thirty-three Gods, he was rather one who always protected and helped. When the Bodhisatta was in need of help, he came to his succour. He protected him from being executed when he was defamed. On that occasion the Bodhisatta's wife had raised her voice to high heaven over this injustice:

> No gods are here! They must be far away.
> No gods who over all the world hold sway.
> Now wild and violent men work their will,
> For here is no one who could say them nay.
>
> (J 347; transl. by W. H. D. Rouse)

Moved by her entreaty, Sakka—the future Anuruddha took action and saved the Bodhisatta.

When the Bodhisatta was a king, he had forbidden animal sacrifices in his kingdom. A bloodthirsty demon resented this and wanted to kill the king, but Sakka appeared and protected the Bodhisatta again (J 347).

In some other cases Sakka wanted to put the Bodhisatta to a test in order to strengthen his virtue. So in the last of the Jātaka tales, the Vessantara Jātaka, Sakka, in the guise of an old brahmin, asked the Bodhisatta for his wife in order to test his joyful generosity (J 547). On another occasion Sakka also wanted to test whether the Bodhisatta was firm in his vow of generosity and asked him for his eyes (J 499). When the Bodhisatta was leading the life of an ascetic, Sakka wanted to test his patience and forbearance and blamed him for his physical ugliness. The Bodhisatta told him of his ugly deeds that had made him so ugly, and he praised the goodness and purity for which he was now striving. Then Sakka said that he would grant him a wish. What the Bodhisatta asked for was freedom from malice, hate, greed and lust; further he wished that he might never hurt anyone. All that, it was explained, was not in Sakka's power to grant, but has to come from one's own moral effort (J 440). Sakka also tested the Bodhisatta's frugality (J 429, 430).

In a third group of accounts, Sakka invited the Bodhisatta to his heaven and showed him the mysteries of the celestial and the hell worlds. This was told in the story of the musician Guttila which we have already recounted (J 243). In the stories of King Nimi (J 541) and of the charitable King Sādhina (J 494), Sakka also invited them to his heaven.

From his lives as a human being, the following episodes have been chosen. When Anuruddha was a court brahmin and counsellor, the king asked him how advantageous actions and justice could be combined by a ruler. Without intellectual pride, the brahmin admitted that he could not answer that question. Instead, he went assiduously in search of one who knew, and he found him in the Bodhisatta (J 515). When he was a royal charioteer, he once wanted to avoid a heavy downpour which was threatening. To speed up the horses, he hit them with the goad. From that time on, whenever the horses came to that particular spot on the road, they would start to gallop as if aware of a danger lurking just there. Seeing this, the charioteer regretted deeply that he had frightened and hurt those noble steeds and he admitted that by having done so he did not fully observe the traditional Kuru virtues (J 276).

All these diverse and colourful stories have a common feature. They show several characteristic qualities of Anuruddha: his strong active striving for virtue, his strength of character, as well as his concern for the welfare of others. They also show that his skill in meditation and his mastery of supernormal faculties had their roots in his experiences during many lives as Sakka, ruler of the gods.

8. The Death of the Buddha and Afterwards

The venerable Anuruddha was present in the last hours before the Buddha's decease, recounted in the Mahāparinibbāna Sutta (DN 16). When the Master knew that death was close, he entered into the full sequence of the meditative absorptions on the fine-material and immaterial levels, and then entered the state of cessation of perception and feeling (*saññā-vedayita-nirodha*).

At that moment Ānanda turned to his brother, the venerable Anuruddha, saying: "Revered Anuruddha, the Blessed One has passed away." But Anuruddha, an Arahant endowed with the divine eye, had been able to gauge the level of meditation into which the Buddha had entered, and he said: "Not so, friend

Ānanda, the Blessed One has not passed away. He has entered the state of cessation of perception and feeling."

The Buddha, however, rising from that attainment of cessation, turned his mind back to the stages of immaterial absorption in their reverse order until he reached the first *jhāna*, then rose up again to the fourth fine-material *jhāna*, and rising from it he instantly passed away into the Nibbāna-element which is without any remainder of the aggregates of existence.

When the Enlightened One had finally passed away, Brahma the High Divinity and Sakka, king of the Thirty-three Gods, honoured the Buddha in verses evoking the law of impermanence. The third to speak was Anuruddha who uttered these verses:

> No movement of the breath, but with a steadfast heart,
> Desireless and tranquil comes the Sage to his end.
> With heart unshaken by any painful feeling,
> Like a flame extinguished, found his mind release.

Many of the monks attending the Buddha's last hours grieved and lamented over the Master's death. But Anuruddha exhorted them and told them that many deities were also present. Among them, too, there were those who lamented and others who contained their grief. But had not the Master always taught them the impermanence of all? And so, just that had happened.

The venerable Anuruddha and the venerable Ānanda spent the rest of the night near the deceased Master. In the morning, Anuruddha asked Ānanda to announce the passing away of the Blessed One to the householders living in the next village, Kusinārā. At once they gathered and prepared the funeral pyre. When, however, eight strong men tried to lift the body up to the pyre, they could not do so. They then went to the venerable Anuruddha and asked for the reason why the body could not be moved. Anuruddha told them that the deities wanted a different ceremony and explained it to them, whereupon all happened just as intended by the deities.

With regard to the procedure of burning the body, the householders turned to the venerable Ānanda for advice. This shows the different competence of the two brothers. Anuruddha was master of otherworldly affairs, while Ānanda was well versed in matters concerning the worldly life (DN 16).

After the Buddha's demise, the guidance of the Order did not go to his next of kin, as for instance the Arahant Anuruddha. The Buddha had not nominated any formal successor, but the natural veneration of the monks and lay people concentrated on the venerable Mahā Kassapa. It was he who initiated the First Council at which five hundred Arahant monks took part in establishing a final text of the Buddha's teachings. Before the Council opened, the venerable Ānanda had not yet attained to Arahantship and this would have excluded him from participating in the Council. It was his brother Anuruddha who urged him to make a determined effort to break through the last fetters and realise final liberation. Within a short time Ānanda succeeded and so as an Arahant could join the other Arahants in the Council. During its sessions, he recited the numerous teachings which he of all monks had best retained in his memory.

In this manner Anuruddha had helped his brother to attain the goal of liberation, for the good of the Sangha and for the good of all seekers looking for a way out of the existential dilemma; and this has remained a blessing for us even today. Anuruddha himself was entrusted at the Council with the preservation of the Aṅguttara Nikāya, according to the commentary to the Dīgha Nikāya.

About the venerable Anuruddha's death nothing else is known except the serene last stanzas of his twenty verses in the "Songs of the Elders":

> The Buddha has my loyalty and love,
> And all the Buddha's ordinance is done.
> Low have I laid the heavy load I bore,
> Cause for rebirth is found in me no more.
> In Veḷuva, in Vajjian land it will be
> That life will reach its final term for me;
> And I beneath bamboo-thicket's shade that day
> Free from all taints, shall wholly pass away. (Th 918–19)

Two Dialogues on Dhamma

by

Bhikkhu Nyanasobhano

WHEEL PUBLICATION NO. 363/364

Bhikkhu Tissa Meets a Sceptic

Outside a Buddhist temple, early on a summer Saturday morning, a monk named Bhikkhu Tissa is sweeping the stone walk. His work is neither slow nor fast, but steady and careful, as if the sweeping of dust and leaves were something important to him. From the road some yards away comes the hum of an approaching automobile. In the morning quiet the hum rises to a rumble, and a shiny sports car passes by. If Bhikkhu Tissa were watching—which he is not—he would notice that the driver momentarily slows down and regards him curiously before disappearing around a curve. Then there is a slight screech of tyres and in a moment the sports car returns and zooms into the driveway by the temple. Mr. Carp, a young man in expensive, casual clothes, climbs out and approaches the monk.

CARP: Hey there, friend.

BHIKKHU: Good morning.

CARP: My name's Carp. I'm a friend of Charlie Prentice. You know him, I think?

BHIKKHU: Oh yes, Mr. Prentice comes by quite often now.

CARP: You are Bhikkhu Tissa, aren't you?

BHIKKHU: Yes, I am.

CARP: Or *Venerable* Tissa, Charlie says. You guys sure have some strange names.

BHIKKHU: Is there anything I can do for you, Mr. Carp?

CARP: Probably not, to tell the truth. I'm on my way down to the beach, and anyway I'm not really interested in Buddhism. But I was reading these books, see?

BHIKKHU: Books on Buddhism?

CARP: Yes.

BHIKKHU: Why were you reading books on Buddhism if you're not interested in it? It sounds like a terrible waste of time.

CARP: Well, I mean—maybe it was! Charlie gave me those books, and let me tell you they were pretty annoying. All that talk about *suffering*. I mean, page after page of misery, old age, death, and so on. It sounds like Buddhism is the most pessimistic religion in the world. I got to thinking about it, and I was wondering why you Buddhists have such a negative attitude toward life and why you dwell on suffering.

BHIKKHU: (*Musing*) You might also say that suffering dwells on us.

CARP: How's that? Anyhow, I saw you just now, and I thought, why not ask the guy about it? So I have a few questions. Unless you're busy, of course.

BHIKKHU: (*Smiling, leaning the broom against a wall*) I'd be glad to try to answer questions about the Dhamma.

CARP: "Dhamma." That's the word that keeps popping up in those books. What does it mean? I forget.

BHIKKHU: Usually it means just the teaching of the Buddha. It also means truth, reality, the way things are, the law of the universe, bare phenomena themselves, the path to deliverance—depending on the context.

CARP: It's pretty important, huh?

BHIKKHU: The word is just a word. What's behind the word is the most important thing in the world.

CARP: I figured you'd say something like that. I'd like to hear about it. Say, could we sit down somewhere?

BHIKKHU: Sure. How about this nice patch of grass over here?

CARP: (*With an attempt at humour*) I guess you don't have any lawn chairs around here!

BHIKKHU: We make do with what we have. I find grass very accommodating.

They sit down in a shady spot. Mr. Carp uncomfortably inspects the area for ants.

CARP: You know, Bhikkhu Tissa, I never met a Buddhist monk before. I understand people treat you monks with all kinds of respect.

BHIKKHU: Depends on the person, depends on the monk.

CARP: You get called "venerable sir" and all that.

BHIKKHU: We get called other things too.

CARP: Yes, I bet you do! But let me get on to my questions. This business of suffering really bothers me. Isn't there enough trouble in the world without you Buddhists harping on it?

BHIKKHU: It's precisely *because* there is trouble in the world that we pay attention to it, or harp on it, if you will.

CARP: Do you think you can do anything about it?

BHIKKHU: Yes. That's the reason Buddhism exists.

CARP: This I want to hear. To me, it seems like we should emphasise the happy side of life. Why should we pay attention to all the misery?

BHIKKHU: If a wasp stings you, do you pay attention to it?

CARP: Well, of course.

BHIKKHU: But what good does that do? Why dwell on it?

CARP: Because I want to get away from it, because I don't want to be stung again.

BHIKKHU: If you don't want to be stung again it would make sense to learn something about wasps, wouldn't it? Where they build their nests, what's likely to upset them, how to keep from annoying them, and so on. There are a great many kinds of suffering in the world, and they all have their own causes and characteristics. If you feel any of these afflictions, or think that you might be prey to them, wouldn't it be wise to take a good look at them and see what might be done about them?

CARP: Yes, that's so, I suppose. But any way you go there's some amount of trouble, so I prefer to accent the positive, so to speak. You've got to take the bitter with the sweet!

BHIKKHU: Would I be wrong in guessing that you have a fair amount of "sweet" in your life?

CARP: It's true, I'm getting along real well. I work for a real-estate development company, organising some new projects. And to tell the truth, I'm doing pretty well at it. Life's good to me, I admit. That's why I object to Buddhism.

BHIKKHU: Are you completely satisfied with the way things are?

CARP: Not completely. Who is? The important thing is to keep totally in command of your life.

BHIKKHU: Permit me to disagree. Nobody keeps totally in command of his life. Consider just your body. You look pretty healthy. But can you keep your body from ever getting sick? Can you keep it from getting old and breaking down? Or from dying?

CARP: No, I can't do that.

BHIKKHU: Or consider your work. Can you be sure your colleagues will treat you fairly?

CARP: (*Grunting*) Those guys? No way!

BHIKKHU: Will your creditors always be tolerant? Will your customers always pay their bills quickly? Will your competitors put up no resistance?

CARP: (*Uncomfortably*) There's a lot of uncertainty in business.

BHIKKHU: There's a lot of uncertainty in social life, in family life, in all spheres of activity. Am I wrong? What do you think?

CARP: No, I can't deny it.

BHIKKHU: Or, to get right down to the most important thing, can you keep totally in control of your own mind?

CARP: I'm a pretty cheerful guy.

BHIKKHU: That's not what I asked, Mr. Carp. When things go wrong around you, can you keep your mind steady and peaceful?

CARP: Of course not. How could that be?

BHIKKHU: If you tell your mind not to get upset or angry or distracted, does it obey you?

CARP: That's a funny way to look at it. But no, I guess my mind pretty much does what it likes. Thoughts and feelings just come boiling up.

BHIKKHU: Then you certainly aren't in command of your mind, are you? And if you can't control your body or your mind or the actions of other people, you can hardly say you're in command of your life.

CARP: It was just a figure of speech.

BHIKKHU: Let's examine this a bit further, if you don't mind. How many people, do you think, can control their lives to any degree?

CARP: Not many probably. You never know what will happen.

BHIKKHU: Right. You never know what will happen. If it's pleasant you will be elated. If it's unpleasant you will be upset and depressed. If someone is kind to you, you'll be gratified. If they cheat you, you'll be angry. Tell me, Mr. Carp, do you see any independence or security in this state of affairs?

CARP: Since you put it like that, not much. I suppose we have to admit we live in insecurity and dependence to a large degree.

BHIKKHU: Would you call this situation pleasant or unpleasant?

CARP: Unpleasant, mostly.

BHIKKHU: The Buddha spoke about sorrow, pain, and insecurity not because he liked them but because he saw them as the key to an understanding of life.

CARP: Pessimistic, like I say.

BHIKKHU: A fact is just a fact. If you're going to come to a good decision about how to act, you need accurate information about the matter at hand. So you look, and you take note of the important details you see, regardless of whether or not they are personally appealing to you.

CARP: What was the Buddha looking for?

BHIKKHU: Ah! A good question. He was looking for a way out.

CARP: A way out of ... dependence and insecurity?

BHIKKHU: Exactly. The word that describes this situation is *dukkha*. This is usually translated as "suffering," but it means a great deal more than that. "Unsatisfactoriness" might be a better word.

CARP: Well, excuse me, Bhikkhu Tissa, but when you get right down to it, *everything* is unsatisfactory to some degree.

BHIKKHU: Indeed?

CARP: Nothing is *completely* dependable. You can't expect that. Everything has flaws.

BHIKKHU: How about permanent? Are pleasure and security permanent?

CARP: Not in my experience. You've got to keep chasing them down. That's what life is all about.

BHIKKHU: Let's see if I can summarise a bit. Nobody—at least, nobody that we know of—can truly control his own body and make it do exactly what he wants. Nobody can tell his mind how to behave when disturbing events occur. Nobody can prevent disasters from happening to him or keep people from doing things he doesn't like. Nobody can make pleasures last or keep good feelings from fading away. So we find ourselves always running after something desirable or away from something frightful. What would you call this state of affairs?

There is a pause while Mr. Carp fidgets, plucks grass blades, laughs.

CARP: Suffering. Okay, suffering or unsatisfactoriness or whatever you want to call it. It goes pretty deep, does it?

BHIKKHU: It is stitched right into the fabric of things. You could even say it's the thread in the fabric itself.

CARP: What a view of life! Now, let me ask, the Buddha was looking for a way out. And he found it, I suppose?

BHIKKHU: He did. The way out that he found is called Dhamma, the word we began with.

CARP: So this Dhamma that the Buddha created can get us out of suffering?

BHIKKHU: The Buddha didn't create it. He only discovered it and made it known. The Dhamma exists whether or not anybody knows it or understands it, just as apples will continue to fall from trees whether or not anyone understands the law of gravity.

CARP: Is Dhamma some kind of god?

BHIKKHU: No. The Dhamma has many aspects, but basically it is just the way things are, the underlying laws of the universe.

CARP: That sounds simple enough. Why isn't it self-evident, then? Why don't people recognise it?

BHIKKHU: Suppose on a dangerous seacoast there were a powerful light, a great beacon in a lighthouse. Would that be self-evident to sailors?

CARP: Certainly.

BHIKKHU: But what if the sailors never came out of their cabins, or had the odd habit of wearing heavy cloths over their heads, or slept all the time?

CARP: They wouldn't see it, then. They would run aground. But what kind of metaphor are you suggesting?

BHIKKHU: Fundamental truth, or Dhamma, is not by its nature hidden or obscure, though countless philosophers have thought so. But there is something that prevents us from seeing the Dhamma. It is called ignorance. This ignorance, this not-knowing, this blankness, covers our minds and distorts our view of reality. The sailors in the ship may never leave the cabin—they may remain simply sunk in ignorance without trying to get out. Or they may intentionally blind themselves with the masks of foolish beliefs and delusions. Or they may sleep all the time, out of laziness and stupidity. So they will not see the light and may even deny that any such thing exists.

CARP: But suppose somebody does see this Dhamma, or sees enough of it to know it's a good thing.

BHIKKHU: Then, if he's sensible, he'll follow it, he'll seek its protection.

CARP: But what kind of protection can Dhamma offer against all this suffering and uncertainty we were just talking about?

BHIKKHU: Above all, the Dhamma offers relief. There is relief from doubt, relief from fear, relief from mental anguish, relief from grief. As we study and practise Dhamma, our ignorance about how the universe works is gradually reduced. We begin to understand cause and effect. We see that certain results follow from certain actions and we learn to govern our actions in order to get happy results. So we gain relief from doubt and begin to have confidence in our ability to make sense of the world. Right now, we may be subject to all kinds of fears about what may happen to us, thinking that some terrible fate may come crashing down on us at any moment. But the Dhamma teaches us that fear is one result of clinging to a permanence that does not really exist. When we are reconciled to the always-changing nature of things, fear can be overcome. Also, we gain relief from mental anguish, another result of clinging and craving, because we train our minds according to Dhamma merely to pay attention to events and objects, not to clutch them as "me" or "mine." If we have no obsession with being a "sufferer," then the suffering itself loses force. Then, as for grief, we have less to endure because we learn that all life is a constant flow and that grief is, in a sense, simply our own unhappy invention. To know how life works is a great protection, because it gives us confidence and helps us avoid suffering.

CARP: These are big promises, Bhikkhu Tissa!

BHIKKHU: These are just possibilities, very real possibilities—but not things that will happen simply because someone calls himself a Buddhist. I don't expect you to believe them.

CARP: You don't?

BHIKKHU: Certainly not. Buddhism holds out great hope to mankind but it does not expect or advise people to believe a set of doctrines without confirmation.

CARP: And what kind of confirmation is necessary?

BHIKKHU: Why, the confirmation of your own mind, your own reason, your own experience. Could anything less satisfy you?

CARP: Well, I believe in my own experience, all right. But why do you bother to tell me about these benefits of the Dhamma?

BHIKKHU: There is a saying that Buddhas only point the way. The Buddha doesn't "save" anybody. He only teaches people how to save themselves. He points out the problems of life and shows how they may be solved. We who are followers of the Buddha try to observe the same principle—we try to point out the way and encourage people to make the journey for themselves.

CARP: So you think that if people will make this journey they will find confirmation of Buddhist teachings for themselves?

BHIKKHU: Yes. You see, the truths the Buddha points out are right here in the body and the mind. Anyone can see them who puts his mind to it, but he has to put his mind to it.

CARP: Can you explain some of these truths? I assure you there's no danger of my believing them without proof!

BHIKKHU: We've already touched on the truth of suffering. As we've noted, suffering or unsatisfactoriness is present in all worldly phenomena to one degree or another. This is one characteristic of existence that the Buddha repeatedly emphasises. Then there is the fact of impermanence.

CARP: Well, nothing lasts forever. Sure, I know that.

BHIKKHU: Excuse me, but the mark of *aniccatā* or impermanence is extremely deep. Anybody can notice gross physical changes—

and these are certainly one aspect of impermanence—but few people realise that everything that exists in the world is whirling in a blur of change, rising and falling every second, flashing in and out of existence, being born and dying, appearing and perishing continually.

CARP: You know, modern physicists describe atoms and subatomic particles in almost the same way—as changing with incredible speed all the time.

BHIKKHU: So they do. But it's not necessary to study physics to understand this. The best laboratory is the mind itself. Have you ever known anything to change faster than your own mind?

CARP: Sometimes I think my head will bust wide open, the way my thoughts run on!

BHIKKHU: Sometimes faster and wilder than you would wish?

CARP: I suppose I've already admitted I don't have much control over my mind. Sometimes it's just a storm of passions, ideas, emotions, memories.

BHIKKHU: Can you remember a time when it wasn't like this?

CARP: No, and that's pretty depressing.

BHIKKHU: It's simply the nature of the mind. Part of our trouble comes from conceiving the notion that the mind is ours, that it is stable and permanent, a self or an instrument of self. But mind is just mind, a collection of impersonal functions. Its nature is continual change. It isn't you and it isn't I.

CARP: I think we're getting into deep waters here!

BHIKKHU: I hope so. The point I want to make is that when you look at it—especially when you look at it—the mind is like a pan of popping popcorn. It just goes on jumping and making a racket and nobody knows what it will do next. It is the best demonstration of impermanence there is. It just keeps changing. No matter how you want it to hold still, it changes. All the aspects of mind are constantly changing: feelings, perceptions, mental formations, and consciousness itself. Wouldn't you agree?

CARP: I guess so. Memories, feelings, all those things keep running on forever.

BHIKKHU: This leads us on to the third mark of existence: non-self, or in Pali, *anattā.*

CARP: I believe I read about that. But it seemed paradoxical to me. I mean, there is no self, but we think there is, only it's just an illusion, and so on.

BHIKKHU: The basic marks of existence aren't obscure in themselves; here again it's our own ignorance, reinforced by craving, that perverts our view. Let's consider non-self in the light of the other two characteristics I've mentioned—unsatisfactoriness and impermanence. Everything in the world is changing, impermanent, not lasting, so it is always, to some degree, liable to suffering or unsatisfactoriness. Anything we like or enjoy we want to keep on enjoying, but we can't because it changes, breaks up, drifts away.

CARP: Like my girl friends!

BHIKKHU: We are always liable to be separated from what we love or united with what we hate.

CARP: If you only knew some of the idiots I have to work with.

BHIKKHU: It's unsatisfactory to be where we don't want to be and it's unsatisfactory to lose what we cherish. But that is the unstable nature of things.

CARP: Wait a minute. I thought of something that doesn't cause suffering! My car. It's a real beauty, you can see.

BHIKKHU: And it never breaks down?

CARP: Never. Of course, I just bought it two weeks ago. But it runs perfectly. No problems!

BHIKKHU: Really?

CARP: Sure. Of course, I've got to watch out for it. The other day in the parking lot some idiot opened his door and banged the side! Took out a chip of paint. Unbelievable. Brand new car! I was furious. I could have killed the guy.

BHIKKHU: I see. Was that a pleasant sensation?

CARP: (*Sheepishly*) Actually I felt lousy. It ruined the afternoon. My nerves are pretty bad when I get into conflict. Okay, I know what you'll say. I admit, that was unsatisfactory, that was suffering. The car's paint is impermanent and impermanent things are unsatisfactory.

BHIKKHU: Well, then, amid all this unsatisfactoriness and impermanence, do you see any real self?

CARP: A self? Sure. I see me. I see my own self.

BHIKKHU: Be careful now, Mr. Carp. What exactly does this self consist of?

CARP: Well, I'd have to say it's my mind.

BHIKKHU: Buddhism analyses "mind" into feelings, perceptions, mental formations, and consciousness. Is your self one or all of these?

CARP: Well, I suppose I'd say all.

BHIKKHU: But haven't we established that the mind and its functions are constantly changing?

CARP: Yeah, I guess so.

BHIKKHU: So, if the mind is constantly changing, where is your self from one moment to the next?

CARP: I don't know.

BHIKKHU: Wouldn't it be changing? But in that case what does this self really amount to? What makes it "you" if from moment to moment it changes into something else? When we say "self" we are really talking about some stable identity, aren't we? But where there is no stability we can't rightly talk about a self. Furthermore, if the mind is your self, if it is your essence, then why can't you control it at will? Why can't you force it to be calm or happy or creative? And if you can't control it, as you admit, if you can't make it stay here or go there, then who does it really belong to? What sort of self is it?

CARP: A pretty poor sort, I must say.

BHIKKHU: Now, this mind, which changes every moment, every instant, which you cannot control at will—does it make you happy? Does it please you?

CARP: Mostly it's a pain, the way my mind runs on.

BHIKKHU: Then if it causes pain, if it's unreliable, if it's constantly in flux, can we honestly call it a self?

CARP: Oh. Wait, now, I'm confused. Perhaps "self" is just a way of speaking.

BHIKKHU: Indeed it is, but what is behind the word? Just a flux of uncontrollable, unreliable conditions.

CARP: Well, Bhikkhu Tissa, I don't know what to say. If you look at it that way, self is a rather flimsy concept.

BHIKKHU: Just so. It's a concept that doesn't accurately reflect the facts.Events occur, one after the other, with terrific speed. We can observe the process. But "self" is merely a concept imposed on top of it. When we Buddhists talk about "non-self" or *anattā*, we mean this bare process of events giving rise to other events.

CARP: Yes, I follow your logic, but still I feel that I am a self or have a self.

BHIKKHU: On a conventional level, "self" is a perfectly useful term. It's necessary for language and communication. I am I and you are you—that's true enough in everyday language. But the trouble arises when we attribute to self a fundamental reality it doesn't possess. By imagining a precious ego, by believing foolishly that we are permanent and satisfactory "selves," we set ourselves up for suffering.

CARP: Because the universe is not permanent or satisfactory?

BHIKKHU: Exactly. Anyone who persists in living contrary to the laws of the universe will continue to experience suffering.

CARP: This is really extraordinary. I'm going to have to think this over. But you haven't convinced me, not at all!

BHIKKHU: These three marks of existence—impermanence, unsatisfactoriness, and non-self—are significant because they indicate the way the universe is, and the sort of conditions we have to deal with. Unfortunately, most of us, out of ignorance, see things incorrectly. We take what is changing as stable; we take what is imperfect and unsatisfactory as satisfactory; we take what is without a self as having a self.

CARP: If what you say is true, then most people are living exactly backward to the way they should be living.

BHIKKHU: Yes, and that in itself is another aspect of dukkha or unsatisfactoriness.

CARP: All right, you Buddhists do have some justification for talking about suffering. But one thing I still don't understand is why people misinterpret the world so grossly. Is it simply out of ignorance?

BHIKKHU: When we talk about ignorance we mean more than the absence of information. We mean self-deception and lack of judgment as well. For example, if we have a problem to solve, we can gather information about the problem and from that information come to a conclusion. But what if the information is faulty? What if we have misunderstood the facts to start with? Then we begin reasoning with false premises, and no matter how clever we are our conclusions will turn out false, too. The problem of understanding life itself depends on properly understanding facts. When we are ignorant and uninstructed we tend to take things at face value. Human nature being what it is, we gravitate toward pleasant objects and shun unpleasant objects. Because we are fond of pleasure, we try to magnify it wherever we see it, and because we hate pain we magnify that. Simply speaking, we run to extremes. We have no special motivation to analyse the objects of our senses as long as they keep us entertained, as they do so well. Moreover, because we live a fair number of years and because there is a continuity in our experience, we fasten onto the notion that we are selves or souls who experience things and have a definite identity. We don't know any better, and without investigation we have no particular reason to question this life of loves and hates and quick assumptions. We rely on our ignorant biases and continue to suffer.

CARP: This ignorance sounds like plain carelessness and stupidity.

BHIKKHU: Yes. To the Buddha, ignorance is not just a neutral not-knowing; it is a very reprehensible defilement, a dangerous and foolish self-deception.

CARP: Now there's a funny old word. "Defilement." It sounds so negative. Who would want to believe in "defilement" nowadays?

BHIKKHU: Well, I ask you, who would want to escape suffering?

CARP: There is a connection?

BHIKKHU: Of course. Ignorance is the basic defilement, the source of all greed, hatred, and delusion. A mind clouded by defilements cannot see reality. Not understanding, not seeing the marks of impermanence, suffering, and non-self, a person acts as if things were quite the contrary. Thus arises conflict with the laws of nature, and misery follows.

CARP: But how exactly does this misery come about?

BHIKKHU: Are you familiar with the Four Noble Truths?

CARP: Oh, them. Yes, I read about them. They sounded depressing at the time.

BHIKKHU: But not now?

CARP: Well, I'm thinking about it.

BHIKKHU: Sometimes people only hear the first noble truth, which states the universal problem—that life passes away, that it breaks up, that health gives way to sickness and life gives way to death, that all experiences and components of ordinary existence are impermanent and flawed. Not that they are necessarily suffering all the time—indeed, they are sometimes full of pleasure—but they are always liable to suffering.

CARP: That is a pretty sobering assessment.

BHIKKHU: The second noble truth is the origin of suffering. Suffering has a cause. This is a deceptively simple statement that contains much meaning. Suffering does not happen spontaneously. It is caused and conditioned by other phenomena. As the primary cause, the Buddha singled out craving. Wherever this craving or obsessive desire springs up, suffering is sure to follow. Why? Because craving leads to grasping and clinging to what is inherently unstable. All delightful objects, experiences, and persons break up and disappear, so whenever we indulge in craving we are bound for disappointment and pain.

CARP: All right, I am with you so far. But how do we get out of this mess?

BHIKKHU: The first two noble truths state the problem. The second two reveal the solution. The third noble truth is called the truth of the cessation or ending of suffering.

CARP: Well, it's about time!

BHIKKHU: The Buddha realised that every phenomenon that arises, arises from causes and conditions, and that when those causes and conditions are removed, the phenomenon must disappear.

Suffering has a cause. The cause is craving. When craving is brought to an end, suffering is also brought to an end.

CARP: But that's easier said than done, I expect.

BHIKKHU: Yes, and that's where the fourth noble truth comes in. The Buddha states that there is a problem, namely suffering; there is a cause of the problem; there is the possibility of eliminating the problem; and finally there is a specific way to eliminate the problem. The fourth noble truth is simply the Noble Eightfold Path, the Buddha's prescription for dealing with the unsatisfactoriness in life. The eight factors of the path are eight virtues or skills which can gradually weaken and ultimately destroy the craving that oppresses us. Right Views means having a correct understanding of the way the universe operates, the way suffering springs up in our lives. Right Intentions means directing our thoughts and intentions toward wholesome things, toward kindness, mental purity, and self-training. Right Speech means refraining from harsh, false, or useless speech. Right Action means acting in a virtuous way, carrying out our intentions, and following the moral precepts. Right Livelihood means earning a living by honest and respectable means, fairly, not cheating anyone, not harming any living creatures. Right Effort means making an effort to guard the mind, to overcome unwholesome mental states such as greed and hatred and to replace them with generosity and loving kindness. Right Mindfulness means developing attention and presence of mind, not being careless or unobservant. Right Concentration means focusing the mind skillfully on objects so as to know them deeply without being distracted. These eight factors summarise the training.

CARP: I hate to criticise, Bhikkhu Tissa, but that word "training" has an unpleasant sound. Life's hard enough. Who wants any more "training" than he has to endure already?

BHIKKHU: What makes you think this training is disagreeable?

CARP: I mean, all those factors, all that discipline. I don't think I'd like to take it all on me.

BHIKKHU: Pardon me, but the purpose is to take it all off you.

CARP: I don't understand.

BHIKKHU: Buddhism as a religion—or as a way of life—aims at lightening your burden, not increasing it. It is the untrained, undisciplined mind that is weighed down and obstructed with woe, just as a person who has no training in finding his way in a jungle is likely to lose the path and struggle miserably through thick vines and thorns. We are so accustomed to carrying unpleasant burdens that we can only think of taking on new, pleasant burdens, instead of putting them all down. The Dhamma is a training in putting down. As such, it liberates and gladdens us.

CARP: Well, now, Bhikkhu Tissa, I've got to say I enjoy some of these "burdens." Why should I get rid of them when they are really the only things that make my life worthwhile?

BHIKKHU: Here we have arrived at an important point, Mr. Carp. Every person has pleasant, unpleasant, and neutral experiences. Naturally we prefer the pleasant. But the burdens I refer to are not the experiences themselves. They are our attachments to those experiences.

CARP: Ah, you're getting subtle on me.

BHIKKHU: Remember, the Buddha identifies craving as the primary cause of our pain, disappointment, and suffering. This craving or mental hunger is a strain or burden on the mind. It causes us to struggle against the natural, changing state of things. For instance, suppose we hunger after some desirable object and try to obtain it. Then we suffer the strain of longing, the worry about getting the object, the fear that somebody else will get it first, and the uncertainty of whether we really have the means to obtain it. If we fail to achieve our ends, our inflamed mind suffers disappointment. If we do get what we want, then we have to protect it, take care of it, see that it is not stolen or destroyed. So we suffer anxiety on account of our craving and attachment. Then we have to deal with the unfaithfulness of our own mind. The mind changes! We may decide we don't like the object after all, so we have the worry of getting rid of it. Or the object turns out to cause us problems of one kind or another. Then our attachment turns to aversion and we suffer the misery of being united with what we don't like. Or suppose we continue to enjoy the object. Not only does the mind change, the object changes. It breaks, it runs away, it rusts, it gets old. Sooner or later we are separated from it, and then we feel grief. Then, not knowing any better, to cover up this grief, our insatiable mind goes lurching after some new object, mental or material. And the wheel keeps turning through the seconds and through the years. And we do not escape.

CARP: Bhikkhu Tissa, there's a lot of truth in what you say. I can't deny it. But how else can a person live, if not by reaching for things? How can anyone be happy?

BHIKKHU: Indeed, we must reach for things, but the right things and in the right way. To put down the burden of craving does not mean to stop acting in the world. It means to cut off our foolish hunger and vanity. The virtuous man, the happy man, is one who follows the middle way, who is moderate in his desires. Buddhism teaches that good results follow good actions and evil results follow evil actions. Events cause and condition other events, so we should act responsibly, knowing that we do, in effect, shape our own future. When we cut off an impulse of blind craving we gain peace in this very moment because the mind is no longer irritated, and we gain benefit in the future because we have set up no painful cycle of grasping and losing. It is advantageous to live simply without superfluous possessions and entanglements, but the most important thing is to root out craving itself.

CARP: So I don't necessarily have to give up things?

BHIKKHU: Ah, Mr. Carp, you must give up what is painful. You must give up what hurts.

CARP: And craving hurts?

BHIKKHU: Just look at your own mind, that's all.

CARP: Do you think I should meditate?

BHIKKHU: I think you should examine yourself and watch the changes in your mind and body.

CARP: Where does all this lead, Bhikkhu Tissa? Does it lead to happiness?

BHIKKHU: Yes, but not happiness as most people have been conditioned to think. True happiness is not the piling up of sense-pleasures. True happiness comes from liberation from the defilements, from clear sight, from an open, generous heart that does not fear the ceaseless change of things.

CARP: What about all this I've read about "supra-mundane wisdom"?

BHIKKHU: Wisdom arises from the practice of Dhamma. It is a tool that helps us reach the goal, but it is not the goal itself.

CARP: The goal is the end of suffering, right?

BHIKKHU: Right. Some people develop what you might call a craving after wisdom—wanting to know the secrets of the workings of things, out of curiosity or pride. This is knowing for its own sake, and it is not useful. In fact, the Buddha refused to answer speculative questions about the origin and the future of the universe, because such questions are distractions from the matter at hand—the problem of suffering and the overcoming of suffering.

CARP: You know, I had the idea that Buddhism was only concerned with very lofty, esoteric things—not the everyday existence of ordinary people. It's somewhat encouraging to hear that Buddhism deals with how to achieve happiness in this world. Not that I necessary believe it, of course.

BHIKKHU: Sometimes people who are too much caught up in the world turn cynical, thinking that there is nothing higher than the gaining and losing of status, objects, or relationships. Not seeing that a higher, worthier, and more peaceful everyday life is possible, they become bogged down in entertainments that fail to satisfy.

CARP: I wonder if you're referring to me, Bhikkhu Tissa. Well, it doesn't matter. I can testify that lots of my unreligious friends just don't believe that any different kind of life exists. You're suggesting that it does.

BHIKKHU: The Dhamma suggests that it does. Now let me return to your charge of pessimism.

CARP: Well, I'm having second thoughts about that.

BHIKKHU: Buddhism deals with the problem of suffering and the cure of suffering. Once we recognise that a disease exists we can treat the disease if we have the medicine at hand. Imagine the joy of health to someone who has never before known health. Imagine the relief of someone who has carried a boulder on his back all his life and now can set it down.

CARP: Yes, I can see that. But really, Bhikkhu Tissa, I don't want to go live in a cave and meditate all the time. I've got to make a living in this world.

BHIKKHU: There's no need to live in a cave. The practice of Dhamma can and should be carried on wherever you find yourself. It is compatible with any kind of respectable livelihood. It depends on mindfully observing our actions from moment to moment, whatever we are doing, and so it can benefit the businessman as well as the monk.

CARP: Well, my friend Charlie Prentice sure seems cheerful lately. But a fellow has got to figure out what is best for him. Tell me, if I wanted to—if a person wanted to practise Buddhism, to follow the Dhamma, what should he do? I'm speaking hypothetically, of course. How does somebody become a Buddhist?

BHIKKHU: Somebody becomes a Buddhist by following the teachings of the Buddha.

CARP: Like the Noble Eightfold Path?

BHIKKHU: Yes. But there's a brief saying that covers it all: to abstain from all evil, to cultivate the good, and to purify the mind—this is the teaching of all the Buddhas.

CARP: That sounds pretty good. Could you explain just a bit?

BHIKKHU: To abstain from all evil means to refrain from all actions that cause harm to oneself or others. It means to follow the Five Precepts: to avoid killing, stealing, sexual misconduct, lying, and taking intoxicants.

CARP: I'm afraid I've been known to break a few of those precepts! Do you mean, for instance, that I shouldn't kill at all, like not stepping on these ants crawling all around here?

BHIKKHU: The precepts protect not only all animals; they protect you as well, because they keep you from doing actions which will coarsen your mind and cause you suffering later on.

CARP: But suppose somebody just can't keep all these precepts perfectly?

BHIKKHU: The precepts are not commandments. The Buddha wasn't a god who laid down absolute rules. The Buddha did, however, perfectly understand the world, and he simply pointed out that when someone keeps the precepts he is acting according to Dhamma and building up protection and happiness for himself and other beings. The closer we can live to the precepts the better it is for us.

CARP: Keeping those precepts would certainly make you think. Now, how about doing good?

BHIKKHU: Avoiding evil is the first step. But beyond that we have to act virtuously and generously. A Buddhist is expected to demonstrate his kindness by helping his fellow beings, by making an effort to have a positive effort on his society. He should show the blessings of the Dhamma in his own conduct.

CARP: And what about purifying the mind?

BHIKKHU: The practitioner restrains his unwholesome impulses by observing the precepts and he becomes a force for good through his own will. And through it all he should strive to cleanse himself of the defilements of greed, hatred, and delusion, and the ignorance that spawns them. He should move steadily, at whatever pace is suitable for him, toward deliverance from all suffering, toward enlightenment.

CARP: What you describe is impressive, really. How can an ordinary guy do such a thing? I'm not really a strong person, I know. I am what I am mainly out of weakness, I guess.

BHIKKHU: Mr. Carp, let me emphasise one thing especially. The Dhamma is the noble path for everyone, weak or strong or in between. Do what you can, because every act of kindness or virtue or mindfulness takes you a step closer to deliverance from sorrow.

CARP: You're really serious about this, aren't you? I wish I could be like that—serious, confident. You know, the trouble is, I'm so restless, I can't sit still. So I go racing here and there all the time. My mind wanders, so I wander too.

BHIKKHU: This wandering is called *saṃsāra*, the cycle of birth and death.

CARP: That's depressing.

BHIKKHU: Indeed it is. And that's why the Dhamma is such a relief. It can free us from that cycle.

CARP: We're all wanderers in a way, aren't we?

BHIKKHU: Yes. You and I and—and even that big red ant crawling up your leg.

CARP: Yeow!

Mr. Carp jumps up and dances around wildly, brushing at his pants.

CARP: Ow! Get off! Get off! These things will bite!

BHIKKHU: Easy now, Mr. Carp. It dropped off.

CARP: It did?

BHIKKHU: It probably considered you an unsteady surface.

CARP: (*Laughing suddenly*) I am! I am an unsteady surface!

Bhikkhu Tissa stands up, smiling.

BHIKKHU: And what will you do about that?

CARP: (*Embarrassed*) Well, I don't know. Say, listen, I've taken up enough of your time. Thanks for explaining things. I'd better get going. I'm heading down to the beach to meet some friends.

BHIKKHU: I hope you have a safe drive.

CARP: Oh, I will, I will. It's a great car, a beauty, you can see. Oh no! No! Did you see that bird? Did you see what that bird just did to my car?

BHIKKHU: Yes, birds will do that.

CARP: (*Shaking his head*) I just had it waxed! You know, that makes me think—oh, never mind. Thanks for your time, Bhikkhu Tissa.

Smiling to himself, Bhikkhu Tissa takes his broom in hand again.

BHIKKHU: I'm glad you dropped by, Mr. Carp.

CARP: Yeah, me too, I guess.

BHIKKHU: If you'll excuse me, I'll get back to my work now.

CARP: (*Hesitantly*) Oh sure, sure. Say, you know, if you need any help around the temple, I wouldn't mind lending a hand sometime.

BHIKKHU: That's kind of you, but we manage pretty well.

CARP: No, I'm serious, I'd be glad to help, anytime. Really!

BHIKKHU: Well then, would you like to sweep? The sidewalk out there needs it.

CARP: (*Startled*) You mean now? But you've only got one broom.

BHIKKHU: Oh, there's another one in the tool shed there.

Bhikkhu Tissa turns away and placidly resumes his sweeping. Mr. Carp fidgets for a moment, then goes and gets the other broom from the shed. He returns and waits awkwardly for instructions, but gets none. Finally he begins sweeping the sidewalk, casting puzzled looks at the monk. At one point he opens his mouth to say something, but shuts it again. Bhikkhu Tissa is no longer paying attention to him. With a bemused expression, Mr. Carp applies himself to sweeping the sidewalk. Little puffs of dust and leaves fly out to either side as the broom finds its rhythm. A morning breeze has now sprung up, swaying the trees above and sending flickers of light and dark, sun and shade, across the sweepers.

Bhikkhu Tissa and the Greater Good

It is noon on a winter day. Bhikkhu Tissa has been a guest for a mid-day meal in the home of a married couple, Leona and Ernest, and now sits with them in the family room, sipping a cup of tea. The windows of the room look out on a snowy landscape. A fire leaps and crackles in the fireplace.

LEONA: Was everything all right, Bhikkhu Tissa?

BHIKKHU: Just fine, thank you.

LEONA: Of course, you know I'm referring to the food, not the state of the universe!

BHIKKHU: Yes, I thought as much. It was delicious.

LEONA: The universe is quite another question, right?

ERNEST: I've got to apologise for my wife, venerable sir. She never stops philosophising!

LEONA: Ernest, my dear husband, I am a woman made for grand ideas!

ERNEST: How well I know. Are you going to bombard this venerable monk with impossible questions?

LEONA: (*Laughing*) Oh, I think he can take care of himself. Anyway, Ernest, you were the one who invited him. You must have something on that oh-so-serious mind of yours.

ERNEST: Well, I did think it might be useful to have a private little discussion about matters of substance.

LEONA: Do you hear that, Venerable? My husband talks like an office memo. Why then do I love him?

BHIKKHU: (*Smiling over his teacup*) Wise men refrain from trying to figure out love.

ERNEST: As you know, I've been getting interested in Buddhism over the last year, and sometimes it seems like it raises more questions than it answers!

BHIKKHU: Oh yes, that often happens at first. I think it's a good sign. If Buddhism is to have a real effect on somebody it must challenge them, make them think of a hundred problems and puzzles they never considered before. The average person all too often takes things for granted, has a careless, habitual way of looking at the world, and idly believes in unexamined concepts. But Buddhism kicks the props entirely out from under such habits and reveals many unanswered questions which have been there all along.

LEONA: Are you referring to big stuff like the meaning of life, and so on?

BHIKKHU: No, just basic laws and relationships that we need to grasp little by little until we can tackle the bigger questions. Sometimes simple intellectual curiosity can start this process. Sometimes it's a single provocative incident.

ERNEST: That's sort of what happened to me—an incident. I've been studying Buddhism for a while, maybe with a little more interest than Leona here ...

LEONA: There he goes, bragging already.

EARNEST: ... and then just recently a question arose that has no end of implications. It has to do with a job offer.

LEONA: Oh, you're going into this, are you? Venerable Tissa, we've talked this over fifty times and I think he's crazy—dear, but crazy. Well, Ernest, tell our guest. Maybe he'll straighten you out.

ERNEST: My field is chemistry, Bhikkhu Tissa, and I've been in and out of academia and private industry over the years. At the moment I've got a teaching position at the college that I like pretty well, though it doesn't pay a lot. Recently I got a very attractive job offer from the research division of a local chemical company. It would mean a sizable increase in salary and a chance to do some creative work in my particular specialty. Professionally it would be a big step up for me, and, as a matter of fact, I know some of the people there and I think we'd get along fine. But I can't make up my mind to take the job. And it's all because of something you said.

BHIKKHU: What was that?

ERNEST: You were talking about the Noble Eightfold Path and you mentioned Right Livelihood. You said one should earn a living without harming others. Now, does this apply to animals?

BHIKKHU: Yes, it does.

ERNEST: I thought so. There's the problem. You see, this company has a research laboratory where they test the effects of their chemicals on animals. I wouldn't be directly connected with that department, I wouldn't do any experiments on animals, but still I'd feel uncomfortably close. And that bothers me.

BHIKKHU: What do they do to the animals there?

ERNEST: Toxicity tests, mostly. That means they poison them—dogs, cats, rabbits, rats, and other animals. They paint chemicals into the eyes of rabbits and see what concentrations will cause ulcers and blindness. They force-feed lethal compounds to groups of dogs and see how long it takes for half of them to die.

BHIKKHU: What happens to the other half?

ERNEST: They might use them again in other tests. More often they kill them all. They "sacrifice" them, to use the euphemism. Sometimes they do autopsies.

LEONA: Ernest, please, you're making me ill.

ERNEST: I got a brief look at the lab when they were giving me a tour of the company. Now, I've known about such labs all my professional life, but I've never worked in one or really paid too much attention. But after studying Buddhism a little, I found that it really upset me to see the animals in cages and the instruments and so on. The guy who was giving me the tour must have noticed because he said, "Don't worry, your office is far away, you won't hear anything." "They make noise?" I said. And he said, "Oh, not so much" and sort of shrugged. Since then I literally haven't been able to sleep. I keep imagining sitting in my office in another part of the building and hearing faint screams coming up through the ventilation ducts or something.

LEONA: This is how he's been going on, Bhikkhu Tissa. I tell him he doesn't have to have anything to do with animal experiments, so why worry about it?

ERNEST: Thinking about the suffering of animals, Bhikkhu Tissa, I find my mind wandering out in wider and wider circles, trying to make sense of a world that seems, well, pretty horrible in many respects. But to begin with, I'd just like to have your opinion about whether or not I should take this job.

BHIKKHU: I wonder if you would really be satisfied if I said, yes, you should, or no, you shouldn't. Sometimes Buddhist teaching has a specific answer to a moral question, sometimes not. In either case what is important is that the student understand the underlying principles himself so that he doesn't just rely on faith in the teacher. You began your reflections with Right Livelihood, so let's pick up there. Right Livelihood means earning a living in a harmless, honest, and inoffensive manner. The Buddha advised his disciples specifically to refrain from dealing in arms, in living beings, in meat, in intoxicants, and in poisons.

LEONA: You know, that covers a whole lot of occupations, venerable sir! I mean—making guns, bombs, all kinds of weapons. And as for living beings and meat, well, you are talking about huge industries there. And do you mean to say that dealing in all kinds of intoxicants is prohibited—beer, wine, and everything? And you could include a host of products under the name of "poisons," everything from nerve gas to bug spray. Do you really believe that everybody working in all of these industries is necessarily evil? Are they all going to suffer some terrible karma? Are they going to hell?

ERNEST: Hold on, Leona, give Bhikkhu Tissa a chance to answer.

BHIKKHU: The Buddha teaches that for our own well-being and the well-being of others we should avoid these classes of occupations. Dealing in arms means just what you think—all kinds of weapons and instruments for killing. Dealing in living beings refers to animals, of course, and it also extends into areas like slavery, or prostitution, or the buying and selling of children or adults in one way or another. "Meat" refers to the bodies of beings after they are killed. And poisons are just as you say—all kinds of toxic products designed to kill.

LEONA: Those are immense categories.

BHIKKHU: The categories are wide because the principle is wide: not to engage in occupations which cause suffering, destruction, and death. Now, you ask whether somebody who works in one of these occupations necessarily suffers misfortune as a result.

LEONA: Yes, what about the perfectly honest owner of a liquor store? Or a sporting goods dealer who sells guns to hunters?

BHIKKHU: *Kamma*, or *karma*, means volitional actions by body, speech, or mind. *Kamma* produces a result for the doer according to its nature as wholesome, unwholesome, or neutral. Acts of killing and harming, for instance, will sooner or later bring painful results for the doer.

LEONA: Yes, I understand that. That's the practical basis for Buddhist moral precepts. But if one doesn't actually kill or harm or steal, and so on, then it seems that one could be engaged in almost any profession.

BHIKKHU: To sell liquor or guns, assuming one does so honestly, may not in itself bring karmic misfortune. But with the factor of Right Livelihood the Buddha recognises the truth that habitual associations strongly influence our thoughts and deeds. There may be someone, for instance, who works in a slaughterhouse, but whose job is not to kill animals but only to grade meat or operate a conveyor belt. He may not actually break the precepts or do evil, but this is nevertheless wrong livelihood because his mind is likely to be harmed by the unwholesome atmosphere. He becomes accustomed to pain and death. He regards the suffering of living beings as unimportant. And thus he sinks further into ignorance and becomes easier prey for mental defilements which will definitely cause him sorrow. The principle is the same for intoxicants or weapons. Dealing with these, a person becomes indifferent to the delusion and destruction that alcohol and drugs cause, or becomes callous about the killing or maiming of living beings by weapons.

LEONA: But these are popular goods and services. There will always be *somebody* to provide them.

BHIKKHU: True, Leona, but it needn't be *you*.

LEONA: Oh, dear, I can see what you think about Ernest's job offer!

BHIKKHU: Maybe you are guessing a little too quickly. Let's analyse the question further. Yes, to do painful experiments on animals in one's work, to wound, poison, or torment them in any way, is certainly a violation of Right Livelihood.

ERNEST: You would condemn such an occupation, then?

BHIKKHU: Yes. To inflict pain on living beings—even for the supposed advantage of other living beings—is cruel and short-sighted.

ERNEST: Ah, well!

BHIKKHU: But I would not exactly on that account advise you to reject your job offer.

ERNEST: I don't understand.

BHIKKHU: I believe you said your job would *not* involve experimenting on animals, and you would not be directly connected with it.

ERNEST: Strictly speaking, no.

BHIKKHU: Then strictly speaking you would not be violating the principle of Right Livelihood. According to Buddhism we are karmically responsible only for what we do intentionally and what we order others to do. Beyond that, it's up to the individual to decide. Right Livelihood is a flexible concept that can guide us regarding professions that were unknown in the Buddha's time. We have to decide how close we can come to occupations that are definitely unwholesome without becoming contaminated. Ultimately, almost every profession is somehow related to every other, so we would likely go crazy if we looked for a job that was not distantly, theoretically, harmful to somebody. Take a big company with many divisions or subsidiaries. Is somebody in one department responsible for what somebody in another department does? Is the typist in New York implicated in the killing of cattle in Texas?

ERNEST: No, that's unreasonable, in my opinion.

BHIKKHU: So, it comes down to this: you must be quite sure and satisfied in your own mind that you are not willingly doing any harmful deeds and that you are not encouraging or condoning the ill-treatment of living beings.

ERNEST: Oh, that's so hard to know...

LEONA: Well and good, Venerable Tissa. But don't we have to balance off harm and benefit? I'm not willing to concede that doing scientific experiments on animals is entirely evil. Think of the lasting benefits to humanity that come of such experiments.

ERNEST: Uh, Leona, at this lab they're presently testing oven-cleaner and hair-spray.

LEONA: Oh. Not the most vital products, I grant you.

ERNEST: And before you go on to cite penicillin or some other wonder drug, I think it's fair to note that medicines can be developed and tested without recourse to live animal subjects. We now have sophisticated techniques of computer-modelling and tissue-culture that are accurate and cause no bloodshed. The fact that animals have been used so much in the past does not prove that discoveries would have been impossible *without* them, only that that has been the habit, or conditioned reflex, of scientific researchers.

LEONA: Maybe, maybe. But, Bhikkhu Tissa, I want to get at the philosophical question here. If some real benefit to humanity can come about through experimenting on animals, even though they suffer, then why not use them? Shouldn't we be concerned with the greater good that will result?

BHIKKHU: I'm glad you raise the question of benefit, Leona, because this is where people often go astray when considering Right Livelihood or those troublesome five precepts. Yes, I agree that we should act for the greater good, but—and here is a question that has sent seekers into the Sangha for centuries—how do we know what the greater good *is*?

LEONA: It's whatever benefits the most people, I guess.

BHIKKHU: Only people? What about animals?

LEONA: Well, people are more important.

BHIKKHU: Indeed? To whom?

LEONA: To people. Okay, I know it sounds self-serving.

BHIKKHU: Leaving animals out for the moment, suppose some action helps us but harms other people. How do you evaluate it? Where is the greater good?

LEONA: I guess you just have to choose.

BHIKKHU: On what basis?

LEONA: Oh, Bhikkhu Tissa, I can see you won't be satisfied with anything less than a moral foundation—a religious foundation!

BHIKKHU: Better to say, a foundation of reality. And the question remains: How do we know the greater good?

ERNEST: Through study of the Dhamma, I would guess.

BHIKKHU: Through study and *practice* of the Dhamma. The Buddha teaches that we should do certain things and avoid other things, but not on his word alone or the words of our teachers or out of respect for tradition. We are told to test these teachings in our own minds and in our own practice and then put our faith in the Dhamma as we see its effects.

LEONA: Yes, I will say that is one of the attractive qualities of Buddhism.

BHIKKHU: Let me ask you, what do you think is the ultimate goal of Buddhism?

LEONA: I know that: to put an end to suffering. But we can't really call that the greater good, can we? We need something more specific.

BHIKKHU: The end of suffering, or *Nibbāna*, is what the entire Dhamma points to. The Buddha said that just as the great ocean has only one taste, the taste of salt, so the Dhamma has only one taste, the taste of liberation. In the Buddhist view, every specific goal—to use your word—must be connected to the ultimate goal to be worthwhile. We have been discussing Right Livelihood. Now, Right Livelihood is not the ultimate goal but in a sense it recapitulates the whole. We want to escape the suffering involved with making a living—the disagreements, difficulties, guilt, anxiety, and so on. To accomplish this we first of all have to place ourselves in conditions where such unpleasantness is least likely to arise; that is, in those occupations which are peaceful, non-threatening, undisturbing to the conscience, and compatible with high ideals. Second, we see to it that we conduct our business or perform our job in a scrupulously fair and honest manner. This frees us from the suffering inherent in trickery and cheating. It helps us get along with our co-workers and the public at large and gives us the security of a good reputation. Finally, by getting our livelihood with energy and effort in a lawful, honest, and harmless manner, we liberate ourselves from self-contempt and the disgust of base money-grabbing, so that one large area of our lives is protected from the worst danger—the danger of our own misguided action. Thus we enjoy the satisfaction of honourable work. This is purification of the mind with regard to livelihood.

ERNEST: It seems that the Buddha overlooked nothing that might contribute to happiness. But still, even if we behave in the manner you suggest, we can't be sure that making a living is going to be free of problems.

LEONA: Yes, *everybody*—good, evil, and average—complains about his or her job. Even in the most blameless work there's some suffering.

BHIKKHU: Very true. Right Livelihood has a beneficial ripple-effect we cannot see the end of, but certainly it will not eradicate *all* suffering. There are, if you remember, seven more factors of the Noble Eightfold Path to develop.

LEONA: (*Laughing*) Ah, I might have known! This Buddhism is nothing if not methodical! There's a sort of—well, a sort of beauty about the way it fits together—like an exquisite watch.

ERNEST: Or like the molecular structure of DNA!

All three laugh.

LEONA: This business of getting through life is certainly complicated. We started with rabbits in cages and now where are we?

ERNEST: One eighth of the way to enlightenment?

LEONA: Oh you! But let's get an answer from the venerable monk. Okay, I see the need for Right Livelihood in a practical sense, but why do we need to link it with anything else? Why buy the whole deal, so to speak?

BHIKKHU: I think, Leona, that you've forgotten what you just said. You noted that even a perfectly blameless livelihood will not remove *all* suffering. Now, how much more suffering is there in life?

LEONA: Oh, heaps and heaps!

BHIKKHU: Are you willing to endure it? Are you ready for it?

LEONA: No, not at all, no, categorically no.

BHIKKHU: Do you think you can escape it simply by wishing to? Do you think that suffering—disease, old age, loss, grief, and so on—will just pass you by?

LEONA: (*Sighing*) No, I don't think that.

BHIKKHU: Well, do you believe *you* have any power in the matter?

LEONA: Maybe. I don't know. I'm not sure.

BHIKKHU: Buddhism teaches that we do have power to reduce and ultimately eliminate suffering. When somebody makes even a small effort to follow the basic precepts he reaps an immediate benefit in the form of a pacified mind. Good qualities—peace-bringing qualities—are strengthened and bad qualities are ever so slightly weakened. When somebody makes a really systematic and conscientious effort to avoid killing, stealing, lying, sexual misconduct, and taking intoxicants, he fortifies himself further. When he pursues the good by acting out of benevolence and compassion he stores up benefit for the future. Then when he tries to purify his mind as well as his deeds he is moving positively to the greater good—Nibbāna, deliverance, the end of sorrow.

ERNEST: I don't doubt what you say, venerable sir, but with all due respect, we are lay people living very much in the world, with many responsibilities and burdens. How can we realistically concern ourselves with getting to Nibbāna?

BHIKKHU: Nibbāna isn't a place to get to. It's not even a state of mind. The Buddha called it simply the end of suffering. This is a goal that should concern everybody regardless of his or her worldly station. The Noble Eightfold Path is a transcendent way that leads out of the world to the inconceivable bliss of Nibbāna, but it is also consistent with an active life *in* the world along the way. I mean by this that the Dhamma protects us now, in our daily problems and challenges, and later, in the kind of future our deeds will lead us to. Some people, when they hear the transcendent promise of the Dhamma, are elated. Others, like you, perhaps, are a little worried, thinking that they are not ready to ascend any spiritual summits. Really, there is no cause for worry. If we apply ourselves to solving immediate problems as the Buddha teaches, then higher goals will simply come into focus in their own time. We need only remind ourselves that there lies ahead of us a greater good which is timeless, steady, and ultimately accessible. Simple moral restraint and deeds of charity and the practice of mindfulness in the household life cannot fail to build a foundation for wisdom.

ERNEST: I have an instinct that what you say is true. That's why I'm trying to order my life at least to the extent of giving wisdom a *chance* to arise. But I'm not sure. Life is often mysterious, like a wandering in the dark.

BHIKKHU: You are right. Life is very mysterious. But in the Buddhist system even that mystery is a suitable theme for meditation. For instance, look out the window here. From where we sit we can't see the ground, only that blank grey sky and a few snowflakes drifting past. If we didn't know better we might think those snowflakes just appear spontaneously in our field of view and whirl out of it again into some kind of oblivion, without a reason, uncaused, absurdly appearing and disappearing.

LEONA: That would be just delusion, just ignorance.

BHIKKHU: But because we have some experience, because we have at one time or another stuck our heads out the window, we know that snow falls from the clouds overhead and it piles up in drifts on the ground beneath. We see where it comes from and where it goes. It's the same with the larger questions of life: investigation destroys ignorance. Somebody might keep moral precepts just out of fear, or tradition, or habit—and there's nothing really wrong with this, it's still a help and protection. But sooner or later most people think, "Why am I really following these rules? Where will they lead me?" If a monk or somebody tells them the purpose is to get rid of suffering, then, if they're intelligent, they want to find out for themselves how and why.

LEONA: Exactly, exactly.

BHIKKHU: The Buddha discovered and made known the path to deliverance. Now, it's a sorry old world we live in, but that path is still open, friends, it is still open.

ERNEST: Perhaps Leona and I are following it already, even without being fully aware. But I would hate to think, Bhikkhu Tissa, that all the mystery must go out of life.

BHIKKHU: Ignorance must go, but mystery in the sense I think you mean comes even more alive in the objects of our experience. Our wonder at the infinite and ineffable is an intuition of Nibbāna itself. Looking here through this plain glass window on emptiness—even though we have no illusions about where those snowflakes come from and where they go, still we find it peaceful and uplifting to gaze out on those random crystals.

ERNEST: Yes, that's true. But why should that be?

Bhikkhu Tissa smiles, says nothing, gazes thoughtfully out the window.

LEONA: Perhaps because—if I might be so bold—because looking out in that dimensionless space we are reminded of our connections to infinite things. I mean, the flake that bumps against our windowpane here is connected to the clouds and the clouds to the whole atmosphere and the atmosphere to the space beyond, with its matter and energy and vast laws of generation and destruction. One can't help feeling part of a cosmic drama, so to speak.

ERNEST: Ah, what a philosopher you are, Leona!

LEONA: And what of it? I think Venerable Tissa would approve. That's what Buddhism teaches, isn't it? Investigation?

BHIKKHU: Yes, and when we investigate we see connections, and when we see connections we are motivated to act in certain ways.

ERNEST: But why act at all? Isn't passive contemplation enough?

BHIKKHU: No. The mindful observation of the world that the Buddha recommends reveals that intentional deeds have results for the doer. We are where we are—in fortune or misfortune, peace or trouble—as a result of what we have done in the past. Where we go in the future depends on what we do now.

LEONA: Are you talking about rebirth? Well, that seems to me like a rather weak motivation, since rebirth is not at all apparent to me. It may very well be true, but I mean to say that I just don't see it in front of me as a reality the same way I see other facts about mind and matter that Buddhism talks about. I've read that *sutta* you referred to where the Buddha says we shouldn't accept any teaching until we see for ourselves that it is true.

BHIKKHU: I see you remember the first part of the *Kālāma Sutta*, but do you remember the second part?

LEONA: The second?

BHIKKHU: After giving specific examples of wrong reasons for believing a teaching, the Buddha goes on to lead the sceptical Kālāmas into the Dhamma. He asks them whether greed, hate, and delusion are wholesome or unwholesome and whether they lead to suffering or not. The Kālāmas make the obvious answer that they are unwholesome and lead to suffering. In response to further questions they agree that the absence of these defilements and the positive cultivation of morality lead to blessing and happiness in this life. If this is so, the Buddha goes on to say, then there are four consolations for whomever is devoted to virtue. First, if there is a future world and if good and bad deeds have results for the doer, then the virtuous person knows himself safe and can expect a happy situation. Second, if there is no rebirth and if deeds have no future effect, then he at least lives happily in this world, without worry. Third, if evil things happen to evildoers, then he, who does no evil, is secure and free from harm. Fourth, if no evil things happen to evildoers, then he in any event will not meet with evil fortune.

LEONA: That's well said. Even a hardened sceptic would have to admire that reasoning. And if one goes *that* far one would have to admit that it would be wise to pay more attention to one's behaviour and even set out on a more systematic path of spiritual practice.

ERNEST: Such as the Noble Eightfold Path, Leona?

LEONA: (*Laughing*) Why yes, now that you mention it. We keep coming back to that, don't we?

BHIKKHU: (*Smiling*) Well, we *should* come back to it. But I hope you understand that this path is a path of practice and self-development and mindful investigation. It's not necessary at the outset to believe in rebirth or other difficult facets of the Dhamma. We need only bear these teachings in mind and watch as the evidence accumulates in our own experience.

LEONA: That's fair, that's certainly fair. I'd say a certain amount has accumulated already. I can see that good and bad deeds have effects here in this present life, and if those effects go beyond, say to a future birth, well, I'm open-minded about the matter. Tell me this, please. These connections we were speaking of—do they exist between animals and human beings? Can human beings be reborn as animals and vice versa?

BHIKKHU: We must first note that according to Buddhism there is no self or soul that is literally born again, but rather a chain of causes or a stream of life that springs up now here, now there, according to conditions. But in ordinary, conventional language we can certainly say that a human being can be reborn as an animal or vice versa. It all depends on the individual's *kamma*, his or her accumulated deeds.

LEONA: Ah, here we have the core of your opposition to cruelty to animals. We are related to them. We may even *become* them.

BHIKKHU: In the Buddhist view all sentient life is related. The differentiations are temporary, fluctuating, and merely provisional. Countless living beings go wandering through the endless cycles of *saṃsāra*, being born high or low, in this world or that, with much suffering or little suffering.

ERNEST: Hence the great Buddhist emphasis on compassion. Yes, I see. We are all part of an organic whole.

BHIKKHU: Yes, all sentient life is organic and inter-related, but you should not make the common, romantic mistake of thinking that this "whole" is *good. Saṃsāra* is, to one degree or another, suffering throughout, and we beings trapped in *saṃsāra* are suffering.

ERNEST: All the more reason for compassion, then!

BHIKKHU: Quite so. And here is a point of Dhamma I want to emphasise especially. One's own ultimate welfare and the welfare of other beings are perfectly harmonious. The life of moral restraint is a life of service to others, because it protects others, soothes them, and inspires them to similar effort. When we follow the path and strive to purify our minds we set incalculable reverberations going in the hearts of other beings. Never doubt that the Dhamma conduces to the greater good, even when circumstances seem to push us toward shabby expediency. The law of *kamma* sees to it that in the long run deeds work out according to their nature, so we should always take the wide view, always strive for detachment in our reflections, so that we can make wise choices.

ERNEST: If one lives as you suggest, being diligent in practising Dhamma, could one be reborn in a heavenly world, a world of bliss?

BHIKKHU: Yes, that's possible.

ERNEST: Wouldn't unadulterated bliss be as good as Nibbāna? Wouldn't that be the end of suffering?

BHIKKHU: No, the so-called heavenly worlds are not perfect refuges for two reasons. First, *all* worldly bliss is adulterated.

There is suffering in even the highest realms. It is very fine and attenuated, but it exists. In the ultimate sense, pleasure itself is suffering, a dis-ease, a kind of irritation to the mind that deprives it of peace. The second reason is that even though life in those planes is said to be very pleasant and long, it is still impermanent: it is going to come to an end; it cannot be relied upon forever; hence there is anxiety and uncertainty even for beings living there.

LEONA: A flawed heaven. How gloomy!

BHIKKHU: Actually, this human world is considered an especially fortunate place to be born. The beings in higher realms are so drenched with pleasure that they have little inducement to strive for deliverance. And the animals and beings in the unhappy lower planes are too unintelligent or too miserable to make spiritual progress. This human world with its puzzling mixture of pleasure and pain often makes people think.

LEONA: Indeed it does that!

BHIKKHU: We really need not speculate about other planes of life when our own provokes us to search for liberation. And now, of course, though the world is full of misery, still we have the priceless treasure of the Dhamma, which the Buddha discovered and made known to cure suffering and free beings from the wheel of birth and death.

ERNEST: Bhikkhu Tissa, it seems the Dhamma is a very demanding teaching.

BHIKKHU: And we are demanding people, are we not? We demand pleasure and security and comfort—and we demand them to be permanent! This is impossible, of course, because the universe is not under our control. So we suffer. And then we demand an end to suffering, preferably through no exertion of our own. We want an escape from old age and illness and death, but, as the Buddha says, this cannot be got by mere wanting, and not to get what one desires, that is suffering, too.

ERNEST: True, true. We are indeed contrary creatures! I see the justice of what you say—we have to make an effort if we really want to accomplish anything. But the question I ask myself is, how much do I want to accomplish?

BHIKKHU: Nobody can answer that question but you.

ERNEST: Considering my limitations I sometimes wonder if I couldn't sort of stop half-way, as it were—just practise basic morality and try to live a modest life and keep out of trouble.

BHIKKHU: The way of Dhamma is a way that goes against the stream of the world and the world's desires. If you cease to struggle against the current, do you think you will just remain stationary?

ERNEST: Well, no, considering the nature of my mind.

LEONA: Going with the flow just won't make it, huh?

BHIKKHU: Going with the flow means succumbing to craving and clinging, which pull us down to suffering. It is said that the Dhamma protects the Dhamma-farer. This means that one who resists craving and clinging, who makes an effort against the worldly stream, becomes stronger by that very effort, just as when we exercise a muscle we strengthen it. By overcoming even small problems with mindfulness and detachment we find ourselves increasingly able—and willing—to surmount spiritual obstacles. I think that if you try to apply the Dhamma in life you will quickly notice within yourself the growth of confidence.

ERNEST: There's something in that. I do feel some confidence—just a little bit!

BHIKKHU: The Buddha said that a follower should examine his teaching in the way that a goldsmith analyses gold—carefully inspecting, refining, testing it before concluding that it is real. So if you have undertaken to practise the Dhamma even a little, then please reflect on the result of that practice and see how you feel about it, see whether you feel cheered and inspired to go a little further.

ERNEST: Here we are—Leona and I—offering a meal to a monk and listening to him preach—something I would have thought ridiculous a year ago! I guess that says something.

LEONA: To me, Bhikkhu Tissa, the Dhamma is appealing because it seems to satisfy both the intellect and the emotions. I've never been a religious person, mainly because I couldn't believe passionately in the supernatural. On the other hand, the materialistic philosophies leave me cold, because they have no understanding of the mind and what for lack of a better word I will call the transcendental. They are earthbound and infinitely depressing. Then there is the swarm of cults and quasi-religions which are *both* hysterical and intellectually incoherent. Whew! It's enough to make me an absolute agnostic. Except ... agnosticism is itself a blind belief! Now I've studied the Dhamma a little bit, and while I don't understand everything, I find it, well, refreshing. As I said, it fits together intellectually and it gives scope to the desire for transcendence, the impulse to become purer or wiser than we now are. Just this morning, before you came, I read a passage in one of Ernest's books that summarised the Dhamma as clear, visible, leading onward—something succinct like that.

BHIKKHU: "Well expounded is the Dhamma by the Exalted One, directly visible, immediately effective, calling one to come and see, leading onward, to be personally realised by the wise."

LEONA: That's it. As clear a statement as I've heard. Now, if it can fulfil that promise...

BHIKKHU: The truths of the Dhamma are for us to examine and confirm. We have to remove the obstructions to our understanding by practising morality and training ourselves in the art of concentration. When the conscience is clear and the mind can hold steady on the objects of attention, then wisdom arises of its own nature. We don't create it.

ERNEST: But wisdom is not the end, is it?

BHIKKHU: No. Wisdom is the sword we use to cut off defilements, to clear a path for ourselves out of the jungle and into the open air.

ERNEST: Buddhism grants us immense freedom of action, doesn't it?

LEONA: And immense responsibility, it seems. If all planes of existence are somehow tied to suffering then probably we should use that freedom of action to get freedom ... of being! Or I might say, if it is *possible* to escape suffering and gain enlightenment, then if we don't *try*, our misery would be really our own fault.

ERNEST: What a predicament. Bhikkhu Tissa, you were right when you said that Buddhism challenges us.

BHIKKHU: The problem of existence and its solution are both contained within the Four Noble Truths. The truth of the omnipresence of suffering in *saṃsāra* and the truth of its arising out of craving point out our plight. The truth of the cessation of suffering and the truth of the way to accomplish that point out the escape from this plight. So you see, there is darkness and light—the darkness of pain and ignorance and confusion, and the light of understanding and deliverance. Life for the intelligent person should be a journey from dark to light.

ERNEST: But how long and how fast?

BHIKKHU: As long as it takes and as fast as you wish.

ERNEST: Well, it's a little frightening, but it's exhilarating, too. In time I might actually be able to make sense out of the universe! Already I feel a certain tension between my miserable old habits of mind and my urge to pursue the Dhamma further. It is sort of dazzling to think that I can walk down the street like anybody else but still be practising mindfulness, or still be reflecting on impermanence, suffering, and non-self. I wonder if I shouldn't be living in a cave or a jungle!

BHIKKHU: You'd still be dealing with the same mind in a cave, Ernest. Better to investigate in your own house—I mean, this very body and mind. The world is to be found there, and liberation from the world. Arising and passing away, suffering, and the empty, flickering personality can be seen and examined within. Wisdom isn't a treasure we can prospect for in the Himalayas; it appears only when conditions are right for it, when the mind is settled, not distracted.

LEONA: When I read the words of the Buddha I get a feeling of immense wisdom, and yet he doesn't answer some questions about the origin of the universe, about what happens to an enlightened person after death, and so on. Now, I'm sure he had good reasons for not answering what might be extraneous questions, but still ...

BHIKKHU: Never forget, Leona, that the Buddha was not out to build a reputation for himself, or to be a human computer spewing information, or to dazzle the ignorant with amazing secrets. He was out to cure suffering. He was a supreme genius, but he never lost sight of his practical purpose: to teach suffering and the way to the ending of suffering. He taught what was necessary. Whatever else he may have *known* it is useless to speculate about. Once, when the Buddha was seated in a forest with a company of monks, he took up a handful of leaves from the ground and showed them to the monks. He asked them which were more numerous, the leaves in his hand or the leaves in the entire forest. The monks reasonably noted that the leaves in his hand were very few compared to those in the entire forest. The Buddha then said that those in his hand were as the truths he had revealed to them, and those in the whole forest were as the truths he knew but had *not* revealed.

LEONA: And why hadn't he revealed them?

BHIKKHU: Because, the Buddha said, they were not useful, they did not lead to dispassion, to tranquillity, to higher knowledge, to enlightenment. Remember, the Buddha had no need to teach at all. He had attained enlightenment, he was free, he had vanquished suffering. There was nothing further he needed to do. Yet he did act, he did exert himself. Why? Simply because of his all-embracing compassion. He taught his followers everything they needed to know about suffering and how to conquer it themselves. He held back nothing of value. Before he died he declared that as a teacher he had never had a "closed fist." He gave unstintingly of the Dhamma that pointed to liberation, entrusting it to his followers who have preserved it and honoured it and offered it as the supreme refuge for a weary world, even to this very day.

ERNEST: That's an encouraging thought. If the Buddha had no personal need to teach anything to anybody yet did teach for the rest of his life, then surely he thought that the teaching would be effective, that his followers, even though they weren't Buddhas, could still attain enlightenment through their own efforts.

BHIKKHU: Yes, indeed. The Buddha is sometimes called the great physician for the ills of the world. He doesn't cure by magic or laying-on of hands or divine power. He prescribes for us the medicine of the Dhamma and instructs us in how to use it.

LEONA: But the patients have to be willing, don't they?

BHIKKHU: Oh yes. Some people complain about the emphasis on suffering in Buddhism; they prefer not to think about it. They suffer, they know they suffer, but they don't realise that suffering is a deep and terrible spiritual disease. Only when they take a close look at their situation do they feel moved to do something about it. It's like a man who smells smoke in his house. If he's intelligent he investigates and sees that his house is on fire. Rather than waiting to be burned, he looks around for an escape and makes use of it promptly—he climbs out a window and slides down the drainpipe. What the Buddha teaches us first of all *is* that our house is on fire—on fire with greed, with hate, with delusion, burning with sickness, old age, death, lamentation, despair.

ERNEST: The truth of suffering, in short.

BHIKKHU: And then the Buddha points out the reasons for this suffering and what can be done about it and how there might be ease and relief for us instead of anxiety and pain. And, more than this, the Buddha shows how our lives may become calmer, wiser, and purer, and how we may in fact achieve what we hardly can imagine: enlightenment, a radiant and unassailable security.

LEONA: (*Sighing*) It's a shame we are not living in the time of the Buddha himself.

BHIKKHU: Ah, but we are, Leona. We are! The Buddha says that whoever sees the Dhamma sees the Buddha. And the Dhamma is not only written in books, it is written in the elements of the world as well.

LEONA: What do you mean?

BHIKKHU: The three characteristics of existence—impermanence, suffering, and non-self—spring up everywhere for the benefit of the diligent meditator. Look at the flames there in the fireplace, snapping and curling and flickering in front of our eyes.

LEONA: Ah, impermanence, yes, of course.

BHIKKHU: Yes, both an instance and an emblem of the changing nature of reality.

ERNEST: Transience and change.

BHIKKHU: And more than that. Don't you see in those wavering sheets of fire and those sputtering little flames something futile and weary? They leap up, they fall back, they smoulder and fail.

ERNEST: An incompleteness, a restlessness. You might call it suffering!

BHIKKHU: And within that chemical reaction we call fire, within that shifting light and heat what's really going on? Is the fire one stable thing and the log another? Does the wood stay the same while the fire just happens to it?

LEONA: No, they're both changing, there's only change. The wood is always changing to something else. You could say it's not being, it's only becoming. Therefore ...

ERNEST: Therefore it's not a self! Just non-self. Well, Bhikkhu Tissa, this is something. Even my own fireplace can instruct me [in] the Dhamma.

BHIKKHU: And why stop there? Out the window there we can see that it's snowing a little harder. There! See that swirl of wind? Look at the flakes spinning against the greyness. What do they suggest to you?

LEONA: Change. Impermanence. And the there's the sadness of it—I don't know why, it's just the wandering, the endless unease. We could call it suffering, sure. And as before, in that change, in that process, I don't see any persisting element. No self. Just like the fire.

BHIKKHU: Just like the fire. And yet the one is blazing hot and the other is icy cold. Still the same truths are manifest in both. Do you see the principle I am getting at?

LEONA: I think I do. All the world is food for contemplation.

BHIKKHU: And above all, do not neglect your own body and mind. That's where craving clings the tightest, that's where ignorance resides.

LEONA: You are assuming, of course, that I'll keep investigating the Dhamma.

BHIKKHU: I am assuming it.

LEONA: (*Smiling*) Well, you're right, I guess. Can't quit now. I'll keep going a little further.

ERNEST: Going toward what, Leona?

LEONA: Why ... Let's call it the greater good, shall we?

ERNEST: Why not?

LEONA: It seems it's possible to live deliberately, and if so, I think one ought to live for the benefit of oneself and others.

ERNEST: And others, yes. Speaking of that. Uh, Leona, talking to this venerable monk has made me sure that I don't want to—I mean, I couldn't possibly accept that job at the chemical company.

LEONA: Oh, Ernest. As for the job ...

ERNEST: No, really, you have to see—I just wouldn't feel ...

LEONA: Peace, husband of mine! There is no dispute.

ERNEST: Say what?

LEONA: (*Smiling, laying a hand on his arm*) Under no circumstances can you accept that job. You are happy where you are. You don't want to be even distantly connected to the suffering of animals. I understand that now. I respect it. Venerable Tissa is skilful, I think, in nudging us in the direction of the Dhamma.

ERNEST: But you were so in favour of the job.

LEONA: (*Shrugging*) Ah, well. Impermanence!

ERNEST: You're a remarkable woman, Leona.

LEONA: It depends on who's doing the remarking! But enough. Let's not weary this tolerant monk any more today, all right? Look, Ernest, the snow is coming down harder. Maybe you had better drive Venerable Tissa home.

ERNEST: You don't have a "home," do you, Bhikkhu Tissa? Just a monastery.

BHIKKHU: There's no real home for any of us short of Nibbāna. But yes, perhaps it's time to go.

ERNEST: Thank you for your time.

BHIKKHU: And thank you for your food.

LEONA: You are the one who's given real food, Bhikkhu Tissa.

ERNEST: We appreciate your teaching.

BHIKKHU: I'm glad you do. But the fire teaches, too. And the snow. And your own hearts.

ERNEST: Shall we go, then?

They rise. Bhikkhu Tissa, wrapped up in his robes, follows Ernest out the door into the sudden cold and light of the snowy day. Leona stands on the doorstep and watches them go down to the car. The wind gusts and the snow falls harder, blurring the landscape and the vanishing figures. At the car, Bhikkhu Tissa turns, smiles, and waves. Or does he wave? She is not sure. Maybe he has pointed at the chaos of snowflakes, or the invisible clouds, or the ghostly horizon of the rooftops. Then the car rolls away. Leona stands gazing after for a moment. The world seems huge and full of silence. Snow—dust blows from the limbs of an oak.

Mettā

The Philosophy and Practice of Universal Love

by

Ācariya Buddharakkhita

WHEEL PUBLICATION NO. 365/366

Introduction

The Pali word *mettā* is a multi-significant term meaning loving kindness, friendliness, goodwill, benevolence, fellowship, amity, concord, inoffensiveness and non-violence. The Pali commentators define *mettā* as the strong wish for the welfare and happiness of others (*parahita-parasukha-karaṇa*). Essentially *mettā* is an altruistic attitude of love and friendliness as distinguished from mere amiability based on self-interest. Through *mettā* one refuses to be offensive and renounces bitterness, resentment and animosity of every kind, developing instead a mind of friendliness, accommodativeness and benevolence which seeks the well-being and happiness of others. True *mettā* is devoid of self-interest. It evokes within a warm-hearted feeling of fellowship, sympathy and love, which grows boundless with practice and overcomes all social, religious, racial, political and economic barriers. *Mettā* is indeed a universal, unselfish and all-embracing love.

Mettā makes one a pure font of well-being and safety for others. Just as a mother gives her own life to protect her child, so *mettā* only gives and never wants anything in return. To promote one's own interest is a primordial motivation of human nature. When this urge is transformed into the desire to promote the interest and happiness of others, not only is the basic urge of self-seeking overcome, but the mind becomes universal by identifying its own interest with the interest of all. By making this change one also promotes one's own well-being in the best possible manner.

Mettā is the protective and immensely patient attitude of a mother who forbears all difficulties for the sake of her child and ever protects it despite its misbehaviour. *Mettā* is also the attitude of a friend who wants to give one the best to further one's well-being. If these qualities of *mettā* are sufficiently cultivated through *mettā-bhāvanā*—the meditation on universal love—the result is the acquisition of a tremendous inner power which preserves, protects and heals both oneself and others.

Apart from its higher implications, today *mettā* is a pragmatic necessity. In a world menaced by all kinds of destructiveness, *mettā* in deed, word and thought is the only constructive means to bring concord, peace and mutual understanding. Indeed, *mettā* is the supreme means, for it forms the fundamental tenet of all the higher religions as well as the basis for all benevolent activities intended to promote human well-being.

The present booklet aims at exploring various facets of *mettā* both in theory and in practice. The examination of the doctrinal and ethical side of *mettā* will proceed through a study of the popular *Karaṇīya Mettā Sutta*, the Buddha's "Hymn of Universal Love." In connection with this theme we will also look at several other short texts dealing with *mettā*. The explanation of *mettā-bhāvanā*, the meditation on universal love, will give the practical directions for developing this type of contemplation as set forth in the main meditation texts of the Theravada Buddhist tradition, the *Visuddhimagga*, the *Vimuttimagga* and the *Paṭisambhidāmagga*.

1. The Karaṇīya Mettā Sutta
Hymn of Universal Love

1. *Karaṇīyam-atthakusalena*
Yan taṃ santaṃ padaṃ abhisamecca
Sakko uju ca sūjū ca
Suvaco c'assa mudu anatimānī

Who seeks to promote his welfare,
Having glimpsed the state of perfect peace,
Should be able, honest and upright,
Gentle in speech, meek and not proud.

2. *Santussako ca subharo ca*
Appakicco ca sallahukavutti
Santindriyo ca nipako ca
Appagabbho kulesu ananugiddho

Contented, he ought to be easy to support,
Not over-busy, and simple in living.
Tranquil his senses, let him be prudent,
And not brazen, nor fawning on families.

3. *Na ca khuddaṃ samācare kiñci*
Yena viññū pare upavadeyyuṃ
Sukhino va khemino hontu
Sabbe sattā bhavantu sukhitattā

Also, he must refrain from any action
That gives the wise reason to reprove him.
(Then let him cultivate the thought:)
May all be well and secure,
May all beings be happy!

4. *Ye keci pāṇabhūt'atthi*
Tasā vā thāvarā vā anavasesā
Dīghā vā ye mahantā vā
Majjhimā rassakānukathūlā

Whatever living creatures there be,
Without exception, weak or strong,
Long, huge or middle-sized,
Or short, minute or bulky,

5. *Diṭṭhā va yeva adiṭṭhā*
Ye ca dūre vasanti avidūre
Bhūtā vā sambhavesī vā
Sabbe sattā bhavantu sukhitattā

Whether visible or invisible,
And those living far or near,
The born and those seeking birth,
May all beings be happy!

6. *Na paro paraṃ nikubbetha*
Nātimaññetha katthaci naṃ kañci
Byārosanā paṭighasaññā
Nāññamaññassa dukkham-iccheyya

Let none deceive or decry
His fellow anywhere;
Let none wish others harm
In resentment or in hate.

7. *Mātā yathā niyaṃ puttaṃ*
Āyusā ekaputtam-anurakkhe
Evam'pi sabbabhūtesu
Mānasaṃ bhāvaye aparimāṇaṃ

Just as with her own life
A mother shields from hurt
Her own son, her only child,
Let all-embracing thoughts
For all beings be yours.

8. *Mettāñ ca sabba-lokasmiṃ*
Mānasaṃ bhāvaye aparimāṇaṃ
Uddhaṃ adho ca tiriyañca
Asambādhaṃ averam-asapattaṃ

Cultivate an all-embracing mind of love
For all throughout the universe,
In all its height, depth and breadth—
Love that is untroubled
And beyond hatred or enmity.

9. *Titthaṃ caraṃ nisinno vā*
Sayāno vā yāvat'assa vigatamiddho

Etaṃ satiṃ adhiṭṭheyya
Brahmam-etaṃ vihāraṃ idhamāhu

As you stand, walk, sit or lie,
So long as you are awake,
Pursue this awareness with your might:
It is deemed the Divine State here.

10. *Diṭṭhiñca anupagamma sīlavā*
Dassanena sampanno
Kāmesu vineyya gedhaṃ
Na hi jātu gabbhaseyyaṃ punar etī'ti

Holding no more to wrong beliefs,
With virtue and vision of the ultimate,
And having overcome all sensual desire,
Never in a womb is one born again.

2. The Background to the Mettā Sutta

The historical background which led the Buddha to expound the *Karaṇīya Mettā Sutta* is explained in the commentary written by Ācariya Buddhaghosa, who received it from an unbroken line of Elders going back to the days of the Buddha himself.

It is told that five hundred monks received instructions from the Buddha in the particular techniques of meditation suitable to their individual temperaments. They then went to the foothills of the Himalayas to spend the four months of the rains retreat by living a life of withdrawal and intensive meditation. In those days, a month or two before the rains retreat started, monks from all parts of the country would assemble wherever the Buddha lived in order to receive direct instruction from the Supreme Master. Then they would go back to their monasteries, forest dwellings or hermitages to make a vigorous attempt at spiritual liberation. This was how these five hundred monks went to the Buddha, who was staying at Sāvatthī in Jeta's Grove in the monastery built by Anāthapiṇḍika.

After receiving instructions they went in search of a suitable place, and in the course of their wandering they soon found a beautiful hillock at the foothills of the Himalayas. This, according to the commentary, "appeared like a glittering blue quartz crystal:

it was embellished with a cool, dense, green forest grove and a stretch of ground strewn with sand, resembling a pearl net or a silver sheet, and was furnished with a clean spring of cool water." The bhikkhus were captivated by the sight. There were a few villages nearby, and also a small market-town ideal as alms-resort. The monks spent a night in that idyllic grove and the next morning went to the market-town for alms.

The residents there were overjoyed to see the monks, since rarely did a community of monks come to spend the retreat in that part of the Himalayas. These pious devotees fed the monks and begged them to stay on as their guests, promising to build each a hut near the grove on the sandy stretch so that they could spend their days and nights plunged in meditation under the ancient boughs of the majestic trees. The bhikkhus agreed and the devotees of the area soon built little huts on the fringe of the forest and provided each hut with a wooden cot, a stool and pots of water for drinking and washing.

After the monks had settled down contentedly in these huts, each one selected a tree to meditate under, by day and by night. Now it is said that these great trees were inhabited by tree-deities who had a celestial mansion built, appropriately using the trees as the base. These deities, out of reverence for the meditating monks, stood aside with their families. Virtue was revered by all, particularly so by deities, and when the monks sat under the trees, the deities, who were householders, did not like to remain above them. The deities had thought that the monks would remain only for a night or two, and gladly bore the inconvenience. But when day after day passed and the monks still kept occupying the bases of the trees, the deities wondered when they would go away. They were like dispossessed villagers whose houses had been commandeered by the officials of visiting royalty and they kept watching anxiously from a distance, wondering when they would get their houses back.

These dispossessed deities discussed the situation among themselves and decided to frighten the monks away by showing them terrifying objects, by making dreadful noises and by creating a sickening stench. Accordingly, they materialised all these terrifying conditions and afflicted the monks. The monks soon grew pale and could no longer concentrate on their subjects of meditation. As the deities continued to harass them, they lost even their basic mindfulness, and their brains seemed to become smothered by the oppressing visions, noise and stench. When the monks assembled to wait upon the senior most Elder of the group, each one recounted his experiences. The Elder suggested: "Let us go, brethren, to the Blessed One and place our problem before him. There are two kinds of rains retreat—the early and the late. Though we will be breaking the early one by leaving this place, we can always take upon ourselves the late one after meeting the Lord." The monks agreed and they set out at once, it is said, without even informing the devotees.

By stages they arrived at Sāvatthī, went to the Blessed One, prostrated at his feet, and related their frightful experiences, pathetically requesting another place. The Buddha, through his supernormal power, scanned the whole of India, but finding no place except the same spot where they could achieve spiritual liberation, told them: "Monks, go back to the same spot! It is only by striving there that you will effect the destruction of inner taints. Fear not! If you want to be free from the harassment caused by the deities, learn this *sutta*. It will be a theme for meditation as well as a formula for protection (*paritta*).

Then the Master recited the *Karaṇīya Mettā Sutta*—the Hymn of Universal Love—which the monks learned by rote in the presence of the Lord. Then they went back to the same place.

As the monks neared their forest dwellings reciting the *Mettā Sutta,* thinking and meditating on the underlying meaning, the hearts of the deities became so charged with warm feelings of goodwill that they materialised themselves in human form and received the monks with great piety. They took their bowls, conducted them to their rooms, caused water and food to be supplied, and then, resuming their normal form, invited them to occupy the bases of the trees and meditate without any hesitation or fear.

Further, during the three months of the rains' residence, the deities not only looked after the monks in every way but made sure that the place was completely free from any noise. Enjoying perfect silence, by the end of the rainy season all the monks attained to the pinnacle of spiritual perfection. Every one of the five hundred monks had become an arahat.

Indeed, such is the power intrinsic in the *Mettā Sutta*. Whoever with firm faith will recite the *sutta*, invoking the protection of the deities and meditating on *mettā*, will not only safeguard himself in every way but will also protect all those around him, and will make spiritual progress that can be actually verified. No harm can ever befall a person who follows the path of *mettā*.

3. Three Aspects of Mettā

The *Mettā Sutta* consists of three parts, each of which focuses on a distinct aspect of *mettā*. The first part (lines 3 to 10) covers that aspect which requires a thorough and systematic application of loving kindness in one's day-to-day conduct. The second part (lines 11 to 20) expresses loving kindness as a distinct technique of meditation or culture of mind leading to *samādhi*—higher consciousness induced by absorption. And the third part (lines 21 to 40) underlines a total commitment to the philosophy of universal love and its personal, social and empirical extensions—loving kindness through all bodily, verbal and mental activities.

Mettā has been identified as that specific factor which "ripens" the accumulated merit (*puñña*) acquired by the ten ways for the acquisition of merit (*dasapuññakiriyavatthu*), such as the practice of generosity, virtue, etc. Again, it is *mettā* which brings to maturity the ten exalted spiritual qualities known as "perfections" (*pāramitā*).

The practice of *mettā* thus can be likened to bringing into being a great tree, from the time the seed is sown to the time the tree is heavily laden with luscious fruits and sends forth its sweet odour far and wide, attracting myriads of creatures to it to enjoy its tasty and nutritious bounty. The sprouting of the seed and the growth of the plant are, as it were, brought about by the first part of the *sutta*. In the second part the tree, robust and developed, is fully covered with fragrant and beautiful flowers, riveting all eyes upon it.

As a pattern of behaviour, the first aspect of *mettā* makes one's life grow like a tree, useful, generous and noble. *Mettā*, as meditation, effects that spiritual efflorescence whereby one's entire life becomes a source of joy for all. The third part envisages in this imagery the fruition of that process of spiritual development whereby one brings about an all-embracing application of spiritual love which can powerfully condition society as a whole and lead one to the heights of transcendental realisation.

The human mind is like a mine holding an inexhaustible storehouse of spiritual power and insight. This immense inner potential of merit can be fully exploited only by the practice of *mettā*, as is clear from the description of *mettā* as that "maturing force" which ripens the dormant merits. In the *Maṅgala Sutta* it is said that only after one has effected an elevating interpersonal relationship (by resorting to good company, etc.) does one choose the right environment for the merits of the past to find fruition. This finding of fruition is exactly what *mettā* does. Mere avoidance of wrong company and living in a cultured environment is not enough; the mind must be cultivated by *mettā*. Hence the allusion to the fruition of past merit.

4. The Ethics of Mettā

Ethics, in the Buddhist context, is right conduct, which brings happiness and peace of mind, and never gives rise to remorse, worry or restlessness of mind. This is the immediate psychological benefit. Right conduct also leads to a happy rebirth, enabling an aspirant to progress further on the onward path to spiritual liberation. It is also the basis for progress in Dhamma here and now. In other words, right speech, right action and right livelihood of the Buddha's Noble Eightfold Path constitute right conduct in the best sense.

Buddhist ethics is twofold: fulfilment of certain virtues (*cāritta*), and precepts of abstinence (*vāritta*). *Cāritta*, as found in the *Mettā Sutta*, is as follows:

> [He] Should be able, honest and upright,
> Gentle in speech, meek and not proud.
> Contented, he ought to be easy to support,
> Not over-busy, and simple in living.
> Tranquil his senses, let him be prudent,
> And not brazen, nor fawning on families.

Vāritta is covered by the next stanza (*gāthā*):

> Also, he must refrain from any action
> That gives the wise reason to reprove him.

Cāritta and *vāritta* are thus practised through *mettā* expressed in bodily and verbal action; the resultant inner happiness and altruistic urge is reflected by the aspirant's *mettā* of mental action, as found in the conclusion of the stanza:

> May all be well and secure,
> May all beings be happy!

The ethics of *mettā* thus provides not only subjective well-being, or the opportunity to progress in Dhamma here and now and to enjoy a happy rebirth in the future, but it means the giving of fearlessness and security—*abhayadāna* and *khemadāna*.

An analysis of the behaviour-pattern and traits commended by the *Mettā Sutta* for meaningful interaction, both with reference to persons individually and to society as a whole, provides ample insight into the great implications of the *sutta* for mental health.

Ability is not just mere efficiency or skill, but means doing a thing well, out of consideration for others, so that one may not cause inconvenience to others. As an able man can become very conceited, the practitioner is advised to be "honest and upright," while being "gentle in speech, meek and not proud" indeed a perfect synthesis and an equilibrium of traits.

He who is contented is "easy to support." Frugality, from consideration of others, is a noble trait. To the extent that one's own needs are cut down as an example to others and as a means not to inconvenience them, to that extent one shows refinement. The more gross and materialistic a person becomes, the more his needs increase. The yardstick to judge the mental health of a given society is thus the diminution of needs, that is to say, the element of satisfaction.

A materialistic and egocentric life is characterised not only by an increase in wants but also by restlessness, showing itself in being over-busy and overactive and lacking in moderation and self-restraint. *Mettā*, which promotes the well-being of all, naturally has to be built on such qualities of sober humanism as are reflected in having a few meaningful and select tasks which conduce to the maximum well-being of all concerned.

Living a simple life as an expression of *mettā* involves a reorientation of one's outlook and conduct, even in our competitive, pleasure-seeking and possession-minded world. A man of simple living is gentle, yet efficient and effective, and has restraint over his sense-faculties, being moderate, frugal and controlled. Mental culture through meditation for such a person becomes natural and effortless: hence the attribute "tranquil in his senses."

Mettā in conduct includes the exercising of prudence, that is to say, practical wisdom. It is only a sagacious and wise person who can really practise *mettā* in all its varied forms in daily life, and through all modes of human relationship. Self-righteousness, arising from a sense of being better or more devout than others, can be (and often is) a masquerade of spiritual practice. To be "not brazen, nor fawning on families" thus is a pointer for the person of *mettā* not to indulge in self-righteousness of any form.

Further, the practitioner of *mettā* is advised to refrain from any action, even social conventions, for which a wise man may reprove him as lacking in prudence or propriety. It is not good enough that one should be good, but one should also appear to be good, in consideration not only of one's own well-being but also of others' well-being. An exemplary life is to be lived for the benefit of all, for the welfare of society.

A person living thus now plunges into the cultivation of the all-embracing mind of *mettā* through definite techniques of meditation as envisaged in the remaining part of the *sutta*.

Mettā is also called a *paritta*—a spiritual formula capable of safeguarding one's well-being, protecting one against all dangers, and rescuing one from mishaps and misfortunes.

When the monks could not stay and meditate in that beautiful forest provided with all facilities because the deities were hostile to them, they had to leave the place. And when they were armed with the protection of the *Mettā Sutta*, which they recited and meditated upon throughout their journey, by the time they reached the place, the deities were full of friendly feelings and already waiting for them. Hostility had been turned into hospitality.

The protection of *paritta* works both subjectively and objectively. Subjectively, as *mettā* cleanses and strengthens the mind, it also awakens the dormant potentials, resulting in the spiritual transmutation of the personality. Transformed by *mettā*, the mind is no longer haunted by greed, hatred, lust, jealousy and those other mind-polluting factors which are one's real enemy and source of misfortune.

Objectively, *mettā* as a thought-force is capable of affecting any mind anywhere, developed or undeveloped. The radiation of *mettā* can not only calm a person or remove the darts of hate from within him, but in some cases can even cure him of severe illness. It is a common experience in Buddhist countries to see how people are cured from all sorts of diseases and freed from misfortunes through the recitation of *paritta*. Thus *mettā* is a real healing power. In this way does *mettā* act as a *paritta*, a healing formula affording safeguards

5. The Psychology of Mettā

The Pali commentaries explain:

One loves all beings:

(a) by the non-harassment of all beings and thus avoids harassment;
(b) by being inoffensive (to all beings) and thus avoids offensiveness;
(c) by not torturing (all beings) and thus avoids torturing;
(d) by the non-destruction (of all life) and thus avoids destructiveness;
(e) by being non-vexing (to all beings) and thus avoids vexing;
(f) by projecting the thought, "May all beings be friendly and not hostile";
(g) by projecting the thought, "May all beings be happy and not unhappy";
(h) by projecting the thought, "May all beings enjoy well-being and not be distressed."

In these eight ways one loves all beings; therefore, it is called universal love. And since one conceives (within) this quality (of love), it is of the mind. And since this mind is free from all thoughts of ill will, the aggregate of love, mind and freedom is defined as universal love leading to freedom of mind.

From the above passage it will be seen that *mettā* implies the "outgrowing" of negative traits by actively putting into practice the correlative positive virtues. It is only when one actively practises non-harassment towards all beings that one can outgrow the tendency to harass others. Similarly, it is with the other qualities of inoffensiveness, non-tormenting, non-destroying and non-vexing in deed, word and thought that one can outgrow the negative traits of being offensive, of tormenting others, of destructiveness and of vexation. Over and above such positive conduct and principled way of life, one further cultivates the mind through that specific technique of meditation called *mettā-bhāvanā,* which generates powerful thoughts of spiritualized love that grow boundless, making consciousness itself infinite and universal.

Thoughts that wish all beings to be friendly and never hostile, happy and never unhappy, to enjoy well-being and never be distressed, imply not only sublimity and boundlessness, but also utter freedom of mind. Hence the appropriateness of the expression "universal love leading to freedom of mind."

As for the meanings of the five aspects opposed by *mettā,* harassment is the desire to oppress or damage; offensiveness is the tendency to hurt or injure; torturing is a synonym of the sadistic tendency to torment, subjecting others to pain or misery; destructiveness is to put an end to or to finish, the trait of the extremist and the iconoclast; vexing is to tax, trouble or cause others worry and strain. Each of these tendencies is rooted in antipathy and malevolence, and provides a contrast with *mettā,* both as a mode of conduct and as a psychological state or attitude of mind.

The substitution of a negative trait by the opposed positive course implies a very developed and mature approach to life. The ability to remain non-harassing, inoffensive, non-torturing, non-destructive and non-vexing means a very refined, beautiful and loving mode of behaviour in a world where interaction between human beings creates so much tension and misery.

According to the *Visuddhimagga, mettā* is a "solvent" that "melts" not only one's own psychic pollutants of anger, resentment and offensiveness, but also those of others. Since it takes the approach of friendship, even the hostile one turns into a friend.

Mettā is characterised as that which "promotes welfare." Its function is to "prefer well-being" rather than ill. It manifests as a force that "removes annoyance" and its proximate cause is the tendency to see the good side of things and beings and never the faults. *Mettā* succeeds when it loves, and it fails when it degenerates into worldly affection.

It will be clear from this analysis that only when one tends to see the good in people, and prefers the welfare of others, and accordingly is inoffensive (to remove any annoyance or hurt) and actively promotes well-being, does *mettā* function as a solvent. It is said that the ultimate purpose of *mettā* is to attain transcendental insight, and if that is not possible, it will at least effect a rebirth in the sublime sphere of the Brahma world, apart from bringing inner peace and a healthy state of mind here and now. Hence the Buddha's assurance in the *Mettā Sutta:*

> Holding no more to wrong beliefs,
> With virtue and vision of the ultimate,
> And having overcome all sensual desire,
> Never in a womb is he born again.

Love wards off ill will, which is the most damaging of emotions. Hence it is said: "For this is the escape from ill will, friends, that is to say, the freedom of mind wrought by universal love" (Dīgha Nikāya, III 234).

In the practice of *mettā* it is important to understand the emotions which nullify *mettā* either by being similar or being dissimilar. The *Visuddhimagga* calls them "the two enemies—the near and the remote." Greed, lust, worldly affection, sensuality—all these are said to be the "near enemies" because they are similar in tendencies. The lustful also sees the "good side" or "beauty," and therefore gets involved. Love should be protected from it lest the masquerades of these emotions deceive the meditator.

Ill will, anger and hatred, being dissimilar emotions, therefore constitute the "remote enemy." The remote enemy can easily be distinguished so one need not be afraid of it, but one should overcome it by projecting a higher force, that of love. But one has to be wary of the near enemy because it creates self-deception, which is the worst thing that can happen to an individual.

It is said that *mettā* begins only when there is zeal in the form of a desire to act. Having commenced through earnest effort, it can be continued only when the five mental hindrances—sensual desire, ill will, sloth and torpor, restlessness and worry, and doubt—are put down. *Mettā* reaches consummation with the attainment of absorption (*jhāna*).

6. Meditation on Mettā

There are various ways of practising *mettā-bhāvanā*, the meditation on universal love. Three of the principal methods will be explained here. These instructions, based on canonical and commentarial sources, are intended to explain the practice of *mettā*-meditation in a clear, simple and direct way so that anyone who is earnest about taking up the practice will have no doubts about how to proceed. For full instructions on the theory and practice of *mettā-bhāvanā* the reader is referred to the *Visuddhimagga*, Chapter IX.

Method 1

Sit down in a comfortable posture in a quiet place—a shrine room, a quiet room, a park, or any other place providing privacy and silence. Keeping the eyes closed, repeat the word "*mettā*" a few times and mentally conjure up its significance—love as the opposite of hatred, resentment, malevolence, impatience, pride and arrogance, and as a profound feeling of good will, sympathy and kindness promoting the happiness and well-being of others.

Now visualise your own face in a happy and radiant mood. Every time you see your face in the mirror, see yourself in a happy mood and put yourself in this mood during meditation. A person in a happy mood cannot become angry or harbour negative thoughts and feelings. Having visualised yourself in a happy frame of mind, now charge yourself with the thought; "May I be free from hostility, free from affliction, free from distress; may I live happily." As you suffuse yourself in this way with the positive thought-force of love, you become like a filled vessel, its contents ready to overflow in all directions.

Next, visualise your meditation teacher, if living; if not, choose some other living teacher or revered person. See him in a happy frame of mind and project the thought: "May my teacher be free from hostility, free from affliction, free from distress; may he live happily."

Then think of other people who are to be revered, and who are also living—monks, teachers, parents and elders, and intensely spread towards each one of them the thought of *mettā* in the manner mentioned already: "May they be free from hostility, free from affliction, free from distress; may they live happily."

The visualisation must be clear and the thought-radiation must be "willed" well. If the visualisation is hurried or the wishing is performed in a perfunctory or mechanical way, the practice will be of little avail, for then it will be merely an intellectual pastime of thinking about *mettā*. One must clearly understand that to think about *mettā* is one thing, and to do *mettā*, to actively project the will-force of loving kindness, is quite another.

Note that only a living person is to be visualised, not a dead one. The reason for this is that the dead person, having changed form, will be out of the focus of *mettā*-projection. The object of *mettā* always is a living being, and the thought-force will become ineffective if the object is not alive.

Having radiated thoughts of *mettā* in the order already mentioned—oneself, the meditation teacher and other revered persons—one should now visualise, one by one, one's dear ones beginning with the members of one's family, suffusing each one with abundant rays of loving kindness. Charity begins at home: if one cannot love one's own people one will not be able to love others.

While spreading *mettā* towards one's own family members, care should be taken to think of a very dear one, like one's husband or wife, at the end of this circle. The reason for this is that the intimacy between husband and wife introduces the element of worldly love which defiles *mettā*. Spiritual love must be the same towards all. Similarly, if one has had a temporary misunderstanding or quarrel with any family member or relative, he or she should be visualised at a later stage to avoid recalling the unpleasant incidents.

Next, one should visualise neutral people, people for whom one has neither like nor dislike, such as one's neighbours, colleagues in one's place of work, bare acquaintances, and so on. Having radiated loving thoughts on everyone in the neutral circle, one should now visualise persons for whom one has dislike, hostility or prejudice, even those with whom one may have had a temporary misunderstanding. As one visualises disliked persons, to each one must mentally repeat: "I have no hostility towards him/her, may he/she also not have any hostility towards me. May he/she be happy!"

Thus, as one visualises the persons of the different circles, one "breaks the barrier" caused by likes and dislikes, attachment and hatred. When one is able to regard an enemy without ill will and with the same amount of goodwill that one has for a very dear friend, *mettā* then acquires a sublime impartiality, elevating the mind upward and outward as if in a spiral movement of ever-widening circles until it becomes all-embracing.

By visualisation is meant "calling to mind" or visualising certain objects, such as a person, a certain area or a direction or a category of beings. In other words it means imagining the people towards whom thoughts of love are to be projected or spread. For instance, you imagine your father and visualise his face in a very happy and radiant mood and project the thought towards the visualised image, mentally saying: "May he be happy! May he be free from disease or trouble! May he enjoy good health." You may use any thought which promotes his well-being.

By radiation is meant, as explained above, the projection of certain thoughts promoting the well-being of those persons towards whom one's mind is directed. A *mettā*-thought is a powerful thought-force. It can actually effect what has been willed. For wishing well-being is willing and thus is creative action. In fact, all that man has created in different fields is the result of what he has willed, whether it is a city or a hydro-electric project, a rocket going to the moon, a weapon of destruction, or an artistic or literary masterpiece. Radiation of thoughts of *mettā*, too, is the development of a willpower that can effect whatever is willed. It is not a rare experience to see diseases cured or misfortunes warded off, even from a great distance, by the application of the thought-force of *mettā*. But this thought-force has to be generated in a very specific and skilful way, following a certain sequence.

The formula for radiating *mettā* that is used here has come down from the ancient *Paṭisambhidāmagga:* "May they be free from hostility, free from affliction, free from distress; may they live happily" (*avera hontu, abyāpajjhā hontu, anīgha hontu, sukhi attānaṃ pariharantu*). The commentarial explanation of these terms is highly significant. "Free from hostility" (*avera*) means absence of hostility whether aroused on account of oneself or others, or on account of oneself because of others or of others because of oneself or others. One's anger towards oneself might take the form of self-pity, remorse or a gripping sense of guilt. It can be conditioned by interaction with others. Hostility combines anger and enmity. "Free from affliction" (*abyāpajjha*) means absence of pain or physical suffering. "Free from distress" (*anīgha*) means the absence of mental suffering, anguish or anxiety, which often follows upon hostility or bodily affliction. It is only when one is free from hostility, affliction and distress that one "lives happily," that is, conducts oneself with ease and happiness. Thus all these terms are interconnected.

By order is meant visualising objects, one after the other, by taking the path of least resistance, in a graduated sequence, which progressively widens the circle and therewith the mind itself. The *Visuddhimagga* is emphatic about this order. According to Ācariya Buddhaghosa, one must start the meditation on *mettā* by visualising oneself, and thereafter a person for whom one has reverence, then one's dear ones, then neutral people, then hostile persons. As one radiates thoughts of love in this order, the mind breaks all barriers between oneself, a revered one, a dear one, a neutral one and a hostile one. Everyone comes to be looked upon equally with the eye of loving kindness.

In the *Visuddhimagga* Ācariya Buddhaghosa gives a very apt analogy for the breaking of the barriers: "Suppose bandits were to come to the meditator who is sitting in a place with a respected, a dear, a neutral, and a hostile or wicked person and demand, 'Friend, we want one of you for the purpose of offering human sacrifice.' If the meditator were to think, 'Let him take this one or that one,' he has not broken down the barriers. And even if he were to think, 'Let none of these be taken, but let them take me,' even then he has not broken down the barriers since he seeks his own harm, and *mettā* meditation signifies the well-being of all. But when he does not see the need for anyone to be given to the bandits and impartially projects the thought of love towards all, including the bandits, it is then that he would break down the barriers."

Method 2

The first method of practising meditation on *mettā* employs the projection of loving thoughts to specific individuals in order of increasing remoteness from oneself. The second method presents an impersonal mode of radiating *mettā* which makes the mind truly all-embracing, as suggested by the Pali term *mettā-cetovimutti,* "the liberation of mind through universal love." The unliberated mind is imprisoned within the walls of egocentricity, greed, hatred, delusion, jealousy and meanness. As long as the mind is in the grip of these defiling and limiting mental factors, for so long it remains insular and fettered. By breaking these bonds, *mettā* liberates the mind, and the liberated mind naturally grows boundless and immeasurable. Just as the earth cannot be rendered "earthless," even so the mind of *mettā* cannot be limited.

After completing the radiation of *mettā* towards selected persons, when the mind breaks the barriers existing between oneself and revered ones, beloved ones, friends, neutral ones and hostile ones, the meditator now embarks on the great voyage of impersonal radiation, even as an ocean-worthy ship voyages through the vast, measureless ocean, nevertheless retaining a route and a goal as well. The technique is as follows.

Imagine the people residing in your house as forming an aggregate, then embrace all of them within your heart, radiating the *mettā* thoughts: "May all those dwelling in this house be free from hostility, free from affliction, free from distress; may they live happily." Having visualised one's own house in this manner, one must now visualise the next house, and all its residents, and then the next house, and the next, and so on, until all the houses in that street are similarly covered by all-embracing loving kindness. Now the meditator should take up the next street, and the next, until the entire neighbourhood or village is covered. Thereafter, extension by extension, direction-wise, should be clearly visualised and spread with *mettā*-rays in abundant measure. In this way the entire town or the city is to be covered; then the district and the entire state should be covered and radiated with thoughts of *mettā.*

Next, one should visualise state after state, starting with one's own state, then the rest of the states in the different directions, the east, south, west and north. Thus one should cover the whole of one's country, geographically visualising the people of this land regardless of class, race, sect or religion. Think: "May everyone in this great land abide in peace and well-being! May there be no war, no strife, no misfortune, no maladies! Radiant with friendliness and good fortune, with compassion and wisdom, may all those in this great country enjoy peace and plenty."

One should now cover the entire continent, country by country, in the eastern, southern, western and northern directions. Geographically imagining each country and the people therein according to their looks, one should radiate in abundant measure thoughts of *mettā*: "May they be happy! May there be no strife and discord! May goodwill and understanding prevail! May peace be unto all!"

Thereafter one should take up all the continents—Africa, Asia, Australia, Europe, North and South America—visualising country by country and people by people, covering the entire globe. Imagine yourself at a particular point of the globe and then project powerful rays of *mettā*, enveloping one direction of the globe, then another, then another and so on until the whole globe is flooded and thoroughly enveloped with glowing thoughts of universal love.

One should now project into the vastness of space powerful beams of *mettā* towards all beings living in other realms, first in the four cardinal directions—east, south, west and north—then in the intermediary directions—northeast, southeast, southwest, northwest—and then above and below, covering all the ten directions with abundant and measureless thoughts of universal love.

Method 3

According to the cosmology of Buddhism there are numberless world-systems inhabited by infinitely varied categories of beings in different stages of evolution. Our earth is only a speck in our world-system, which again is a minute dot in the universe with its innumerable world-systems. Towards all beings everywhere one should radiate thoughts of boundless love. This is developed in the next method of practice, the universalization of *mettā*.

The universalization of *mettā* is effected in these three specific modes:

1. generalised radiation (*anodhiso-pharaṇa*),
2. specified radiation (*odhiso-pharaṇa*),
3. directional radiation (*disa-pharaṇa*).

According to the *Paṭisambhidāmagga*, the generalised radiation of *mettā* is practised in five ways, the specified radiation in seven ways, and the directional radiation in ten ways. These ten directional ways may be combined with the five categories of general radiation and with the seven categories of specified radiation, as we will show. In each of these modes of practice, any of the four phrases of the standard *mettā* formula—"May they be free from hostility, free from affliction, free from distress; may they live happily"—may be used as the thought of radiation. Thus four types of thought applied to five, seven, and 120 objects of *mettā* amount to 528 modes of radiation. Any of these can be used as a vehicle for attaining absorption (*jhāna*) through the technique of *mettā-bhāvanā*. (See Vism IX.58)

Generalised Radiation

The five ways of generalised radiation are as follows:

1. "May all beings *(sabbe sattā)* be free from hostility, free from affliction, free from distress; may they live happily."
2. "May all those that breathe (*sabbe pāṇā*) be free from hostility, free from affliction, free from distress; may they live happily."
3. "May all creatures (*sabbe bhūtā*) be free from hostility, free from affliction, free from distress; may they live happily."
4. "May all those with individual existence (*sabbe puggalā*) be free from hostility, free from affliction, free from distress; may they live happily."
5. "May all those who are embodied (*sabbe attabhāvapariyapannā*) be free from hostility, free from affliction, free from distress; may they live happily."

Specified Radiation

The seven ways of specified radiation are as follows:

1. "May all females (*sabbā itthiyo*) be free from hostility, free from affliction, free from distress; may they live happily."
2. "May all males (*sabbe purisā*) be free from hostility, free from affliction, free from distress; may they live happily."
3. "May all the Noble Ones (*sabbe ariyā*) be free from hostility, free from affliction, free from distress; may they live happily."
4. "May all worldlings (*sabbe anariyā*) be free from hostility, free from affliction, free from distress; may they live happily."

5. "May all gods (*sabbe devā*) be free from hostility, free from affliction, free from distress; may they live happily."
6. "May all human beings (*sabbe manussā*) be free from hostility, free from affliction, free from distress; may they live happily."
7. "May all those in states of woe (*sabbe vinipātikā*) be free from hostility, free from affliction, free from distress; may they live happily."

Directional Radiation

The ten ways of directional radiation involve sending thoughts of *mettā* to all beings in the ten directions. This method, in its basic form, is applied to the class of beings (*sattā*), the first of the five generalised objects of *mettā*. But it can be developed further by extending *mettā* through each of the five ways of generalised radiation and the seven ways of specified radiation, as we will see.

I.

1. "May all beings in the eastern direction be free from hostility, free from affliction, free from distress; may they live happily."
2. "May all beings in the western direction be free from hostility, free from affliction, free from distress; may they live happily."
3. "May all beings in the northern direction be free from hostility, free from affliction, free from distress; may they live happily."
4. "May all beings in the southern direction be free from hostility, free from affliction, free from distress; may they live happily."
5. "May all beings in the northeastern direction be free from hostility, free from affliction, free from distress; may they live happily."
6. "May all beings in the southwestern direction be free from hostility, free from affliction, free from distress; may they live happily."
7. "May all beings in the northwestern direction be free from hostility, free from affliction, free from distress; may they live happily."
8. "May all beings in the southeastern direction be free from hostility, free from affliction, free from distress; may they live happily."

9. “May all beings below (in the downward direction) be free from hostility, free from affliction, free from distress; may they live happily.”
10. “May all beings above (in the upward direction) be free from hostility, free from affliction, free from distress; may they live happily.”

II.

1–10. “May all those that breathe life in the eastern direction ... above be free from hostility, free from affliction, free from distress; may they live happily.”

III.

1–10. “May all creatures in the eastern direction ... above be free from hostility, free from affliction, free from distress; may they live happily.”

IV.

1–10. “May all those with individual existence in the eastern direction ... above be free from hostility, free from affliction, free from distress; may they live happily.”

V.

1–10. “May all those who are embodied in the eastern direction ... above be free from hostility, free from affliction, free from distress; may they live happily.”

VI.

1–10. “May all females in the eastern direction ... above be free from hostility, free from affliction, free from distress; may they live happily.”

VII.

1–10. “May all males in the eastern direction ... above be free from hostility, free from affliction, free from distress; may they live happily.”

VIII.

1–10. "May all Noble Ones in the eastern direction ... above be free from hostility, free from affliction, free from distress; may they live happily."

IX.

1–10. "May all worldlings in the eastern direction ... above be free from hostility, free from affliction, free from distress; may they live happily."

X.

1–10. "May all gods in the eastern direction ... above be free from hostility, free from affliction, free from distress; may they live happily."

XI.

1–10. "May all human beings in the eastern direction ... above be free from hostility, free from affliction, free from distress; may they live happily."

XII.

1–10. "May all those in states of woe in the eastern direction ... above be free from hostility, free from affliction, free from distress; may they live happily."

Explanation

In this technique of universalizing *mettā*, each of the five categories of generalised radiation refers to the total dimension of animate, sentient, or organic existence, belonging to the three mundane spheres, namely, the *kāmaloka,* the sphere of sensory existence where desire is the primal motivation; the *rūpaloka,* the realm of the radiant Brahma gods with subtle form; and the *arūpaloka,* the realm of the formless beings with pure mental life. Whether it is a "being," or that which "breathes," or a "creature," or that which has "individual existence," or that which "is embodied"—all refer to the totality of animate existence, the distinction being that each term expresses comprehensively a certain aspect of life in its entirety.

While visualising each category one should keep in mind the specific aspect expressed by its designation. If one trains the mind in the manner of a "mental drill" after having exercised it with the first two methods, the meaning of the five unspecified or generalised terms will become clear. By the time one has completed the two methods, the consciousness will be sufficiently developed and all-embracing. And with such a consciousness, when each of these universal concepts is grasped, the universalization becomes effortless. It may be pointed out that visualisation of each of these is no longer of individual objects, but of a concept which is total and all-embracing. The radiation in this case becomes a "flowing out" of love in abundant measure towards the conceptualised mental object—all beings, all creatures, etc.

Each of the seven categories of specified radiation comprehends a part of the total range of life, and in combination with the others expresses the whole. *Itthi* refers to the female principle in general, incorporating all females among the *devas*, human beings, animals, demons, spirits and denizens of hell. *Purisa* means the male principle evident in all the spheres of existence, and both *itthi* and *purisa* together comprehend the entirety. Again, from another angle, the *ariyas* or the spiritually transformed seers, and the anariyas or worldlings bound to the wheel of becoming, comprehend the totality. Ariyas are those who have entered the transcendental path; they are to be found in the human world and the celestial worlds and therefore they constitute the tip of the pyramid of sentient existence. Worldlings are in all the spheres of existence and constitute the body of the pyramid from the base to the tip, so to say. Likewise, the three categories of *deva, manussa* and *vinipātika*—gods, human beings, and those fallen into states of woe—comprehend the totality in terms of cosmological status. *Devas*, the radiant celestial beings, comprise the upper layer, human beings the middle layer, and *vinipātikas* the lower layer of the cosmological mound.

The "mental drill" in terms of directional radiation, the radiation of *mettā* to the above twelve categories of beings in the ten directions, makes the universalization of *mettā* a most exhilarating experience. As one mentally places oneself in a particular direction and then lets love flow out and envelop the entire region, one literally transports the mind to the sublimest heights leading to *samādhi*, concentrated absorption of the mind.

When one projects this total wish for others to dwell happily, free from hostility, affliction and distress, not only does one elevate oneself to a level where true happiness prevails, but one sets in motion powerful vibrations conducing to happiness, cooling off enmity, relieving affliction and distress. It will be seen, therefore, that universal love simultaneously infuses well-being and happiness and removes the mental and physical suffering caused by the mental pollutants of hostility, enmity and anger.

7. The Blessings of Mettā

> Monks, when universal love leading to liberation of mind is ardently practised, developed, unrelentingly resorted to, used as one's vehicle, made the foundation of one's life, fully established, well consolidated and perfected, then these eleven blessings may be expected. What eleven?
>
> "One sleeps happily; one wakes happily; one does not suffer bad dreams; one is dear to human beings; one is dear to non-human beings; the gods protect one; no fire or poison or weapon harms one; one's mind gets quickly concentrated; the expression of one's face is serene; one dies unperturbed; and even if one fails to attain higher states, one will at least reach the state of the Brahma world.
>
> Monks, when universal love leading to liberation of mind is ardently practised, developed, unrelentingly resorted to, used as one's vehicle, made the foundation of one's life, fully established, well consolidated and perfected, then these eleven blessings may be expected.
>
> Aṅguttara Nikāya, 11:16

Mettā cetovimutti—universal love leading to liberation of mind—signifies the attainment of *samādhi*, absorption based upon meditation on *mettā*. Since *mettā* liberates the mind from the bondage of hatred and anger, selfishness, greed and delusion, it constitutes a state of liberation. Every time one practises *mettā*, for however short a period, one enjoys a measure of freedom of mind. Measureless freedom of mind, however, is to be expected only when *mettā* is fully developed into *samādhi*.

The various applications of *mettā*, as indicated by the terms "practised, developed," etc., signify a well-structured force brought about not only by specific hours of meditation, but also by converting all one's deeds, words and thoughts into acts of *mettā*.

By "practised" (*āsevita*) is meant the ardent practice of *mettā*, not as a mere intellectual exercise, but by committing oneself wholeheartedly to it and making it life's guiding philosophy, something which conditions one's attitudes, outlook and conduct.

By "developed" (*bhāvita*) is implied the various processes of inner culture and mental integration effected by the practice of meditation on universal love. Since meditation brings about unification of mind by integrating the various faculties, it is called development of mind. The Buddha taught that the entire mental world is developed by the practice of meditation on universal love, leading to mind's liberation and the transformation of the personality.

"Unrelentingly resorted to" (*bahulīkata*) emphasises repeated practice of *mettā* all through one's waking hours, in deed, word and thought, and maintaining the tempo of *mettā*-awareness throughout. Repeated action means generation of power. All the five spiritual powers, namely, faith, vigour, mindfulness, concentration and wisdom, are exercised and cultivated by the repeated practice of *mettā*.

"Used as one's vehicle" (*yānikata*) signifies a "total commitment" to the ideal of *mettā* as the only valid method for the solution of interpersonal problems and as an instrument for spiritual growth. When *mettā* is the only "mode of communication," the only vehicle, life automatically is a "divine abiding" as mentioned in the *Mettā Sutta*.

"Made the foundation of one's life" (*vatthukata*) is making *mettā* the basis of one's existence in all respects. It becomes the chief resort, the haven, the refuge of one's life, making one's refuge in the Dhamma a reality.

"Fully established" (*anuṭṭhita*) refers to a life that is firmly rooted in *mettā*, has anchorage in *mettā* under all circumstances. When *mettā* is effortlessly practised, not even by error does one violate the laws of universal love.

"Well consolidated" (*paricita*) means one is so habituated to *mettā* that one remains effortlessly immersed in it, both in meditation as well as in one's day-to-day conduct.

"Perfected" (*susamāraddha*) indicates a mode of completeness through total adherence and development, leading to that fully integrated state in which one enjoys perfect well-being and spiritual felicity, indicated by the passage detailing the eleven blessings of *mettā*.

The benefits of *mettā* are indeed great and comprehensive. For a follower of the Buddha this is one supreme instrument that can be wielded with advantage everywhere.

8. The Power of Mettā

The subjective benefit of universal love is evident enough. The enjoyment of well-being, good health, peace of mind, radiant features, and the affection and goodwill of all are indeed great blessings of life accruing from the practice of *mettā*-meditation. But what is even more wonderful is the impact which *mettā* has on the environment and on other beings, including animals and *devas*, as the Pali scriptures and commentaries illustrate with a number of memorable stories.

Once the Buddha was returning from his alms-round together with his retinue of monks. As they were nearing the prison, in consideration of a handsome bribe from Devadatta, the Buddha's evil and ambitious cousin, the executioner let loose the fierce elephant Nālāgiri, which was used for the execution of criminals. As the intoxicated elephant rushed towards the Buddha trumpeting fearfully, the Buddha projected powerful thoughts of *mettā* towards it. Venerable Ānanda, the Buddha's attendant, was so deeply concerned about the Buddha's safety that he ran in front of the Buddha to shield him, but the Buddha asked him to stand aside since the projection of love itself was quite sufficient. The impact of the Buddha's *mettā*-radiation was so immediate and overwhelming that by the time the animal neared the Buddha it was completely tamed as though a drunken wretch had suddenly become sober by the magical power of a spell. The tusker, it is said, bowed down in reverence in the way trained elephants do in a circus.

The *Visuddhimagga* records the case of one landlord of Pātaliputra (modern Patna), Visākha by name. It seems he had heard that the island of Sri Lanka was a veritable garden of Dhamma with its innumerable shrines and stupas adorning the isle. And blessed with a favourable climate, the people were highly righteous, following the Teaching of the Buddha with great fervour and sincerity.

Visākha decided to visit Sri Lanka and spend the rest of his life there as a monk. Accordingly, he made over his great fortune to his wife and children and left home with a single gold coin. He stopped for some time at the port town of Tamralipi (modern Tamluk) waiting for a ship, and during that time engaged himself in business and made a thousand gold coins.

Eventually he reached Sri Lanka and went to the capital city of Anurādhapura. There he went to the famous Mahāvihāra and asked the abbot's permission to enter the Sangha. As he was led to the chapter house for the ordination ceremony, the purse containing the thousand gold coins dropped out from under his belt. When asked, "What is it?" he said, "I have a thousand gold coins, sir." When he was told that a monk cannot possess any money, he said, "I don't want to possess it but I wanted to distribute it among all who come for this ceremony." Accordingly he opened his purse and strewed the entire yard of the chapter house, saying, "Let no one who has come to witness Visākha's ordination depart empty-handed."

After spending five years with his teacher, he now decided to go to the famous Cittalapabbata forest, where a good number of monks with supernatural powers lived. Accordingly, he went to the jungle-monastery of Cittalapabbata. On his way he came to a fork in the road and stood wondering which way to turn. Since he had been practising *mettā*-meditation assiduously, he found a certain *deva* living in the rock there, holding out a hand pointing the road to him. After reaching the Cittalapabbata jungle-monastery, he occupied one of the huts.

Having stayed there for four months, as he was thinking of leaving the next morning, he heard somebody weeping, and when he asked, "Who is that?" the *deva* living in the manila tree at the end of the walkway said, "Venerable sir, I am Maniliya (i.e., belonging to the manila tree)."

"Why are you weeping?"

"Because you are thinking of going away from here."

"What good does my living here do you?"

"Venerable sir, so long as you live here, the *devas* and other non-human beings treat each other with kindness. When you are gone, they will again start their wrangling and quarrels."

"Well, if my living here makes all of you live at peace, it is good." And so he stayed on for another four months. It is said that when he again thought of going, again the deity wept. So this Elder stayed on permanently and attained Nibbāna there. Such is the impact of *mettā-bhāvanā* on others, even among invisible beings.

There is also the famous story of the cow. It seems that a cow was giving milk to her calf in a forest. A hunter wanting to kill her flung a spear which, when it struck her body, bounced off like a palm leaf. So mightily powerful is *mettā*—loving kindness. This is not the case of one who has developed *mettā-samādhi.* It is a simple case of the consciousness of love for the offspring.

Indeed, the power of *mettā* can never be told enough. The commentaries to the Pali Canon are replete with stories, not only of monks, but also of ordinary people who overcame various dangers, including weapons and poison, through the sheer strength of *mettā*—selfless love.

But let not *mettā* be mistaken as a mere sentiment. It is the power of the strong. If the leaders from different walks of life were to give *mettā* a fair trial, no principle or guideline to action would be found to possess greater efficiency or fruitfulness in all spheres.

In everything man is the ultimate unit. If man decides to substitute *mettā* as a policy of action for aggression and ill will, the world will turn into a veritable abode of peace. For it is only when man shall have peace within himself, and boundless goodwill for others, that peace in the world will become real and enduring.

Dāna:
The Practice of Giving

Selected Essays

by

Susan Elbaum Jootla,
Lily de Silva, M.O' C. Walshe,
Nina van Gorkom, Ācariya Dhammapāla

Edited by

Bhikkhu Bodhi

WHEEL PUBLICATION NO. 367/368/369

Introduction

Bhikkhu Bodhi

The practice of giving is universally recognized as one of the most basic human virtues, a quality that testifies to the depth of one's humanity and one's capacity for self-transcendence. In the teaching of the Buddha, too, the practice of giving claims a place of special eminence, one which singles it out as being in a sense the foundation and seed of spiritual development. In the Pali *suttas* (discourses) we read time and again that "talk on giving" (*dānakathā*) was invariably the first topic to be discussed by Buddha in his "graduated exposition" of the Dhamma. Whenever the Buddha delivered a discourse to an audience of people who had not yet come to regard him as their teacher, he would start by emphasizing the value of giving. Only after his audience had come to appreciate this virtue would he introduce other aspects of his teaching, such as morality, the law of *kamma*, and the benefits in renunciation, and only after all these principles had made their impact on the minds of his listeners would he expound to them that unique discovery of the Awakened Ones, the Four Noble Truths.

Strictly speaking, giving does not appear in its own right among the factors of the Noble Eightfold Path, nor does it enter among the other requisites of enlightenment (*bodhipakkhiyā dhammā*). Most probably it has been excluded from these groupings because the practice of giving does not by its own nature conduce directly and immediately to the arising of insight and the realization of the Four Noble Truths. Giving functions in the Buddhist discipline in a different capacity. It does not come at the apex of the path, as a factor constituent of the process of awakening, but rather it serves as a basis and preparation which underlies and quietly supports the entire endeavour to free the mind from the defilements.

Nevertheless, though giving is not counted directly among the factors of the path, its contribution to progress along the road to liberation should not be overlooked or underestimated. The prominence of this contribution is underscored by the place which the Buddha assigns to giving in various sets of practices he has laid down for his followers. Besides appearing as the first topic in the graduated exposition of the Dhamma, the practice of giving also figures as the first of the three bases of meritorious deeds (*puññakiriyavatthu*), as the first of the four means of benefiting others (*saṅgahavatthu*), and as the first of the ten *pāramis* or "perfections." The latter are the sublime virtues to be cultivated by all aspirants to enlightenment, and to the most exalted degree by those who follow the way of the Bodhisatta aimed at the supreme enlightenment of perfect Buddhahood.

Regarded from another angle, giving can also be identified with the personal quality of generosity (*cāga*). This angle highlights the practice of giving, not as the outwardly manifest act by which an object is transferred from oneself to others, but as the inward disposition to give, a disposition which is strengthened by outward acts of giving and which in turn makes possible still more demanding acts of self-sacrifice. Generosity is included among the essential attributes of the *sappurisa*, the good or superior person, along with such other qualities as faith, morality, learning and wisdom. Viewed as the quality of generosity, giving has a particularly intimate connection to the entire movement of the Buddha's path. For the goal of the path is the destruction of greed, hate and delusion, and the cultivation of generosity directly debilitates greed and hate, while facilitating that pliancy of mind that allows for the eradication of delusion.

The present *Wheel* publication has been compiled in order to explore in greater depth this cardinal Buddhist virtue, the practice of giving, which in writings on applied Buddhism is so often taken for granted that it is usually passed over without comment. In this issue four practising Buddhists of today, all of whom combine a textual knowledge of the Buddha's teachings with a personal commitment to the path, set forth their understanding of the various aspects of giving and examine it in relation to the wider body of Dhamma practice.

The collection concludes with a translation of an older document—the description of the Bodhisatta's practice of giving by the medieval commentator, Ācariya Dhammapāla. This has been extracted from his *Treatise on the Pāramis*, found in his commentary to the Cariyāpiṭaka.

The Practice of Giving[1]

Susan Elbaum Jootla

Giving (*dāna*) is one of the essential preliminary steps of Buddhist practice. When practised in itself, it is a basis of merit or wholesome *kamma*. When coupled with morality, concentration and insight, it leads ultimately to liberation from *saṃsāra*, the cycle of repeated existence. Even those who are well-established on the path to emancipation continue to practise giving as it is conducive to wealth, beauty and pleasure in their remaining lifetimes. Bodhisattas complete the *dānapārami* or perfection of giving to the ultimate degree by happily donating their limbs and their very lives to help other beings.

Like all good deeds, an act of giving will bring us happiness in the future, in accordance with the kammic law of cause and effect taught by the Buddha. Giving yields benefits in the present life and in lives to come whether or not we are aware of this fact, but when volition is accompanied by understanding, we can greatly increase the merits earned by our gifts.

The amount of merit gained varies according to three factors: the quality of the donor's motive, the spiritual purity of the recipient, and the kind and size of the gift. Since we have to experience the results of our actions, and good deeds lead to good results and bad deeds to bad results, it is sensible to try to create as much good *kamma* as possible. In the practice of giving, this would mean keeping one's mind pure in the act of giving, selecting the worthiest recipients available, and choosing the most appropriate and generous gifts one can afford.

---

1. The inspiration and basic material for this essay come from *The Perfection of Generosity* (*Dāna Pārami*), by Saya U Chit Tin, published as No. 3 in the Dhamma Series of the Sayagi U Ba Khin Memorial Trust, U.K., Splatts House, Heddington near Calne, Wiltshire, England. I am deeply grateful to Saya U Chit Tin and to all the other teachers associated with the International Meditation Centres at Heddington, U.K. and Rangoon, Burma.

The Factor of Volition

The volition of the donor before, during and after the act of generosity is the most important of the three factors involved in the practice of giving: "If we have no control over our minds we will not choose proper gifts, the best recipient ... we will be unable to prepare them properly. And we may be foolish enough to regret having made them afterwards."[2] Buddhist teaching devotes special attention to the psychological basis of giving, distinguishing among the different states of mind with which one may give. A fundamental distinction is made between acts of giving that lack wisdom and those that are accompanied by wisdom, the latter being superior to the former. An example of a very elementary kind of giving would be the case of a young girl who places a flower on the household shrine simply because her mother tells her to do so, without having any idea of the significance of her act.

Generosity associated with wisdom before, during and after the act is the highest type of giving. Three examples of wise giving are: giving with the clear understanding that according to the kammic law of cause and effect, the generous act will bring beneficial results in the future; giving while aware that the gift, the recipient and the giver are all impermanent; and giving with the aim of enhancing one's efforts to become enlightened. As the giving of a gift takes a certain amount of time, a single act of giving may be accompanied by each of these three types of understanding at a different stage in the process.

The most excellent motive for giving is the intention that it strengthen one's efforts to attain Nibbāna. Liberation is achieved by eliminating all the mental defilements (*kilesa*), which are rooted in the delusion of a controlling and lasting "I." Once this illusion is eradicated, selfish thoughts can no longer arise. If we aspire to ultimate peace and purity by practising generosity, we will be developing the *dānapārami*, the perfection of giving, building up a store of merit that will bear its full fruit with our attainment of enlightenment. As we progress towards that goal, the volition involved in acts of giving will assist us by contributing towards the

2. U Chit Tin, *The Perfection of Generosity*, Introduction.

pliancy of the mind, an essential asset in developing concentration and wisdom, the prime requisites of liberation.

Ariyas—noble ones, those who have attained any of the four stages of holiness—always give with pure volition because their minds function on the basis of wisdom. Those below this level sometimes give carelessly or disrespectfully, with unwholesome states of mind. The Buddha teaches that in the practice of giving, as in all bodily and verbal conduct, it is the volition accompanying the act that determines its moral quality. If one is offering something to a monk, doing so without adopting a respectful manner would not be proper. Throwing a coin to a beggar in order to get rid of him would also be considered a defilement of giving. One should think carefully about the relevance and the timing of a gift for it to bring the best results. A gift given through an intermediary—for example, having a servant give food to a monk rather than giving it by one's own hand—also detracts from the value of the gift. When one gives without realizing that one must experience the results of one's deeds, an act of giving again diminishes in meritorious potency.

If one only plans on giving a donation but does not fulfil one's plan, the merit earned will be very slight. Thus we should always follow up our intentions of generosity expeditiously, unless something intervenes to prevent our doing so. If, after having given a gift, we should subsequently regret our action, much of the merit of the deed will be lost.

A moral person gives politely and respectfully. Whether the gift is spontaneous or planned, he or she will make sure that the timing and contents of the gift are appropriate for the receiver. Many housewives in Buddhist countries regularly invite a few monks to their homes to receive alms food early in the day. Before feeding the family, these women always offer the food to the bhikkhus with their own hands.

One might contribute to a certain cause from fear that friends would disapprove if one did not give. Giving in response to such social pressure will have weak, though still beneficial, results. Charitable actions undertaken to gain a good reputation are also selfish and hence not a very valuable kind of giving. Nor can it be praiseworthy when one gives merely to return a favour or in expectation of a reward. The former is like repaying a debt, the latter analogous to offering a bribe.

The Recipient of Gifts

The purity of the recipient is another factor which helps determine the kammic fruitfulness of a gift. The worthier the receiver, the greater the benefits that will come to the donor; hence it is good to give to the holiest people available. The Buddha teaches that the worthiest recipients of gifts are the ariyas, the noble ones, such as the Buddha himself and those of his disciples who have reached the supramundane paths and fruits; for it is their purity of mind, attained by wisdom, that makes the act of giving capable of yielding abundant benefits. Therefore, to earn the maximum merit, we should give as much as we can and as often as possible, to the noble ones. Gifts to a bhikkhu who strives for the state of a noble one, or to a Buddhist meditator who lives by the Five Precepts, will also yield bountiful results.

When ariyas accept offerings, they do so to provide an opportunity for the donor to earn merit. Non-returners and Arahats in particular, who have attained the two highest stages of sanctity, have eliminated desire for sense objects. Thus when they are given gifts their minds remain detached from the objects presented and are filled with compassion for the giver.

The story of Sīvali in the *Dhammapada* Commentary[3] is an example of the great merit which even a small gift can yield when presented to the Saṅgha led by the Buddha. At the time of Vipassī Buddha, the citizens of a country were competing with their king to see who could make the greatest offering to the Buddha and Saṅgha. The citizens had obtained everything for their offering except fresh honey, and they sent out several messengers, each with plenty of money, to buy the missing ingredient.

One of these men met a villager who happened to be bringing a newly harvested honeycomb into the city for sale. The messenger was only able to buy it from the peasant when he had offered his entire allowance of a thousand pieces of money, which was far more than a single honeycomb was worth. The villager said: "Are you crazy? This honey isn't worth a farthing but you offer me a thousand pieces of money for it. What is the explanation for

3. E.W. Burlingame, trans. *Buddhist Legends* (London: Pali Text Society, 1969), 2:212-16.

this?" The other man told him that the honey was worth so much to him because it was the final item on the menu for the citizens' offering to the Buddha. The peasant spontaneously replied, "If that is the case, I will not sell it to you for a price; if I may receive the merit of the offering, I will give it to you." The citizens were impressed with the faith of this man who so readily gave up a windfall and enthusiastically agreed that he should receive the merit of the offering.

Because of this simple gift at the time of Vipassī Buddha, the villager was reborn numerous times in celestial planes and then became the prince who inherited the throne of Benares. In his final lifetime, he became the Elder Sīvali and attained Arahatship as a disciple of the present Buddha. Even after that, his gift of the honeycomb continued to bear fruit. To honour the one who had made the sweet gift aeons before, the gods provided lodging and food for the Buddha and five hundred of his monks, including Sīvali, when for several days they had been walking along a deserted road.

The practice of giving is also beneficial when directed to someone who is not spiritually advanced. If the donor's intention is good, then even though the receiver is immoral, the donor will earn merit and further, by his act of giving, he will strengthen within himself his own disposition to renunciation. A gift mentally offered to the noble Saṅgha but physically presented to a monk who is morally corrupt will still bear great fruit. To be sure, we should not pretend that a bad person is good, but we must be most careful of our own attitude while giving, as our attitude is the factor over which we have most control.

The Objects to be Given

The third factor involved in giving is the gift itself, which can be either material or immaterial. *Dhammadāna*, the gift of the noble teaching, is said by the Buddha to excel all other gifts (Dhp 354). Those who expound his teachings—monks who preach sermons or recite from the *Tipiṭaka*, teachers of meditation—frequently share the Truth, thus practising the highest kind of generosity. Those of us who are not qualified to teach the Dhamma can give the gift of Dhamma in other ways. We can donate Dhamma books or pay for the translation or publication of a rare or new manuscript propagating the Buddha-word. We can discuss the Dhamma informally and encourage others to keep precepts or to take up meditation. We might write an explanation of some aspect of the Dhamma for the benefit of others. Giving cash or labour to a meditation centre or helping support a meditation teacher can also be considered the gift of the Dhamma, as the purpose of the centre and the teacher is the transmission of the Buddha's teaching.

The most common type of gift is material things. A material object need not have a high monetary value for it to bring great results, as the story of Sīvali and honeycomb illustrates. If a poor man gives a monk the cup of rice that was to be his only food for the day, the man is making a great donation which may bear abundant fruit, while if a prosperous merchant, knowing in advance that the monk was coming for alms, were to give the same small portion of rice, he would reap meager fruits. We should try to give things whose quality is at least as good as those we use ourselves, like the people in Burma, who buy the best fruits on the market as gifts for the monks although these fruits are much too expensive for them to consume themselves.

Gifts to the Saṅgha may consist of food, robes, medicine or monasteries, each of which has a wide range. The limits are set by the rules of the Vinaya which the Buddha established, as and when required, to keep the Bhikkhu Saṅgha pure and strong. Lay people who understand the monks' rules can earn vast merit by donating the proper things at the proper time to the order of monks and nuns.

A story about Visākhā, the Buddha's chief woman lay disciple, offers a delightful illustration of the results of large-scale charity.[4] When Visākhā was to be married, elaborate preparations and gifts were arranged by her father. He gave her five hundred cartloads each of money, of gold, silver and copper vessels, of silk clothes, of ghee and rice, and of farm implements. Then he decided that she must also take cattle with her. He gave orders to his men to allow out of their pen just as many animals as would fill a particular lane. When the cows had filed out and stood close together in that

4. *Buddhist Legends*, 2:67-68.

road, he had the corral closed, saying, "These cattle are enough for my daughter." However, after the gate had been latched securely, powerful bulls and milk cows jumped over the barrier to join the animals going with Visākhā. Her father's servants could not keep them inside no matter how hard they tried.

All these cattle came to Visākhā because, in a former lifetime long ago at the time of Buddha Kassapa, she had given a generous gift of five kinds of dairy products to a company of 20,000 monks and novices. As the youngest of the seven daughters of King Kiki of Benares, she continued to urge the monks to take more milk, curds, ghee, etc., even when they said they had eaten enough. That gift earned her the merit of having such a large number of cattle go along with her at her marriage in the lifetime when she was Visākhā, and no one could prevent this merit from bearing its fruit.

Material gifts of a religious nature would include contributions towards the erection of a new temple or shrine, gold leaf to help gild the umbrella of a shrine, or the purchase of a Buddha statute for a temple. The recipients of such gifts are the general public—whoever comes to the temple or worships before the Buddha image.

Mundane gifts to the citizens of one's town would include donations to various welfare organizations, a contribution to a hospital or public library, keeping a neighbourhood park neat and clean. If one does not merely contribute funds for such projects but provides physical labour as well, the kammic results will be even greater. Gifts of this sort can be quite meritorious if preceded, accompanied, and followed by pure mental volitions.

The Perfection of Giving

There is a mode of giving which completely disregards the qualities of the recipient and even the mundane fruits of the merit acquired by giving. Such generosity springs from the motive of renunciation, the thought of eliminating one's attachments to one's possessions, and thus aims at giving away the dearest and most difficult gifts. Bodhisattas give in this manner whenever the opportunity presents itself, strictly in order to fulfil the *dānapārami*, the "perfection of giving," which is the first of the ten perfections they must cultivate to the highest degree in order to attain Buddhahood. A Bodhisatta's work to complete the perfection of giving demands much more of him than other beings could emulate. Many *jātaka* stories relate how the Bodhisatta who was to become the Buddha Gotama gave things away with absolutely no thought of himself or of the mundane benefits that might follow. A Bodhisatta's only concern in practising generosity is to fulfil the requirements for Buddhahood.

The Basket of Conduct[5] contains ten stories of the Bodhisatta's former lives. In one of these lifetimes, he was a Brahmin named Saṅkha who saw a Paccekabuddha, or non-teaching enlightened one, walking barefoot on a desert path. Saṅkha thought to himself, "Desiring merit, seeing one eminently worthy of a gift of faith, if I do not give him a gift, I will dwindle in merit." So the Brahmin, who had a very delicate constitution, presented his sandals to the Paccekabuddha even though his own need for them was greater (Cp 1.2).

Another time the Bodhisatta was a great emperor named Mahā-Sudassana. He had criers proclaim several times every day, in thousands of places throughout his empire, that anyone who wanted anything would be given it if he just came there and asked. "If there came a mendicant beggar, whether by day or by night, receiving whatever goods he wanted, he went away with hands full." Mahā-Sudassana gave with completely open-handed generosity, "without attachment, expecting nothing in return, for the attainment of Self-Awakening" (Cp 1.4).

A Bodhisatta must give more difficult gifts than material goods to fulfil the highest form of the perfection of generosity. He must freely give the parts of his body, his children, his wife, and even his own life. As King Sivi, our Bodhisatta plucked out both his eyes with his bare hands and gave them to Sakka, the king of the gods. Sakka had come to Sivi in the guise of a blind old man, just to provide him with the opportunity to make this remarkable gift. Sivi did this with no hesitation prior to the act, nor with any reluctance during the act, nor with any hint of regret afterwards. He said that this gift was made "for the sake of Awakening itself. The two eyes were not disagreeable to me. Omniscience was dear to me, therefore I gave the eyes" (Cp 1.8).

---

5. Cariyāpiṭaka, translated by I.B. Horner, included in *Minor Anthologies of the Pali Canon*, Part III (London: Pali Text Society, 1975).

As Prince Vessantara, the Bodhisatta gave the auspicious, powerful royal elephant to the people of a rival kingdom merely because they had requested it. As a result of this liberality, he and his wife and two small children were banished to a remote mountain. They lived there in the forest, Vessantara tending his son and daughter in their hut while his wife spent the days gathering the wild fruits on which they lived. One day a traveller chanced by and asked the Bodhisatta to give him the children. Vessantara gave them away without any hesitation at all. Later he gave away his virtuous wife too. "Neither child was disagreeable to me, the Lady Maddī was not disagreeable. Omniscience was dear to me, therefore I gave away those who were dear" (Cp 1.9). It should be noted that at that time, a man's children and wife were generally considered his property. Ages before, the Lady Maddī had aspired to be the wife of the Bodhisatta and to share whatever trials he had to undergo along the path to Buddhahood. The result of her own *kamma* complemented Prince Vessantara's volition and led to her being given away. Their children must also have been experiencing the results of their own past deeds when they had to leave their parents.

Another time the Bodhisatta took birth as a wise hare. That existence came to an end when, joyously, he jumped into a fire after inviting a famished brahmin (again, Sakka in disguise) to eat him roasted. Because of the purity of the Bodhisatta's mind while making his highest gift of his entire body and life, the blazing fire did not hurt him as it burned his flesh. In relating the story he said that, in fact, the fire had calmed him and brought him peace as if it had been cool water, because he had accomplished the complete perfection of giving.

The Ultimate Goal of Giving

The goal of the Buddhist path is emancipation from the suffering of repeated existence in *saṃsāra*. The Buddha taught that uprooting ignorance and the mental defilements it nurtures will bring us to Nibbāna, the utter cessation of suffering. Unwholesome mental tendencies make us cling to what we mistakenly take to be our "selves," they keep us struggling to satisfy our insatiable sense desires with objects that are inherently transitory and thus unsatisfying.

The Buddha said that the practice of giving will aid us in our efforts to purify the mind. Generous gifts accompanied by wholesome volition help to eradicate suffering in three ways. First, when we decide to give something of our own to someone else, we simultaneously reduce our attachment to the object; to make a habit of giving can thus gradually weaken the mental factor of craving, one of the main causes of unhappiness. Second, giving accompanied by wholesome volition will lead to happy future births in circumstances favourable to encountering and practising the pure Dhamma. Third, and most important, when giving is practised with the intention that the mind becomes pliant enough for attainment of Nibbāna, the act of generosity will help us develop virtue, concentration and wisdom (*sīla, samādhi, paññā*) right in the present. These three stages make up Buddha's Noble Eightfold Path, and perfecting the path leads to the extinction of suffering.

If we give in the hope of winning luxury in future lives, we may attain our aim providing that we adhere to the principles of virtuous conduct. According to the Buddha, however, the motivation of working for liberation is far superior to that of aiming at mundane happiness in future births. This is because a gift made with the desire for pleasure is accompanied in part by the unwholesome psychological root craving (*taṇhā*). The merits earned by such gifts are exhausted in transient pleasure, and such mundane happiness keeps us revolving in the round of rebirth, which in the deepest sense is always *dukkha*, subject to suffering. Giving associated with craving cannot contribute to the one form of happiness that does not perish. The happiness that releases from the round comes only with the full elimination of craving. Gifts untainted by craving and attachment can only be made during a *Buddha-sāsana*, the period when the teachings of a Buddha are available. So when we give now, during such a time, we should do so with the aim of putting an end to craving. With the end of craving, suffering ceases, and that is liberation.

May the merits of this gift
of the Dhamma
be shared by all beings!

Giving in the Pali Canon

Lily de Silva

Dāna, giving, is extolled in the Pali Canon as a great virtue. It is, in fact, the beginning of the path to liberation. When the Buddha preaches to a newcomer he starts his graduated sermon with an exposition on the virtues of giving (*dānakathā*, Mv 1:7.5). Of the three bases for the performance of meritorious deeds (*puññakiriyavatthu*), giving is the first, the other two being virtue and mental culture (AN 8:36). It is also the first of the ten *pāramitā* perfected by a Buddha. Therefore on the march towards liberation as an Arahant or a Buddha, one initially has to practise *dāna*.

Function of Giving

Giving is of prime importance in the Buddhist scheme of mental purification because it is the best weapon against greed (*lobha*), the first of the three unwholesome motivational roots (*akusalamūla*). Greed is wrapped up with egoism and selfishness, since we hold our personalities and our possessions as "I" and "mine." Giving helps make egoism thaw; it is the antidote to cure the illness of egoism and greed. "Overcome the taint of greed and practise giving," exhorts the *Devatā Saṃyutta* (SN 1:35 v. 86). The *Dhammapada* admonishes us to conquer miserliness with generosity (*jine kadariyaṃ dānena*, Dhp 223).

It is difficult to exercise this virtue of giving proportionate to the intensity of one's greed and selfishness. As such the *Devatā Saṃyutta* equates giving to a battle (*dānañ ca yuddhañ ca samānam āhu*, SN 1:33 v. 97). One has to fight the evil forces of greed before one can make up one's mind to give away something dear and useful to oneself. The *Laṭukikopama Sutta* illustrates how a man lacking in spiritual strength finds it hard to give up a thing he has been used to (MN 66.8). A small quail can come to death when it gets entangled in a useless, rotten creeper. Though weak, a rotten creeper is a great bond for a small bird. But even an iron chain is not too big a bond for a strong elephant. Similarly, a poor wretched man of weak character would find it difficult to part with his shabby meagre belongings, while a strong-charactered king will even give up a kingdom once convinced of the dangers of greed.

Miserliness is not the only hindrance to giving. Carelessness and ignorance of the working of *kamma* and survival after death are equally valid causes (*maccherā ca pamādā ca evaṃ dānaṃ na dīyati,* SN 1:32 v. 85). If one knows the moral advantages of giving, one will be vigilant to seize opportunities to practise this great virtue. Once the Buddha said that if people only knew the value of giving as he does, they would not take a single meal without sharing their food with others (It 1:26).

Qualities of the Donor

The *suttas* (e.g., DN 5.13) employ a number of terms to describe the qualities of a donor. He is a man with faith (*saddhā*), he has faith in the nobility of a morally sound life, in the teachings of *kamma* and survival after death. He believes in the possibility of the moral and spiritual perfection of man. In short, he is not a materialist, and he has faith in the Buddha, the Dhamma and the Saṅgha. He is not merely a giver (*dāyako*), he is a lordly giver (*dānapati*). The commentary explains the concept of "lordly giver" in the following words: "He who himself enjoys delicious things but gives to others what is not delicious is a donor who is a slave to the gifts he gives. He who gives things of the same quality as he himself enjoys is one who is like a friend of the gift. He who satisfies himself with whatever he can get but gives delicacies to others is a lordly giver, a senior and a master of the gifts given."

The donor is also described as one who keeps an open house for the needy (*anāvaṭadvāro*). He is like a wellspring (*opānabhūto*) for recluses, Brahmins, the destitute, wayfarers, wanderers and beggars. Being such a one he does meritorious deeds. He is munificent (*muttacāgo*) and is interested in sharing his blessings with others (*dānasaṃvibhāgarato*). He is a philanthropist who understands the difficulties of the poor (*vadaññū*). He is open-handed and is ready to comply with another's request (*payatapāṇī*). He is one fit to be asked from (*yācayogo*). He takes delight in distributing gifts to the needy (*vossaggarato*), and has a heart bent on giving (*cāgaparibhāvitacitto*). Such are the epithets used in the *suttas* to describe the qualities of the liberal-minded.

A noble giver is one who is happy before, during and after giving (AN 6:37). Before giving he is happy anticipating the opportunity to exercise his generosity. While giving he is happy that he is making another happy by fulfilling a need. After giving he is satisfied that he has done a good deed. The *suttas* list generosity as one of the important qualities that go to make a gentleman (AN 8:35). The Buddha compares the man who righteously earns his wealth and gives of it to the needy to a man who has both eyes, where as the one who only earns wealth but does no merit is like a one-eyed man (AN 3:29). The wealthy man who enjoys his riches by himself without sharing is said to be digging his own grave (Sn 102).

The Donations

Practically anything useful can be given as a gift. The *Cullaniddesa* (Nidd II 523)[6] gives a list of fourteen items that are fit to be given for charity. They are robes, alms food, dwelling places, medicine and other requisites for the sick, food, drink, cloths, vehicles, garlands, perfume, unguent, beds, houses and lamps. It is not necessary to have much to practise generosity, for one can give according to one's means. Gifts given from one's meagre resources are considered very valuable (*appasmā dakkhiṇā dinnā sahassena samaṃ mitā*, SN 1:32 v. 89; *dajjāppasmim pi yācito*, Dhp 224). If a person leads a righteous life even though he ekes out a bare existence on gleanings, looks after his family according to his means, but makes it a point to give from his limited stores, his generosity is worth more than a thousand sacrifices (SN 1:32 v. 92). Alms given from wealth righteously earned is greatly praised by the Buddha (AN 6:45; It 3:25; AN 5:41). A householder who does so is said to be one who is lucky here and hereafter. In the *Māgha Sutta* of the *Suttanipāta* (Sn 3.5) the Buddha highly appreciates Māgha who says that he earns through righteous means and liberally gives of it to the needy.

Even if one gives a small amount with a heart full of faith one can gain happiness hereafter. The *Vimānavatthu* supplies ample examples. According to the *Ācāmadāyikā-vimānavatthu*, the alms given consisted of a little rice crust, but as it was given with

6. PTS Pali edition. There is no English translation of this work.

great devotion to an eminent Arahant, the reward was rebirth in a magnificent celestial mansion. The *Dakkhiṇāvibhaṅga Sutta* (MN 142.9–13) states that an offering is purified on account of the giver when the giver is virtuous, on account of the recipient when the recipient is virtuous, on account of both the giver and the recipient if both are virtuous, by none if both happen to be impious. *Dhammadāna*, the dissemination of the knowledge of the Dhamma, is said to excel all other forms of giving (*sabbadānaṃ dhammadānaṃ jināti*, Dhp 354).

The *Aṅguttara Nikāya* mentions five great gifts which have been held in high esteem by noble-minded men from ancient times (AN 8:39). Their value was not doubted in ancient times, it is not doubted at present, nor will it be doubted in future. The wise recluses and Brahmins had the highest respect for them. These great givings comprise the meticulous observance of the Five Precepts. By doing so one gives fearlessness, love and benevolence to all beings. If one human being can give security and freedom from fear to others by his behaviour, that is the highest form of *dāna* one can give, not only to mankind, but to all living beings.

The Donee

The *suttas* also describe the person to whom alms should be given (AN 8:39). Guests, travellers and the sick should be treated with hospitality and due consideration. During famines the needy should be liberally entertained. The virtuous should be first entertained with the first fruits of fresh crops. There is a recurrent phrase in the *suttas* (DN 5.13; 23.32) describing those who are particularly in need of public generosity. They are recluses (*samaṇa*), Brahmins (*brāhmaṇa*), destitutes (*kapaṇa*), wayfarers (*addhika*), wanderers (*vaṇibbaka*) and beggars (*yācaka*). The recluses and Brahmins are religious persons who do not earn wages. They give spiritual guidance to the laity and the laity is expected to support them. The poor need the help of the rich to survive and the rich become spiritually richer by helping the poor. At a time when transport facilities were meagre and amenities for travellers were not adequately organized, the public had to step in to help the wayfarer. Buddhism considers it a person's moral obligation to give assistance to all these types of people.

In the *Aṅguttara Nikāya* the Buddha describes, with sacrificial terminology, three types of fires that should be tended with care and honour (AN 7:44). They are *āhuneyyaggi, gahapataggi* and *dakkhiṇeyyaggi*. The Buddha explained that *āhuneyyaggi* means one's parents, and they should be honoured and cared for. *Gahapataggi* means one's wife and children, employees and dependents. *Dakkhiṇeyyaggi* represents religious persons who have either attained the goal of Arahantship or have embarked on a course of training for the elimination of negative mental traits. All these should be cared for and looked after as one would tend a sacrificial fire. According to the *Mahāmaṅgala Sutta*, offering hospitality to one's relatives is one of the great auspicious deeds a lay person can perform (Sn 262–63).

King Kosala once asked the Buddha to whom alms should be given (SN 3:24). The Buddha replied that alms should be given to those by giving to whom one becomes happy. Then the king asked another question: To whom should alms be offered to obtain great fruit? The Buddha discriminated the two as different questions and replied that alms offered to the virtuous bears great fruit. He further clarified that offerings yield great fruit when made to virtuous recluses who have eliminated the five mental hindrances (*nīvaraṇa*) and cultivated moral habits, concentration, wisdom, emancipation and knowledge and vision of emancipation (*sīla, samādhi, paññā, vimutti, vimuttiñāṇadassana*).

In the *Sakka Saṃyutta* (SN 11.16) Sakka asked the same question from the Buddha: Gifts given to whom bring the greatest results? The Buddha replied that what is given to the Saṅgha bears the greatest results. Here the Buddha specifies that what he means by "Saṅgha" is the community of those upright noble individuals who have entered the path and who have established themselves in the fruit of saintship, and who are endowed with morality, concentration and wisdom. It is important to note that "Saṅgha" according to the Vinaya means a sufficient group of monks to represent the Order of monks for various ecclesiastical purposes (Mv 9:4.1). But in the *suttas* "Saṅgha" means the four pairs of noble individuals or the eight particular individuals (*cattāri purisayugāni, aṭṭha purisapuggalā*), i.e., those who are on the path to stream-entry, once-returning, non-returning, and Arahantship, and those who have obtained the fruits thereof.

The *Māgha Sutta* (Sn 3.5) gives a detailed account of the virtues of the Arahant to show to whom alms should be offered by one desiring merit. The *Brāhmaṇa Saṃyutta* (SN 7:13) maintains that offerings bear greatest results when they are made to those who know their previous lives, who have seen heavens and hells, who have put an end to birth and who have realized ultimate knowledge. Thus the Saṅgha comprising morally perfect, worthy personages as described in the *suttas* constitutes the field of merit (*puññakkhetta,* MN 65:34). Just as seeds sown in fertile well-watered fields yield bountiful crops, alms given to the virtuous established on the Noble Eightfold Path yield great results (AN 8:34; 3:57). The *Dhammapada* maintains that fields have weeds as their blemish; lust, hatred, delusion and desire are the blemishes of people, and therefore what is given to those who have eliminated those blemishes bears great fruit (Dhp 356–59). The results of generosity are measured more by the quality of the field of merit represented by the recipient than by the quantity and value of the gift given.

The *Aṅguttara Nikāya* (AN 9:20) records a fabulous alms-giving conducted by the Bodhisatta when he was born as a brahmin named Velāma. Lavish gifts of silver, gold, elephants, cows, carriages, etc., not to mention food, drink and clothing, were distributed among everybody who came forward to receive them. But this open-handed munificence was not very valuable as far as merit was concerned because there were no worthy recipients. It is said to be more meritorious to feed one person with right view, a stream-enterer (*sotāpanna*), than to give great alms such as that given by Velāma. It is more meritorious to feed one once-returner than a hundred stream-enterers. Next in order come non-returners, Arahants, Paccekabuddhas and Sammāsambuddhas. Feeding the Buddha and the Saṅgha is more meritorious than feeding the Buddha alone. It is even more meritorious to construct a monastery for the general use of Saṅgha of the four quarters of all times. Taking refuge in the Buddha, Dhamma and Saṅgha is better still. Abiding by the Five Precepts is even more valuable. But better still is the cultivation of *mettā*, loving-kindness, and, best of all, the insight into impermanence, which leads to Nibbāna.

The Motivation for Giving

The *suttas* record various motives for exercising generosity. The *Aṅguttara Nikāya* (AN 8:31) enumerates the following eight motives:

1. *Āsajja dānaṃ deti:* one gives with annoyance, or as a way of offending the recipient, or with the idea of insulting him.[7]
2. *Bhayā dānaṃ deti:* fear also can motivate a person to make an offering.
3. *Adāsi me ti dānaṃ deti:* one gives in return for a favour done to oneself in the past.
4. *Dassati me ti dānaṃ deti:* one also may give with the hope of getting a similar favour for oneself in the future.
5. *Sādhu dānan ti dānaṃ deti:* one gives because giving is considered good.
6. *Ahaṃ pacāmi, ime na pacanti, na arahāmi pacanto apacantānaṃ adātun ti dānaṃ deti:* "I cook, they do not cook. It is not proper for one who cooks not to give to those who do not cook." Some give urged by such altruistic motives.
7. *Imaṃ me dānaṃ dadato kalyāṇo kittisaddo abbhug-gacchatī ti dānaṃ deti:* some give alms to gain a good reputation.
8. *Cittālaṅkāra-cittaparikkhāratthaṃ dānaṃ deti:* still others give alms to adorn and beautify the mind.

Favouritism (*chanda*), ill will (*dosa*) and delusion (*moha*) are also listed as motives for giving. Sometimes alms are given for the sake of maintaining a long-standing family tradition. Desire to be reborn in heaven after death is another dominant motive. Giving pleases some and they give with the idea of winning a happy frame of mind (AN 8:31).

But it is maintained in the *suttas* (AN 7:49) that alms should be given without any expectations (*na sāpekho dānaṃ deti*). Nor should alms be given with attachment to the recipient. If one

7. Though the PTS translation reads "one gives alms on one's own accord," the accuracy of this translation is questionable. The *sutta* seems to record motives for giving in ascending order of refinement. If the PTS translation is accepted, the order is disturbed. Moreover, *āsajja* is the gerund of *āsādeti*, which means to strike, offend, assail, insult.

gives with the idea of accumulating things for later use, that is an inferior act of giving. If one gives with the hope of enjoying the result thereof after death, that is also an inferior act of giving. The only valid motive for giving should be the motive of adorning the mind, to rid the mind of the ugliness of greed and selfishness.

The Manner of Giving

The *suttas* (e.g., AN 5:148) lay much emphasis on the manner of giving. The attitude of the donor in the act of giving makes a world of difference for the goodwill between the donor and recipient irrespective of whether the gift given is big or small. *Sakkaccaṃ dānaṃ deti:* alms should be given in such a way that the donee does not feel humiliated, belittled or hurt. The needy ask for something with a sense of embarrassment, and it is the duty of the donor not to make him feel more embarrassed and make his already heavy burden still heavier. *Cittikatvā dānaṃ deti:* alms should be given with due consideration and respect. The recipient should be made to feel welcome. It is when a gift is given with such warmth that a cohesive mutually enriching friendliness emerges between the donor and donee. *Sahatthā deti:* one should give with one's own hand. The personal involvement in the act of giving is greatly beneficial. This promotes rapport between the donor the donee and that is the social value of giving. Society is welded in unity with care and concern for one another when generosity is exercised with a warm sense of personal involvement. *Na apaviddhaṃ deti*: one should not give as alms what is only fit to be thrown away. One should be careful to give only what is useful and appropriate. *Na anāgamanadiṭṭhiko deti:* one should not give in such a callous manner so as to make the donee not feel like coming again.

Giving with faith (*saddhāya deti*) is much extolled in the *suttas* (AN 5:148). Especially when offering alms to the clergy one should do so with due deference and respect, taking delight in the opportunity one has got to serve them. One should also give at the proper time to meet a dire need (*kālena deti*). Such timely gifts are most valuable as they relieve the anxiety and stress of the suppliant. One should give with altruistic concerns, with the sole intention of helping another in difficulty (*anuggahacitto dānaṃ deti*). In the act of giving one should take care not to hurt oneself or another (*attānañ ca parañ ca anupahacca dānaṃ deti*). Giving with understanding and discretion is praised by the Buddha (*viceyyadānaṃ sugatappasatthaṃ*). If a gift contributes to the well-being of the donee it is wise to give. But if the gift is detrimental to the welfare of the donee one should be careful to exercise one's discretion. Giving as described above is highly commended as noble giving (*sappurisadāna*). More than what is given, it is the manner of giving that makes a gift valuable. One may not be able to afford a lavish gift, but one can always make the recipient feel cared for by the manner of giving.

The Value of Giving

Many *suttas* enumerate the various benefits of giving. Giving promotes social cohesion and solidarity. It is the best means of bridging the psychological gap, much more than the material economic gap, that exists between haves and have-nots. The *Māgha Sutta* maintains that hate gets eliminated when one is established in generosity (Sn 506). The one with a generous heart earns the love of others and many associate with him (AN 5:34). Giving also cements friendships (Sn 187).

It is maintained that if a person makes an aspiration to be born in a particular place after giving alms, the aspiration will be fulfilled only if he is virtuous, but not otherwise (AN 8:35). According to one *sutta* (AN 8:36), if one practises giving and morality to a very limited degree and has no idea about meditation, one obtains an unfortunate birth in the human world. One who performs meritorious deeds such as giving and morality to a considerable degree, but does not understand anything about meditation, meets a fortunate human birth. But those who practise giving and morality to a great extent without any knowledge of meditation find rebirth in one of the heavens. They excel other deities in the length of life, beauty, pleasure, fame and the five strands of sense pleasures.

The *Aṅguttara Nikāya* (AN 7:54) enumerates a number of this-worldly benefits of giving. The generous person, and not the miser, wins the sympathy of others. Arahants approach him, accept alms and preach to him first. A good reputation spreads about him. He can attend any assembly with confidence and dignity. He is reborn in a state of happiness after death. Another *sutta* (AN 5:35) adds that a generous person wins popularity; people of noble character associate with him and he has the satisfaction of having fulfilled a lay person's duties (*gihidhammā anapeto hoti*).

It is said that an almsgiver bestows on others life, beauty, happiness, strength and intelligence. Having bestowed them on others, he becomes a beneficiary of them himself (AN 5:37). The same idea is expressed by the succinct statement that one reaps what one sows (*yādisaṃ vapate bījaṃ tādisaṃ harate phalaṃ*, SN 11:10 v. 903).

Giving with faith results in the attainment of riches and beauty whenever the fruition of the gift occurs. By giving alms with due deference one gains, in addition, children, wives, subordinates and servants who are obedient, dutiful and understanding. By giving alms at the proper time not only does one obtain great wealth but also timely fulfilment of needs. By giving alms with the genuine desire to help others, one gains great wealth and the inclination to enjoy the best of sense pleasures. By giving alms without hurting oneself and others, one gains security from dangers such as fire, floods, thieves, kings and unloved heirs (AN 5:148).

Alms given to recluses and Brahmins who follow the Noble Eightfold Path yield wonderful results just as seeds sown on fertile, well-prepared, well-watered fields produce abundant crops (AN 8:34). Alms given without any expectations whatsoever can lead to birth in the Brahma-world, at the end of which one may become a non-returner (AN 7:49).

The *Dakkhiṇāvibhaṅga Sutta* (MN 142.6) enumerates a list of persons to whom alms can be offered and the merit accruing therefrom in ascending order. A thing given to an animal brings a reward a hundredfold. A gift given to an ordinary person of poor moral habit yields a reward a thousandfold; a gift given to a virtuous person yields a reward a hundred thousandfold. When a gift is given to a person outside the dispensation of Buddhism who is without attachment to sense pleasures, the yield is a hundred thousandfold of crores. When a gift is given to one on the path to stream-entry the yield is incalculable and immeasurable. So what can be said of a gift given to a stream-enterer, a once-returner, a non-returner, an Arahant, a Paccekabuddha, and a Fully Enlightened Buddha?

The same *sutta* (MN 142.8) emphasizes that a gift given to the Saṅgha as a group is more valuable than a gift offered to a single monk in his individual capacity. It is said that in the distant future there will be Buddhist monks who wear only a yellow collar as a distinguishing clerical mark, who are immoral and of evil character. If a gift is offered even to such monks in the name of the Order, it yields much more merit than a gift given to a monk in his individual capacity. But it should be observed that this statement is contradictory to ideas expressed elsewhere, that what is given to the virtuous is greatly beneficial but not what is given to the immoral. It is evident here that a later interpolation cannot be altogether ruled out.

The Buddha once explained that it is a meritorious act even to throw away the water after washing one's plate with the generous thought: "May the particles of food in the washing water be food to the creatures on the ground." When that is so, how much more meritorious it is to feed a human being! But the *sutta* hastens to add that it is more meritorious to feed a virtuous person (AN 7:49).

Another *sutta* (AN 6:37) maintains that it is not possible to estimate the amount of merit that accrues when an offering is endowed with six particular characteristics. Three of the characteristics belong to the donor while three belong to the donee. The donor should be happy at the thought of giving prior to making the offering. He should be pleased at the time of making the offering, and he should be satisfied after the offering is made. Thus the nobility of thought—without a trace of greed before, during and after the offering—makes a gift truly great. The recipients also should be free from lust, hatred and delusion, or they should have embarked on a course of training for the elimination of these mental depravities. When an almsgiving is endowed with these qualities of the donor and donee, the merit is said to be as immeasurable as the waters in the ocean.

Once Visākhā gave a learned explanation of the benefits she expected from her munificence when the Buddha questioned her as to what she saw as the advantages of her great generosity (Mv 8:15.12–14). She said that when she hears that a particular monk or nun has attained any of the fruit of recluseship, and if that monk or nun has visited Sāvatthī, she would be certain that he or she has partaken of the offerings she constantly makes. When she reflects that she has contributed in some measure to his or her spiritual distinction, great delight (*pāmujja*) arises in her. Joy (*pīti*) arises in the mind that is delighted. When the mind is joyful the body relaxes (*kāyo passambhissati*). When the body relaxes a sense of ease (*sukha*) is experienced which helps the mind to be concentrated (*cittaṃ samādhiyissati*). That will help development of the spiritual faculties (*indriya-bhāvanā*), spiritual powers (*balabhāvanā*), and factors of enlightenment (*bojjhaṅgabhāvanā*). These are advantages she hopes for by her munificence. The Buddha was so pleased with her erudite reply that he exclaimed "Sādhu! Sādhu! Sādhu!" in approbation.

It is evident that giving alone is not sufficient for one to make an end of suffering. Anāthapiṇḍika, who was pronounced by the Buddha as the foremost among almsgivers, became only a stream-enterer. It is specifically said that *dāna* has to be fortified by *sīla*, morality, if it is to produce good results. Though Anāthapiṇḍika practised unblemished virtue, it is nowhere stated that he practised mental culture or meditation (*bhāvanā*). Therefore, in spite of all his magnanimous munificence, he had to remain a stream-enterer.

The *Ghaṭīkāra Sutta* (MN 81.19) records a unique alms-giving where even the donor was not present. Ghaṭīkāra the potter was the chief benefactor of the Buddha Kassapa. He was a non-returner who did not want to enter the Order as he was looking after his blind, aged parents. He had greatly won the trust of the Buddha by the nobility of his conduct and devotion. One day the Buddha Kassapa went to his house on his alms round but Ghaṭīkāra was out. He asked the blind parents where the potter had gone. They replied that he had gone out, but invited the Buddha to serve himself from the pots and pans and partake of a meal. The Buddha did so. When Ghaṭīkāra returned and inquired who had taken from the food, the parents informed him that the Buddha had come and they had requested him to help himself to a meal. Ghaṭīkāra was overjoyed to hear this as he felt that the Buddha had so much trust in him. It is said that the joy and happiness (*pītisukha*) he experienced did not leave him for two weeks, and the parents' joy and happiness did not wane for a whole week.

The same *sutta* reports that on another occasion the roof of the Buddha Kassapa's monastery started leaking. He sent the monks to Ghaṭīkāra's house to fetch some straw, but Ghaṭīkāra was out at that time. The monks came back and said that there was no straw available there except what was on the roof. The Buddha asked the monks to get the straw from the roof there. Monks started stripping the straw from the roof and the aged parents of Ghaṭīkāra asked who was removing the straw. The monks explained the matter and the parents said, "Please do take all the straw." When Ghaṭīkāra heard about this he was deeply moved by the trust the Buddha reposed in him. The joy and happiness that arose in him did not leave him for a full fortnight and that of his parents did not subside for a week. For three months Ghaṭīkāra's house remained without a roof with only the sky above, but it is said that the rain did not wet the house. Such was the great piety and generosity of Ghaṭīkāra.

As mentioned at the beginning of this essay, *dāna* is the first of the meritorious deeds. It is also one of the four benevolent ways of treating others (*cattāri saṅgahavatthūni,* AN 8:34). But it is noteworthy that in the lists of virtues required for liberation such as those included among the thirty-seven requisites of enlightenment (*bodhipakkhiyā dhammā*), *dāna* never occurs as a required virtue. Instead of *dāna*, *cāga* or generosity is included in some of the lists, such as the five qualities—faith, virtue, learning, generosity and wisdom. Perhaps there is a slight difference between *dāna* and *cāga* when considered as virtues ingrained in the mind. *Dāna* is the very practical act of giving; *cāga* is the generous attitude ingrained in the mind by the repeated practice of *dāna*. The word *cāga* literally means giving up, abandonment, and it is an indication that the close-fisted selfish grip one has on one's possessions is loosened by *cāga*. It is possible to give alms even out of negative motives such as favouritism (*chanda*), ill will (*dosa*), fear (*bhaya*), delusion (*moha*), desire for a good reputation, etc., but *cāga* is the positive virtue of a generous disposition.

Buddhism teaches a gradual process of emptying oneself. It starts with giving away one's external possessions. When the generous dispositional trait sets in and is fortified by the deepening insight into the real nature of things, one grows disenchanted with sense pleasures (*nibbindati*). At this stage one gives up household life and seeks ordination. Next comes the emptying of sensory inputs by guarding the sense doors. Through meditation (*bhāvanā*) one empties oneself of deep-seated defilements and fills oneself with positive noble qualities. But this whole process of bailing out negativities starts with *dāna*, the practice of giving.

Giving from the Heart

M.O' C. Walshe

Giving comes very naturally to some people. They enjoy giving and are unhappy if they cannot do so. And though it is obvious that one can give foolishly, it is in general a very good and meritorious thing to give. This is recognized in, probably, all religions: in Christianity we are told that it is more blessed to give than to receive, and in Islam there is a positive injunction to give part of one's wealth to the poor.

Perhaps, however, we ought to start by squarely facing a point which may worry some people: the question of giving to the Saṅgha. In a phrase which lay Buddhists may frequently hear chanted, or even chant themselves, the Saṅgha is described as *anuttaraṃ puññakkhettaṃ lokassa*, "an unequalled field of merit-making for the world," meaning that the merit to be gained by giving to the Saṅgha is unequalled. Well of course, not all the lay people who hear or join in such chanting know what the words mean, but of those who do, Westerners who are Buddhists or Buddhist sympathizers, sometimes react to this notion with a degree of indignation, considering the words tactless or worse! In fact some, whose conditioning was at least partly under the influence of the Lutheran Christian tradition, are reminded of the abuses to which Martin Luther objected in the Church of his day, when "good deeds" were very largely associated in the popular mind with maintaining priests and monks, who in some cases at least were idle and corrupt, in the style to which they were accustomed.

Such misgivings are perhaps understandable, but can be countered by a proper explanation, and will in any case not take root provided the Saṅgha is patently seen to be well conducted (*supaṭipanno*). The traditional Buddhist community consists of four groups: monks, nuns, male and female lay followers. Though the original order of nuns has died out, there are women who have undertaken the holy life and live virtually as nuns, and there is every indication that their numbers will grow. The relation between the first two groups and the latter two is one of symbiosis. After all, the Saṅgha has a priceless gift to give, the gift of the Dhamma. *Sabbadānaṃ dhammadānaṃ jināti:* "The gift of Dhamma excels all other gifts" (Dhp 354). Members of the Saṅgha also have an inescapable obligation to live according to the Vinaya and to strive continuously for enlightenment. It is in fact only by so doing that they can claim to be "an unequalled field of merit-making," and if they fail in this obligation they are letting down not only themselves but also the laity who support them. A monk or nun who cannot observe the rules should, and in certain cases must, leave the Order. This could be regarded, at least in part, as the price to be paid for abusing the generosity of lay supporters.

It was mentioned above that, according to the Bible, it is more blessed to give than to receive. It is interesting to note that, just as in the practice of *mettā-bhāvanā*, the meditation on universal love, there is given an actual method for fulfilling that difficult Judaeo-Christian injunction "love thy neighbour as thyself," so too Buddhism can give a precise technical meaning to this biblical statement. If we receive something pleasant, this in Buddhism is considered to be *vipāka*, the result of previous meritorious conduct. It is nice while it lasts, but when it is finished, its virtue is exhausted. To give, however, is *kusala kamma*, skilled action, which will be productive of some pleasant *vipāka* or result for the giver. In this way it can be clearly seen to be more "blessed" to give than to receive. True, this "blessing" remains purely mundane and limited, being "merit-making for the world" (*lokassa*). But as all our actions are habit-forming, giving once inclines us to give again, so that the result tends to be cumulative. Also, of course, this kind of *kusala kamma* can lead on to other things, and it is not for nothing that *dāna* is listed as the first among the ten *pāramis* or "perfections," coming even before *sīla* or morality. It is, after all, possible for an immoral person to be generous!

The late Dr. I.B. Horner selected ten *jātaka* stories to illustrate the ten perfection, in a little book that is widely used as an introductory Pali reader, and she used the delightful story of the self-sacrificing hare (J 316) to illustrate the perfection of giving. Strangely enough, though, to the Western mind at least, the most popular *jātaka* story on this theme is the very last, the *Vessantara Jātaka* (J 547), in which the Bodhisatta gives everything away including, finally, his wife and children—a distinctly dubious moral, one might think! But in Theravāda Buddhist countries this story has been singled out and is regularly made the subject of special readings and sermons for the edification of the laity.

Giving is something that comes from the heart, and as I have said, there are people who enjoy giving for its own sake—which is fine provided the giving is balanced with wisdom. There are of course other people who are reluctant givers, and they are often the same people who find it difficult to say "please," "thank you," "I'm sorry," and so on. For all such types the *brahmavihāra* meditations on love and compassion would be beneficial, to enable them to open up their hearts.

Recently, in Britain, we have had a magnificent example of the power of giving from the heart, and from what to many must have seemed an unexpected source. Moved by the plight of the starving people in Ethiopia, the rock star Bob Geldof organized the fantastic international Live Aid concert which raised millions of pounds—in its way, and with the aid of modern technology, the most spectacular act of generosity in history, touching the hearts of millions, and transcending the boundaries not only of politics and religions, but also that gulf that exists between those addicted to this particular form of entertainment and those who dislike it.

It is perhaps hardly necessary to point out that *dāna* has to be exercised with discretion, and is as much subject to the rule of the middle way as everything else. It is not the best way to bring up a child, for instance, to give it everything it wants—or thinks it wants. Contrary to some trendy theories recently current, it does no harm to frustrate a spoilt brat occasionally! Nor, of course, is it the highest kind of giving if one expects something in return—even a nice rebirth in some heavenly realm! That is a kind of giving which is basically rooted in attachment and is therefore of limited kammic value.

In point of fact, one of the true benefits to the giver is precisely that the act of spontaneous giving is a very fine way of helping to overcome attachment. And that is the intended point of the Vessantara story. We Westerners think of the unfortunate wife and family the Bodhisatta "sacrificed" (though, of course, there was a happy ending in the story and they came back to him!) but the intention is to regard them as objects of attachment, to be given up as such. As a matter of fact, despite the popularity of this particular story, modern scholars consider that it was not originally a Buddhist tale at all, and was somewhat unskilfully adapted to provide a "Buddhist" moral.

The more we consider the question of *dāna*, the more aspects emerge, and we see that there are many ways of giving, skilfully or otherwise. We may conclude with an amusing canonical example of the alleged results of relatively unskilful giving. In the *Pāyāsi Sutta* (DN 23) we read of the debate between the sceptic Prince Pāyāsi, who did not believe in an afterlife, and the Venerable Kumāra Kassapa. After listening to a brilliant series of parables from the monk, Pāyāsi declares himself converted, and decides to establish a charity "for ascetics and Brahmins, wayfarers, beggars and the needy," and he appoints the young Brahmin Uttara to organize the distribution. (N.B. This is the correct version—there is an error in the Rhys Davids translation at this point.) Uttara complains that the food and clothing he is called upon to distribute are of such poor quality that Pāyāsi would not touch them himself, and Pāyāsi finally gives him leave to supply "food as I eat and clothes as I wear." At the conclusion of the *sutta*, we are told of the rewards the two men received after death. Pāyāsi, who had established the charity grudgingly, was indeed reborn in a heavenly world, but in the very lowest, that of the Four Great Kings, where he was lodged in the empty Serīsaka mansion (*vimāna*). Here indeed, he was visited by the Venerable Gavampati, an Arahant who made a habit of taking his siesta in the lower heavens. And so the story was brought back to earth. But Uttara, who had reorganized the charity and given from the heart, was born in a higher heaven, among the Thirty-three Gods.

Probably few Westerners will give in order to be reborn among the Thirty-three Gods, and perhaps the only reward some people look to is an easing of the conscience: being aware of some particular need—of which the case of Ethiopia is the outstanding current example—people feel unable to live with themselves if they do not give something. This is certainly better than hoping for a heavenly reward, but an easy conscience, too, may perhaps sometimes be purchased a little too easily. Best let the giving itself be its own reward, and leave it at that!

Generosity: The Inward Dimension

Nina van Gorkom

> As from a heap of flowers many a garland is made, even so many good deeds should be done by one born a mortal.
>
> Dhp 53

The giving away of useful or pleasant things is an act of generosity. However, if we only pay attention to the outward deeds we do not know whether or not we are being sincerely generous. We should learn more about the mind which motivates our deeds. True generosity is difficult. While we are giving, our thoughts may not all be good and noble. Our motives for giving may not all be pure. We may give with selfish motives—expecting something in return, hoping to be liked by the receiver of our gift, wanting to be known as a generous person. We may notice that there are different thoughts at different moments, some truly generous, and others having different motives.

The Buddha taught that there is no lasting mind or soul which undergoes different experiences. Our experiences themselves are different moments of consciousness, which arise one at a time and then fall away immediately. Each moment of consciousness that arises and falls away is succeeded by the next moment of consciousness. Our life is thus a series of moments of consciousness arising in succession. Gradually we can learn to distinguish different types of consciousness. There is consciousness which is unwholesome or unskilful and there is consciousness which is wholesome or skilful, and besides these there are other types of consciousness, which are neither wholesome nor unwholesome. Only one type of consciousness occurs at a time, but each type is accompanied by several mental factors. Unwholesome types of consciousness are accompanied by unwholesome mental factors, such as attachment, stinginess, jealousy or aversion. Wholesome types of consciousness are accompanied by beautiful mental factors, such as generosity, kindness or compassion.

Three of the unwholesome mental factors are "roots of evil."[8] These are the strong foundation of unwholesome types of consciousness: attachment or greed, aversion or anger, and ignorance.

Each of these unwholesome factors has many shades and degrees. We may know that there is attachment when we are greedy for food or desire to acquire someone else's property. However, we may not realize that there is also attachment when we enjoy natural scenery or beautiful music. In society attachment of a subtle kind is considered good, provided we do not harm others. The unwholesome has a wider range than what we call in conventional language "immoral." It can include states that are weaker than the immoral. We cannot force ourselves not to like beautiful things; there are conditions for the arising of attachment. But we can learn to know the difference between the moments, which are wholesome, and the moments, which are unwholesome. A degree of selfishness persists even in moments of subtle attachment. These are different from selfless moments of consciousness accompanied by generosity, when we do not think of our own enjoyment. There is attachment time and again, when we stand up, move around, reach for things, eat or go to sleep. We think of ourselves and want to acquire pleasant things for ourselves. We expect other people to be nice to us, and this is also a form of attachment.

We may wonder whether attachment to relatives is wholesome. Attachment to relatives is not wholesome; it is different from pure loving-kindness, which is wholesome. When we cling to the pleasant feeling we derive from the company of relatives or dear friends, there is attachment. When we are genuinely concerned for someone else we do not think of ourselves, and then there is wholesome consciousness. We are so used to living with attachment that we may have never considered the difference between the moments of attachment and the moments of unselfish love. The different types of consciousness succeed one another so rapidly that so long as we have not developed understanding of them, we do not notice that they have changed.

---

8. See Nyanaponika Thera, *The Roots of Good and Evil* (Wheel No. 251/253).

The unwholesome root of aversion also has many degrees. It can manifest as slight uneasiness or as coarse anger or hate. Aversion does not arise at the same time as attachment. When there is attachment, consciousness likes the object that is experienced, and when there is aversion, consciousness dislikes the object. Attachment arises with certain types of consciousness, not with all types, and so does aversion.

Ignorance is an unwholesome root that arises with all types of unwholesome consciousness. It is the root of all evil. Ignorance does not know what is wholesome and what is unwholesome, it does not know anything about what is real. Whenever there is attachment or aversion, at the same time there is also ignorance.

The three beautiful roots are: non-attachment or generosity, non-aversion or kindness, and understanding or wisdom. Each type of wholesome consciousness is rooted in non-attachment and non-aversion, and it may be rooted in understanding as well. Each of these beautiful roots has many degrees. Without the assistance of non-attachment and non-aversion wholesome consciousness could not arise motivating acts of generosity. Attachment cannot exist at the same time as generosity. When one is truly generous one gives impartially and does not restrict one's generosity to people one likes or to the members of one's family. The purpose of all kinds of wholesomeness should be to eliminate defilements, to get rid of selfishness. The Buddha taught the wisdom that can eradicate the clinging to the idea of self, but if one does not learn to get rid of stinginess and clings to one's possessions, one cannot give up the clinging to self.

When we see that true generosity is beneficial and that selfishness and stinginess are harmful, we would like to have more moments of generosity. However, in spite of our wishes, we notice that unwholesome types of consciousness often arise. Then we are disappointed with ourselves. We should acquire understanding of what conditions the arising of unwholesome consciousness. We must have been full of attachment, aversion and ignorance in the past, even in past lives. Such tendencies have become deeply rooted; they have been accumulated. What is past has gone already, but the unwholesome tendencies that have been accumulated can condition the arising of unwholesome consciousness at the present time.

We have accumulated not only tendencies to evil but also inclinations to the wholesome. That is why there can also be moments of generosity and kindness at the present time. When an unwholesome type of consciousness arises we accumulate more unwholesomeness; when a wholesome type arises we accumulate more wholesomeness.

The Buddha taught different ways of developing wholesomeness, and when we learn about these ways there are already conditions for more wholesomeness. We find opportunity for generosity not only while we are giving but also before the actual giving, when we try to obtain the things we intend to give, and afterwards when we recollect our giving. When we are honest with ourselves we can notice that before, during and after the giving, opportunities for generosity are often spoilt by unwholesome consciousness. We may get tired when we have to buy or prepare the gift, and then aversion arises. While we are giving the gift the receiver may be ungrateful and fail to respond to our gift in the way we expected, and then we may be disappointed.

However, when we have right understanding of what wholesomeness is, we should be concerned only with developing wholesome states of mind and not with the reactions of other people. Wholesomeness is wholesomeness and nobody else can change the wholesome consciousness that arises. Before we learnt about the Buddha's teachings we did not consider generosity in this way, we did not pay attention to the moments of consciousness. Through the Buddha's teachings we learn about things as they really are. After the act of giving the opportunity to recollect our generosity with wholesome consciousness can be wasted by unwholesome consciousness. At first we may have been generous, but afterwards we may find that the gift was too expensive and regret having spent our money.

The Buddha taught that there is no self that can exert power over the different types of consciousness that arise; they arise because of their appropriate conditions. Through his teachings we can learn about the different types of consciousness and about our accumulated tendencies. Thus there will be more understanding of what is real, and this too is wholesome. When one has accumulated the tendency to stinginess it is difficult to be generous, but through the understanding of what the Buddha taught inclinations can be changed.

We read in the commentary to the *Sudhābhojana Jātaka*[9] about a monk in the Buddha's time who practised the utmost generosity. He gave away his food, and if he received drink sufficient to fill the hollow of his hand, he would, free from greed, still give it away. But formerly he used to be so stingy that "he would not give so much as a drop of oil on the tip of a blade of grass." In one of his past lives, when he was named Kosiya, he lived as a miser. One day he had a craving for rice porridge. When his wife suggested that she would cook porridge not only for him but also for all the inhabitants of Benares, he felt "just as if he had been struck on the head with a stick." Then his wife offered to cook for a single street, or only for the attendants in his house, only for the family, only for the two of them, but he turned down all her offers. He wanted porridge cooked for himself alone, in the forest, so that nobody else could see it. The Bodhisatta, who was at that time the god Sakka, wanted to convert him and came to him with four attendants disguised as brahmins. One by one they approached the miser and begged for some of his porridge. Sakka spoke the following stanza, praising generosity (J 535 v. 387):

> From little one should little give,
> from moderate means likewise,
>
> From much give much:
> of giving nothing no question can arise,
>
> This then I tell you, Kosiya,
> give alms of that is thine:
>
> Eat not alone;
> no bliss is his that by himself shall dine,
>
> By charity you may ascend
> the noble path divine.

Kosiya reluctantly offered them some porridge. Then one of the brahmins changed into a dog. The dog made water and a drop of it

9. *The Jātaka or Stories of the Buddha's Former Births*, Vol. V, Story 535. London: Pali Text Society, 1981.

fell on Kosiya's hand. Kosiya went to the river to wash and then the dog made water in Kosiya's cooking pot. When Kosiya threatened him he changed into a "blood horse" and pursued Kosiya. Then Sakka and his attendants stood in the air and Sakka preached to Kosiya out of compassion and warned him of an unhappy rebirth. Kosiya came to understand the danger of stinginess. He gave away all his possessions and became an ascetic.

We may find it difficult to part with our possessions, but when we die we cannot take them with us. Life is short: thus when we have an opportunity for generosity we should use it in order to combat selfishness. Each moment of generosity now will condition the arising of generosity in the future.

Good deeds bring about pleasant results and bad deeds bring unpleasant results. This is the law of *kamma* and its fruit, of cause and effect.[10] A deed (*kamma*) can produce results in the form of rebirth. Wholesome *kamma* can produce a happy rebirth and unwholesome *kamma* can produce an unhappy rebirth. Besides the human plane of existence, there are other planes which are happy or unhappy. Birth in the human plane or in a heavenly plane is a happy rebirth conditioned by wholesome *kamma*; birth in a hell plane, as a ghost or as an animal is an unhappy rebirth conditioned by unwholesome *kamma*. *Kamma* can also produce results in the form of pleasant or unpleasant sense experiences arising in the course of life. Seeing and hearing are types of consciousness that are results of *kamma*. We see and hear pleasant or unpleasant objects according to the *kamma* that produces these experiences.

Stinginess can bring about—either in this life or in a future life—the very result we fear: loss of possessions. Generosity can bring about pleasant results, such as prosperity. However, when we perform acts of generosity we should not cling to pleasant results; clinging is unwholesome. *Kamma* will produce its appropriate result whether we think of it or not. While we are giving we can have right understanding of *kamma* and its results, without clinging. We may do good deeds with the understanding of what wholesomeness is. As we have seen, understanding is a beautiful root which may or may not accompany wholesome consciousness. When understanding accompanies the wholesome consciousness, it increases the degree

10. See *Kamma and Its Fruit* (Wheel No. 221/224).

of wholesomeness. We cannot make understanding arise at will; it arises when there are conditions for it. Learning what the Buddha taught is a condition for greater understanding.

There are still other ways of practising generosity, even when we do not have things to give. The appreciation of other people's good deeds is also a type of generosity. When we notice that someone else is doing a good deed we can appreciate his wholesomeness, and we may express this with words of approval and praise. We may be stingy not only with regard to our possessions but also with regard to words of praise. Gradually one can learn to be generous in appreciating the wholesomeness of others.

In Thailand I had an opportunity to learn about this way of generosity, which I had not heard before. I received a book that was printed on the occasion of the birthday of Her Majesty Queen Sirikit of Thailand. This book mentioned many of her good works, such as promoting the teaching of Buddhism, supporting temples, improving the standard of living of the people in the provinces by setting up different projects for them. When one reads this one can sincerely admire and rejoice in the good works of Her Majesty. In Thailand I also often heard the Thais saying, "*anumodana*," which means "thanks," with the inclination of their head and clasped hands. This they do when they respect and appreciate the wholesomeness of others, usually on occasions of presenting food to the monks or giving books on the Buddhist teachings. It can become a wholesome custom to express one's appreciation on such occasions.

When we know about this way of generosity we may remember to speak about others with wholesome consciousness. In the development of wholesomeness one has to be farsighted. One should realize that whatever wholesomeness or unwholesomeness one accumulates today will produce its effects in the future, even in future lives. One can become more adept in evaluating the circumstances one is in and the friends one has. One will then be able to judge whether or not one's surroundings and friends are favourable for the development of wholesomeness. One will know what kind of speech should be avoided, what kind of speech cultivated. Often conversation tends to be about the bad qualities of others or about useless matters, which are not helpful for the development of wholesomeness. Since we often become engaged in conversation with others, we should learn how to turn the conversation into an opportunity for wholesomeness.

Another way of generosity is the "sharing" of one's wholesome deeds with others. This does not mean that other people can receive the pleasant results of our good deeds. The Buddha taught that beings are "heirs" to their deeds. We each receive the results of the deeds we have done ourselves. Sharing wholesomeness with others means that our good deeds can be the condition for the arising of wholesome consciousness in others when they rejoice in our good deeds. We can share wholesomeness even with beings in other planes of existence, provided they are in planes where they can receive the benefits.

The commentary to the *Without the Walls Sutta*[11] narrates that King Bimbisāra offered a meal to the Buddha and omitted to dedicate his merits to other beings. Ghosts, his relatives in a former life, had hoped for this in vain, and because they were disappointed, in their despair they made a horrible screeching noise throughout the night. The Buddha explained to King Bimbisāra why the ghosts had screeched. Then King Bimbisāra made another offering and uttered the dedication, "Let this be for those relatives." The ghosts benefited from his gifts immediately; they had wholesome states of consciousness and their sufferings were allayed. Lotus-covered pools were generated for them in which they could bathe and drink, and they took on the colour of gold. Heavenly food, heavenly clothing and heavenly palaces manifested spontaneously for their use. This story illustrates that one can share one's good deeds with departed ones. If one's departed relatives are not able to receive the merit, other beings can.

It is understandable that we are sad when we lose loved ones, but if we know how to develop what is wholesome we can find great consolation. Instead of becoming filled with sadness and aversion, we should dedicate our good deeds to all those who are able to rejoice in them, then our consciousness will be wholesome. It can become our custom to share wholesomeness with others; we need not even specify to whom we wish to dedicate it.

11. In *The Illustrator of Ultimate Meaning* (Paramatthajotikā), *Commentary to the Minor Readings* (Khuddakapātha). London: Pali Text Society, 1960.

It is a Buddhist custom when a meal or robes are offered to monks to pour water over one's hands while the monks recite words of blessing, in order to give expression to one's intention to dedicate this deed to other beings. The water symbolizes a river, which fills the ocean, and even so a wholesome deed is so plentiful that it can also be shared with others.

Good deeds are usually classified as threefold: as generosity, morality, and mental development. This threefold classification should not be considered a rigid one. Morality, or abstinence from evil deeds, can also be seen as an aspect of generosity, as an act of kindness to others. When we abstain from evil deeds we give other beings the opportunity to live in peace, free from harm. If we want to develop generosity, we should not neglect mental development—the development of wholesome states of mind. We should know when consciousness is unwholesome and when wholesome in order to develop generosity and other good qualities. Knowing more about one's different types of consciousness is mental development.

The "stream-winner" is the noble person at the first stage of enlightenment. He has developed right understanding of the different mental and physical phenomena that appear at the present moment and has seen realities as they are. With the attainment of enlightenment he experiences Nibbāna, the unconditional reality, for the first time. At the moment of enlightenment the wrong view of self is eradicated, and with it stinginess too is destroyed. Stinginess can never arise again, and he thus has perfect generosity. An ordinary person may be able to suppress stinginess temporarily, for example, at the time of giving, but stinginess is bound to arise again so long as its accumulated tendency remains. The stream-winner, through right understanding, has eradicated the tendency to stinginess and can never be overcome by it any more.

Learning from Buddha's teachings how to develop wholesomeness and to eradicate defilements is the greatest blessing. Therefore the teaching of the Dhamma, the Buddha's teaching, should be considered as the giving of the highest gift. In learning what the Buddha taught and in developing wholesomeness we correct our views about what is worthwhile striving for and what is not, about what is real and what is mere illusion. Before we heard about the Buddha's teachings we may have considered the enjoyment of pleasant sense objects to be the goal of our life. After we learn the Buddha's teachings we may gradually come to see that selfish attachment gives unrest of mind and that it is harmful to ourselves and others. We may come to understand that wholesomeness is beneficial both for ourselves and for others, that it brings peace of mind.

Our outlook on what is worthwhile in life can change. We correct our views about reality when we understand what wholesome *kamma* is and what unwholesome *kamma* is, when we understand that *kamma* brings its appropriate result. We correct our views when we understand that not a self but different types of consciousness, wholesome or unwholesome, motivate our deeds, when we understand that these types of consciousness arise because of different conditioning factors. There are many degrees of correcting one's views. By developing understanding of realities the wrong view of self can be eradicated, and thereby perfect generosity can emerge. The effect of learning the Dhamma should be that we become less selfish and more generous, that we have more genuine concern for other people.

The Perfection of Giving[12]

Ācariya Dhammapāla

The perfection of giving is to be practised by benefiting beings in many ways—by relinquishing one's happiness, belongings, body, and life to others, by dispelling their fear, and by instructing them in the Dhamma. Herein, giving is threefold by way of the object to be given: the giving of material things (*āmisadāna*), the giving of fearlessness (*abhayadāna*), and the giving of the Dhamma (*dhammadāna*). Among these, the object to be given can be twofold: internal and external. The external gift is tenfold: food, drink, garments, vehicles, garlands, scents, unguents, bedding, dwellings, and lamps. These gifts, again, become manifold by analysing each into its constituents, e.g., food into hard food, soft food, etc. The external gift can also become sixfold when analysed by way of sense objects: visible forms, sounds, smells, tastes, tangibles, and non-sensory objects. The sense objects, such as visible forms, become manifold when analysed into blue, etc. So too, the external gift is manifold by way of divers valuables and belongings, such as gems, gold, silver, pearls, coral etc.; fields, land, parks, etc.; slaves, cows, buffaloes, etc.

When the Great Man (the Bodhisatta) gives an external object, he gives whatever is needed to whomever stands in need of it; and knowing by himself that someone is in need of something, he gives it even unasked, much more when asked. He gives generously, not ungenerously. He gives sufficiently, not insufficiently, when there is something to be given. He does not give because he expects something in return. And when there is not enough to give sufficiently to all, he distributes evenly whatever can be shared. But he does not give things that issue in affliction for others, such as weapons, poisons, and intoxicants. Nor does he give amusements which are harmful and lead to negligence. And he does not give unsuitable food or drink to a person who is sick,

12. From the Cariyāpiṭaka Aṭṭhakathā, translated by Bhikkhu Bodhi in *The Discourse on the All-Embracing Net of Views: The Brahmajāla Sutta and its Commentaries* (BPS, 1978), pp. 289–96, pp. 322–23.

even though he might ask for it, and he does not give what is suitable beyond the proper measure.

Again, when asked, he gives to householders things appropriate for householders, and to monks things appropriate for monks. He gives to his mother and father, kinsmen and relatives, friends and colleagues, children, wife, slaves and workers, without causing pain to anyone. Having promised an excellent gift, he does not give something mean. He does not give because he desires gain, honour, or fame, or because he expects something in return, or out of expectation of some fruit other than the supreme enlightenment. He does not give detesting the gift or those who ask. He does not give a discarded object as a gift, not even to unrestrained beggars who revile and abuse him. Invariably he gives with care, with a serene mind, full of compassion. He does not give through belief in superstitious omens: but he gives believing in *kamma* and its fruits.

When he gives he does not afflict those who ask by making them do homage to him, etc.; but he gives without afflicting others. He does not give a gift with the intention of deceiving others or with the intention of injuring; he gives only with an undefiled mind. He does not give a gift with harsh words or a frown, but with words of endearment, congenial speech, and a smile on his face.

Whenever greed for a particular object becomes excessive, due to its high value and beauty, its antiquity, or personal attachment, the Bodhisatta recognizes his greed, quickly dispels it, seeks out some recipients, and gives it away. And if there should be an object of limited value that can be given and a suppliant expecting it, without a second thought he bestirs himself and gives it to him, honouring him as though he were an uncelebrated sage. Asked for his own children, wife, slaves, workers, and servants, the Great Man does not give them while they are as yet unwilling to go, afflicted with grief. But when they are willing and joyful, then he gives them. But if he knows that those who ask for them are demonic beings—ogres, demons, or goblins—or men of cruel disposition, then he does not give them away. So too, he will not give his kingdom to those intent on the harm, suffering, and affliction of the world, but he would give it away to righteous men who protect the world with Dhamma.

This, firstly, is the way to practise the giving of external gifts.

The internal gift should be understood in two ways. How? Just as a man, for the sake of food and clothing, surrenders himself to another and enters into servitude and slavery, in the same way the Great Man, wishing for the supreme welfare and happiness of all beings, desiring to fulfil his own perfection of giving, with a spiritually-oriented mind, for the sake of enlightenment, surrenders himself to another and enters into servitude, placing himself at the disposal of others. Whatever limbs or organs of his might be needed by others—hands, feet, eyes, etc.—he gives them away to those who need them, without trembling and without cowering. He is no more attached to them, and no more shrinks away (from giving them to others), than if they were external objects. Thus the Great Man relinquishes an internal object in two ways: for the enjoyment of others according to their pleasure; or while fulfilling the wishes of those who ask, for his own self-mastery. In this matter he is completely generous, and thinks: "I will attain enlightenment through non-attachment." Thus the giving of the internal gift should be understood.

Herein, giving an internal gift, he gives only what leads to the welfare of the recipient, and nothing else. The Great Man does not knowingly give his own body, limbs, and organs to Māra or to the malevolent deities in Māra's company, thinking: "Let this not lead to their harm." And likewise, he does not give to those possessed by Māra or his deities, or to madmen. But when asked for these things by others, he gives immediately, because of the rarity of such a request and the difficulty of making such a gift.

The giving of fearlessness is the giving of protection to beings when they have become frightened on account of kings, thieves, fire, water, enemies, lions, tigers, other wild beasts, dragons, ogres, demons, goblins, etc.

The giving of the Dhamma is an unperverted discourse on the Dhamma given with undefiled mind; that is, methodical instruction conducive to good in the present life, to good in the life to come, and to ultimate deliverance. By means of such discourses, those who have not entered the Buddha's Dispensation enter it, while those who have entered it reach maturity therein.

This is the method: In brief, he gives a talk on giving, on virtue, and on heaven, on the unsatisfactoriness and defilement in sense pleasures, and on the benefit in renouncing them. In detail, to those whose minds are disposed towards the enlightenment of disciples (*sāvakabodhi*) he gives a discourse establishing and purifying them (in progress towards their goal) by elaborating upon the noble qualities of whichever among the following topics is appropriate: going for refuge, restraint by virtue, guarding the doors of the sense-faculties, moderation in eating, application to wakefulness, the seven good *dhammas*; application to serenity (*samatha*) by practising meditation on one of the thirty-eight objects (of serenity meditation); application to insight (*vipassanā*) by contemplating the objects of insight-interpretation such as the material body, the progressive stages of purification (*visuddhipaṭipadā*), the apprehension of the course of rightness (*sammattagahaṇa*), the three kinds of clear knowledge (*vijjā*) the six kinds of direct knowledge (*abhiññā*), the four discriminations (*paṭisambhidā*), and the enlightenment of a disciple.

So too, for beings whose minds are disposed towards the enlightenment of paccekabuddhas and perfectly enlightened Buddhas, he gives a discourse establishing and purifying them in the two vehicles (leading to these two types of enlightenment) by elaborating upon the greatness of the spiritual power of those Buddhas, and by explaining the specific nature, characteristic, function, etc., of the ten *pāramis* in their three stages. Thus the Great Man gives the gift of the Dhamma to beings.

When he gives a material gift, the Great man gives food thinking: "May I, by this gift, enable beings to achieve long life, beauty, happiness, strength, intelligence, and the supreme fruit of unsullied bliss." He gives drink wishing to allay the thirst of sensual defilements; garments to gain the adornment of shame and moral dread and the golden complexion (of a Buddha); vehicles for attaining the modes of psychic potency and the bliss of Nibbāna; scents for producing the sweet scent of virtue; garlands and unguents for producing the beauty of the Buddha-qualities; seats for producing the seat on the terrace of enlightenment; bedding for producing the bed of a Tathāgata's rest; dwellings so he might become a refuge for beings; lamps so he might obtain the five eyes.[13] He gives visible forms for producing the fathom-wide aura

13. The five eyes are the fleshy eye (*maṃsacakkhu*); the divine eye

(surrounding a Buddha); sounds for producing the Brahmā-like voice (of a Buddha); tastes for endearing himself to all the world; and tangibles for acquiring a Buddha's elegance.

He gives medicines so he might later give the ageless and deathless state of Nibbāna. He gives slaves the gift of freedom so he might later emancipate beings from the slavery of the defilements. He gives blameless amusements and enjoyments in order to produce delight in the true Dhamma. He gives his own children as a gift in order that he might adopt all beings as his children by granting them an ariyan birth. He gives his wives as a gift in order that he might become master over the entire world. He gives gifts of gold, gems, pearls, coral, etc. in order to achieve the major marks of physical beauty (characteristic of a Buddha's body), and gifts of the diverse means of beautification in order to achieve the minor features of physical beauty.[14] He gives his treasuries as a gift in order to obtain the treasury of the true Dhamma; the gift of his kingdom in order to become the king of the Dhamma; the gift of monasteries, parks, ponds, and groves in order to achieve the *jhānas*, etc.; the gift of his feet in order that he might be marked with the auspicious wheels; the gift of his hands in order that he might give to beings the rescuing hand of the true Dhamma to help them across the four floods;[15] the gift of his ears, nose, etc. in order to obtain the spiritual faculties of faith, etc.; the gift of his eyes in order to obtain the universal eye; the gift of his flesh and blood with the thought: "May my body be the means of life for all the world! May it bring welfare and happiness to all beings at all times, even on occasions of merely seeing, hearing, recollecting, or ministering to me!" And he gives the gift of his head in order to become supreme in all the world.

(*dibbacakkhu*), by which he sees beings pass away and re-arise in accordance with their *kamma*; the wisdom eye (*paññācakkhu*), by which he sees the specific and general characteristics of things; the Buddha-eye (*buddhacakkhu*), by which he sees the propensities and dispositions of beings; and the universal eye (*samantacakkhu*), his knowledge of omniscience.

14. The thirty-two major and eighty minor characteristics of a Great Man's body.

15. The four floods of sensual desire, desire for existence, wrong views, and ignorance.

Giving thus, the Great Man does not give unwillingly, nor by afflicting others, nor out of fear, moral shame, or the scolding of those in need of gifts. When there is something excellent, he does not give what is mean. He does not give extolling himself and disparaging others. He does not give out of desire for the fruit, nor with loathing for those who ask, nor with lack of consideration. Rather, he gives thoroughly, with his own hand, at the proper time, considerately, without discrimination, filled with joy throughout the three times.[16] Having given, he does not become remorseful afterwards. He does not become either conceited or obsequious in relation to the recipients, but behaves amiably towards them. Bountiful and liberal, he gives things together with a bonus (*saparivāra*). For when he gives food, thinking; "I will give this along with a bonus," he gives garments, etc., as well. And when he gives garments, thinking: "I will give this along with a bonus," he gives food, etc., as well. The same method with gifts of vehicles, etc. And when he gives a gift of one of the sense objects, such as visible forms, he gives the other sense objects also as a bonus.

The gift of visible forms should be understood thus: Having gained something, such as a flower, garment, or relic of a blue, yellow, red, or white colour, etc., considering it in terms of its visible form, thinking to make a gift of a visible form, he offers it to a worthy recipient together with its base.

The gift of sounds should be understood by way of the sounds of drums, etc. It is certainly not possible to give a sound as one gives a cluster of lotuses, tearing it out by its bulb and roots and placing it in the hands. But one gives a gift of sound by giving its base. Thus he makes a gift of sound by presenting a musical instrument, such as drums or tom toms, to the Triple Gem; or by giving medicine for the voice, such as oil and molasses, to preachers of the Dhamma; or by announcing a lecture on the Dhamma, chanting the scriptures, giving a discourse on the Dhamma, holding a discussion, or expressing appreciation for the good deeds of others.

The gift of scents is made when, after getting a delightfully scented object, such as scented roots, powdered scent, etc.,

16. The "three times" are before presenting the gift, while giving it, and after giving it.

considering it in terms of its scent, thinking to make a gift of scent, he offers it to the Triple Gem. He relinquishes a scented object such as *agaru* or sandalwood, for the purpose of making an offering of scent.

The gift of tastes is made when, after getting a delightfully flavoured object, such as flavoured roots, etc., considering it in terms of its taste, thinking to make a gift of taste, he gives it to worthy recipients. Or he relinquishes a flavourful object, such as grain, cows, etc.[17]

The gift of tangibles should be understood by way of beds, chairs, etc., and by way of coverlets and mantels, etc. For having gained some soft, delightful, blameless tangible object, such as a bed, chair, cushion, pillow, undergarment, or upper garment, considering it in terms of its tangible qualities, thinking to make a gift of a tangible item, he gives it to worthy recipients; having gained the aforesaid tangible objects, he relinquishes them.

The gift of mental objects (*dhammadāna*) should be understood by way of nutriment, drink, and life, since it is the mental-object base which is here intended.[18] Having gained a delightful object such as nutriment, considering it as part of the mental-object base, thinking to make a gift of a non-sensory object, he gives nutriment—i.e., ghee, butter, etc., or a drink—i.e., the eight kinds of drink such as mango juice, etc.; or, considering it a gift of life, he gives a ticket-meal or a fortnightly meal, etc., gets doctors to wait upon the sick and afflicted, liberates animals from a net, has a fishing net or bird-cage destroyed, releases prisoners from prison, causes an injunction to be given forbidding the slaughter of animals, or undertakes any action of a similar nature for the sake of protecting the life of beings.

This entire accomplishments in giving he dedicates to the welfare and happiness of the whole world, and to his own unshakable emancipation through supreme enlightenment. He

17. Doubtlessly the commentator means cows as a source for the "five delicacies"—milk, curd, butter, ghee and cream of ghee—not as a source of beef steak.

18. *Dhamma* here, as the context indicates, means the sixth type of object, not the Buddha's teaching. The class of object includes the nutritive essence of food and the life faculty, hence the explanation that follows in the text.

dedicates it to the attainment of inexhaustible desire (for the good), inexhaustible concentration, ingenuity, knowledge, and emancipation. In practising the perfection of giving the Great Being should apply the perception of impermanence to life and possessions. He should consider them as shared in common with many, and should constantly and continuously arouse great compassion towards beings. Just as, when a house is blazing, the owner removes all his property of essential value and himself as well without leaving anything important behind, so does the Great Man invariably give, without discrimination and without concern.

When the Great Man has made a mental determination to completely relinquish whatever possessions come his way, whether animate or inanimate, there are four shackles to giving (which he must overcome), namely, not being accustomed to giving in the past, the inferiority of the object to be given, the excellence and beauty of the object, and worry over the loss of the object.

1. When the Bodhisatta possesses objects that can be given and suppliants are present, but his mind does not leap up at the thought of giving and he does not want to give, he should conclude: "Surely, I have not been accustomed to giving in the past, therefore a desire to give does not arise now in my mind. So that my mind will delight in giving in the future, I will give a gift. With an eye for the future let me now relinquish what I have to those in need." Thus he gives a gift—generous, open-handed, delighting in relinquishing, one who gives when asked, delighting in giving and in sharing. In this way the Great Being destroys, shatters, and eradicates the first shackle to giving.
2. Again, when the object to be given is inferior or defective, the Great Being reflects: "Because I was not inclined to giving in the past, at present my requisites are defective. Therefore, though it pains me let me give whatever I have as a gift even if the object is low and inferior. In that way I will, in the future, reach the peak in the perfection of giving." Thus he gives whatever kind of gift he can—generous, open-handed, delighting in relinquishing, one who gives when asked, delighting in giving and in sharing. In this way the Great Being destroys, shatters and eradicates the second shackle to giving.

3. When a reluctance to give arises due to the excellence or beauty of the object to be given, the Great Being admonishes himself: "Good man, haven't you made the aspiration for the supreme enlightenment, the loftiest and most superior of all states? Well then, for the sake of enlightenment, it is proper for you to give excellent and beautiful objects as gifts." Thus he gives what is excellent and beautiful—generous, open-handed, delighting in relinquishing, one who gives when asked, delighting in giving and in sharing. In this way the Great Man destroys, shatters and eradicates the third shackle to giving.
4. When the Great Being is giving a gift, and he sees the loss of the object being given, he reflects thus: "This is the nature of material possessions, that they are subject to loss and to passing away. Moreover, it is because I did not give such gifts in the past that my possessions are now depleted. Let me then give whatever I have as a gift, whether it be limited or abundant. In that way I will, in the future, reach the peak in the perfection of giving." Thus he gives whatever he has as a gift—generous, open-handed, delighting in relinquishing, one who gives when asked, delighting in giving and in sharing. In this way the Great Being destroys, shatters and eradicates the fourth shackle to giving

Reflecting upon them thus in whatever way is appropriate is the means for dispelling the harmful shackles to the perfection of giving. The same method used for the perfection of giving also applies to the perfection of virtue and the other perfections.

Satipaṭṭhāna Vipassanā

Insight through Mindfulness

by

Ven. Mahasi Sayadaw

WHEEL PUBLICATION NO. 370/371

Introduction

On the personal request of the Honourable U Nu, Prime Minister, and Thado Thiri Thudhamma Sir U Thwin, President of the Buddha Sāsanānuggaha Association, the Venerable Mahāsi Sayādaw, Bhadanta Sobhana Mahāthera, came down from Shwebo to Rangoon on 10th November 1949. The Meditation Centre at the Thathana Yeiktha, Hermitage Road, Rangoon, was formally opened on 4th December 1949, when the Mahāsi Sayādaw began to give to fifteen devotees a methodical training in the right system of Satipaṭṭhāna Vipassanā.

From the first day of the opening of the Centre a discourse on the exposition of Satipaṭṭhāna Vipassanā, its purpose, the method of practise, the benefits derived therefrom, etc., has been given daily to each batch of devotees arriving at the Centre almost every day to undertake the intensive course of training. The discourse lasts usually for one hour and thirty minutes, and the task of talking almost daily in this manner inevitably caused a strain. Fortunately, the Buddha Sāsanānuggaha Association came forward to relieve the situation with an offer of the donation of a tape recorder, and the discourse given on 27th July 1951 to a group of fifteen devotees undertaking the training was taped. Thereafter this taped discourse has been in constant daily use preceded by a few preliminary remarks spoken by the Mahāsi Sayādaw.

Then, owing to the great demand of many branch meditation centres of the Mahāsi Satipaṭṭhāna Vipassanā, as well as of the public, this discourse was published in book form in 1954. The book has now run into its sixth edition. As there is also a keen interest and eager demand among many devotees of other nationalities who are unacquainted with Burmese, the discourse is now translated into English.

U Pe Thin (translator)
Mahāsi Yogi
December 1957

Satipaṭṭhana Vipassanā

Insight through Mindfulness

Namo Buddhassa
(Honour to the Fully Enlightened One)

On coming across the Teaching of the Buddha, it is most important for everyone to cultivate the virtues of moral conduct (*sīla*), concentration (*samādhi*), and wisdom (*paññā*). One should undoubtedly possess these three virtues.

For lay people the minimal measure of moral conduct is the observance of the Five Precepts. For bhikkhus it is the observance of the *Pātimokkha,* the code of monastic discipline. Anyone who is well-disciplined in moral conduct will be reborn in a happy realm of existence as a human being or a *deva* (god).

However, this ordinary form of mundane morality (*lokiya-sīla*) will not be a safeguard against relapse into the lower states of miserable existence, such as hell, the animal realm, or the realm of *petas* (ghosts). It is therefore desirable to cultivate the higher form of supramundane morality (*lokuttara-sīla*). When one has fully acquired the virtue of this morality, one will be secure from relapse into the lower states and will always live a happy life by being reborn as a human being or a *deva.* Everyone should therefore make it his duty to work for supramundane morality.

There is every hope of success for anyone who strives sincerely and in real earnestness. It would indeed be a pity if anyone were to fail to take advantage of this fine opportunity of being endowed with higher qualities, for such a person will undoubtedly be a victim sooner or later of his own bad karma, which will pull him down to the lower states of miserable existence in hell, the animal realm, or the sphere of *petas,* where the span of life lasts for many hundreds, thousands or millions of years. It is therefore emphasised here that coming across the Teaching of the Buddha is the unique opportunity to work for path morality (*magga-sīla*) and fruition morality (*phala-sīla*).

It is not, however, advisable to work for moral conduct alone. It is also necessary to practise *samādhi* or concentration. *Samādhi* is the fixed or tranquil state of mind. The ordinary or undisciplined mind is in the habit of wandering to other places. It cannot be kept under control, but follows any idea, thought or imagination, etc. In order to prevent this wandering, the mind should be made to attend repeatedly to a selected object of concentration. On gaining practice, the mind gradually abandons its distractions and remains fixed on the object to which it is directed. This is *samādhi.*

There are two kinds of concentration: mundane concentration (*lokiya-samādhi*) and supramundane concentration (*lokuttara-samādhi*). Of these two, the former consists in the mundane absorptions, such as the four *rūpa jhānas*—the absorptions pertaining to the world of form—and the four *arūpa jhānas*—the absorptions pertaining to the formless world. These can be attained by the practice of tranquillity meditation (*samathabhāvanā*) with such methods as mindfulness of breathing, loving kindness (*mettā*), *kasiṇa* meditation, etc. By virtue of these attainments one will be reborn in the plane of the *brahmās.* The life-span of a *brahma* is very long and lasts for one world cycle, two, four, or eight world cycles, up to a limit of 84,000 world cycles, as the case may be. But at the end of his lifespan, a *brahma* will die and be reborn as a human being or a *deva.*

If one leads a virtuous life all the time, one may lead a happy life in a higher existence, but as one is not free from the defilements of attachment, aversion, and delusion, one may commit demeritorious deeds on many occasions. One will then be a victim of one's bad *kamma* and be reborn in hell or in other lower states of miserable existence. Thus mundane concentration also is not a definite security. It is desirable to work for supramundane concentration, the concentration of the path (*magga*) and the fruit (*phala*). To acquire this concentration it is essential to cultivate wisdom (*paññā*).

There are two forms of wisdom: mundane and supramundane. Nowadays, knowledge of literature, art, science, or other worldly affairs is usually regarded as a kind of wisdom, but this form of wisdom has nothing to do with any kind of mental development (*bhāvanā*). Nor can it be regarded as of real merit, because many weapons of destruction are invented through these kinds of knowledge, which are always under the influence of attachment, aversion, and other evil motives. The real spirit of mundane wisdom, on the other hand, has only merits and no demerits of any kind.

True mundane wisdom includes the knowledge used in welfare and relief work, which causes no harm; learning to acquire the knowledge of the true meaning or sense of the scriptures; and the three classes of knowledge of development for insight (*vipassanā-bhāvanā*), such as knowledge born of learning (*suttamaya-paññā*), knowledge born of reflection (*cintāmaya-paññā*), and wisdom born of meditative development (*bhāvanāmaya-paññā*). The virtue of possessing mundane wisdom will lead to a happy life in higher states of existence, but it still cannot prevent the risk of being reborn in hell or in other states of miserable existence. Only the development of supramundane wisdom (*lokuttara-paññā*) can decidedly remove this risk.

Supramundane wisdom is the wisdom of the path and fruit. To develop this wisdom it is necessary to carry on the practice of insight meditation (*vipassanā-bhāvanā*) out of the three disciplines of morality, concentration, and wisdom. When the virtue of wisdom is duly developed, the necessary qualities of morality and concentration will also be acquired.

The Development of Wisdom

The method of developing this wisdom is to observe materiality (*rūpa*) and mentality (*nāma*)—the two sole elements existing in a living being—with a view to knowing them in their true nature. At present, experiments in the analytical observation of materiality are usually carried out in laboratories with the aid of various kinds of instruments, yet these methods cannot deal with the mind. The method of the Buddha does not require any kind of instruments or outside aid. It can successfully deal with both materiality and mentality. It makes use of one's own mind for analytical purposes by fixing bare attention on the activities of materiality and mentality as they occur within oneself. By continually repeating this form of exercise, the necessary concentration can be gained, and when concentration is keen enough, the ceaseless course of arising and passing away of materiality and mentality will be vividly perceptible.

The living being consists solely of the two distinct groups of materiality and mentality. The solid substance of body as it is now found belongs to the group of materiality. According to the usual enumeration of material phenomena, there are altogether twenty-eight kinds in this group, but in short it may be noted that the body is a mass of materiality. For example, it is the same as a doll made of clay or wheat, which is nothing but a collection of particles of clay or flour. Materiality changes its form (*ruppati*) under physical conditions of heat, cold, etc., and because of this changeableness under contrary physical conditions, it is called *rūpa* in Pali. It does not possess any faculty of knowing an object.

In the *Abhidhamma*, the elements of mentality and materiality are classified as "states with object" (*sārammaṇa-dhammā*) and "states without object" (*anārammaṇa-dhammā*), respectively. The element of mentality has an object, holds an object, knows an object, while that of materiality does not have an object, does not hold an object, and does not know an object. It will thus be seen that the *Abhidhamma* has directly stated that materiality has no faculty of knowing an object. A yogi also perceives in like manner that "materiality has no faculty of knowing".

Logs and pillars, bricks and stones, and lumps of earth are a mass of materiality. They do not possess any faculty of knowing. It is the same with the materiality which makes up a living body—it has no faculty of knowing. The materiality in a dead body is the same as that of a living body—it does not possess any faculty of knowing. People, however, have a common idea that the materiality of a living body possesses the faculty of knowing an object and that it loses this faculty only at death. This is not really so. In actual fact, materiality does not possess the faculty of knowing an object in either a dead or a living body.

What is it then that knows objects now? It is mentality, which comes into being depending on materiality. It is called *nāma* in Pali because it inclines (*namati*) towards an object. Mentality is also spoken of as thought or consciousness. Mentality arises depending on materiality: depending on the eye, eye-consciousness (seeing) arises; depending on the ear, ear-consciousness (hearing) arises; depending on the nose, nose-consciousness (smelling) arises; depending on the tongue, tongue-consciousness (tasting) arises; depending on the body, body-consciousness (sense of touch) arises. There are many kinds of sense of touch, either good or bad.

While touch has a wide field of action in running throughout the whole length of the body, inside and outside, the senses of seeing, hearing, smelling, and tasting come into being in their own particular spheres—the eye, ear, nose, and tongue—each of which occupies a very small and limited area of the body. These senses of touch, sight, etc., are nothing but the elements of mind. There also comes into being mind-consciousness—thoughts, ideas, imaginings, etc.—depending on the mind-base. All of these are elements of mind. Mind knows an object, while materiality does not know an object.

Seeing

People generally believe that in the case of seeing, it is the eye which actually sees. They think that seeing and the eye are one and the same thing. They also think: "Seeing is I", "I see things", "The eye, seeing, and I are one and the same person". In reality this is not so. The eye is one thing and seeing is another, and there is no separate entity such as "I" or "ego". There is only the reality of seeing coming into being depending on the eye.

To give an example, it is like the case of a person who sits in a house. The house and the person are two separate things: the house is not the person, nor is the person the house. Similarly, it is so at the time of seeing. The eye and seeing are two separate things: the eye is not seeing, nor is seeing the eye.

To give another example, it is just like the case of a person in a room who sees many things when he opens the window and looks through it. If it is asked, "Who is it that sees? Is it the window or the person that actually sees?" the answer is, "The window does not possess the ability to see; it is only the person who sees". If it is again asked, "Will the person be able to see things on the outside without the window?" the answer will be, "It is not possible to see things through the wall without the window. One can only see through the window". Similarly, in the case of seeing, there are two separate realities of the eye and seeing. The eye is not seeing, nor is seeing the eye, yet there cannot be an act of seeing without the eye. In reality, seeing comes into being depending on the eye.

It is now evident that in the body there are only two distinct elements of materiality (eye) and mentality (seeing) at every moment of seeing. In addition, there is also a third element of materiality—the visual object. At times the visual object is noticeable in the body and at times it is noticeable outside the body. With the addition of the visual object there will then be three elements, two of which (the eye and the visual object) are materiality and the third of which (seeing) is mentality. The eye and the visual object, being materiality, do not possess the ability to know an object, while seeing, being mentality, can know the visual object and what it looks like. Now it is clear that there exist only the two separate elements of materiality and mentality at the moment of seeing, and the arising of this pair of separate elements is known as seeing.

People who are without the training in and knowledge of insight meditation hold the view that seeing belongs to or is "self", "ego", "living entity", or "person". They believe that "seeing is I", or "I am seeing", or "I am knowing". This kind of view or belief is called *sakkāya-diṭṭhi* in Pali. *Sakkāya* means the group of materiality (*rūpa*) and mentality (*nāma*) as they exist distinctively. *Diṭṭhi* means a wrong view or belief. The compound word *sakkāya-diṭṭhi* means a wrong view or belief in self with regard to *nāma* and *rūpa*, which exist in reality.

For greater clarity, we will explain further the manner of holding the wrong view or belief. At the moment of seeing, the things which actually exist are the eye, the visual object (both materiality), and seeing (mentality). *Nāma* and *rūpa* are reality, yet people hold the view that this group of elements is self, or ego, or a living entity. They consider that "seeing is I", or "that which is seen is I", or "I see my own body". Thus this mistaken view is taking the simple act of seeing to be self, which is *sakkāya-diṭṭhi*, the wrong view of self.

As long as one is not free from the wrong view of self, one cannot expect to escape from the risk of falling into the miserable realms of the hells, the animals or the *petas*. Though one may be leading a happy life in the human or *deva* world by virtue of one's merits, yet one is liable to fall back into the miserable states of existence at any time, when one's demerits operate. For this reason, the Buddha pointed out that it is essential to work for the total removal of the wrong view of self:

"Let a monk go forth mindfully to abandon view of self" (*sakkāya-diṭṭhippahānāya sato bhikkhu paribbaje*).

To explain: Though it is the wish of everyone to avoid old age, disease, and death, no one can prevent their inevitable arrival. After death, rebirth follows. Rebirth in any state of existence does not depend on one's own wish. It is not possible to avoid rebirth in the hell realm, the animal realm or the realm of the *petas* by merely wishing for an escape. Rebirth takes place in any state of existence as the consequence of one's own deeds: there is no choice at all. For these reasons, the round of birth and death, *saṃsāra*, is very dreadful. Every effort should therefore be made to acquaint oneself with the miserable conditions of *saṃsāra*, and then to work for an escape from *saṃsāra*, for the attainment of Nibbāna.

If an escape from *saṃsāra* as a whole is not possible for the present, an attempt should be made for an escape at least from the round of rebirth in the hell realms, the animal realm, and the *peta* realm. In this case it is necessary to work for the total removal within oneself of *sakkāya-diṭṭhi*, which is the root cause of rebirth in the miserable states of existence. *Sakkāya-diṭṭhi* can only be destroyed completely by the noble path and fruit: the three supramundane virtues of morality, concentration, and wisdom. It is therefore imperative to work for the development of these virtues. How should one do the work? By means of noting or observing one must go out from the jurisdiction of defilements (*kilesa*). One should practise by constantly noting or observing every act of seeing, hearing, etc., which are the constituent physical and mental processes, till one is freed from *sakkāya-diṭṭhi*, the wrong view of self.

For these reasons advice is always given here to take up the practice of *vipassanā* meditation. Now yogis have come here for the purpose of practising *vipassanā* meditation who may be able to complete the course of training and attain the noble path in no long time. The view of self will then be totally removed and security will be finally gained against the danger of rebirth in the realms of the hells, animals, and *petas*.

In this respect, the exercise is simply to note or observe the existing elements in every act of seeing. It should be noted as "seeing, seeing" on every occasion of seeing. By the terms "note" or "observe" or "contemplate" is meant the act of keeping the mind fixedly on the object with a view to knowing it clearly.

When this is done, and the act of seeing is noted as "seeing, seeing", at times the visual object is noticed, at times consciousness of seeing is noticed, at times the eye-base, the place from which one sees, is noticed. It will serve the purpose if one can notice distinctly any one of the three. If not, based on this act of seeing there will arise *sakkāya-diṭṭhi,* which will view it in the form of a person or as belonging to a person, and as being permanent, pleasurable, and self. This will arouse the defilements of craving and attachment, which will in turn prompt deeds, and the deeds will bring forth rebirth in a new existence. Thus the process of dependent origination operates and the vicious circle of *saṃsāra* revolves incessantly. In order to prevent the revolving of *saṃsāra* from this source of seeing, it is necessary to note "seeing, seeing" on every occasion of seeing.

Hearing, Etc.

Similarly, in the case of hearing, there are only two distinct elements, materiality and mentality. The sense of hearing arises depending on the ear. While the ear and sound are two elements of materiality, the sense of hearing is the element of mentality. In order to know clearly any one of these two kinds of materiality and mentality, every occasion of hearing should be noted as "hearing, hearing". So also, "smelling, smelling" should be noted on every occasion of smelling, and "tasting, tasting" on every occasion of tasting.

The sensation of touch in the body should be noted in the very same way. There is a kind of material element known as bodily sensitivity throughout the body, which receives every impression of touch. Every kind of touch, either agreeable or disagreeable, usually comes in contact with bodily sensitivity, and from this there arises body-consciousness, which feels or knows the touch on each occasion. It will now be seen that at every moment of touching there are two elements of materiality—the bodily sensitivity and the tangible object—and one element of mentality—knowing of touch.

In order to know these things distinctly at every moment of touching, the practice of noting as "touching, touching" has to be carried out. This merely refers to the common form of sensation of touch. There are special forms which accompany painful or disagreeable sensations, such as feeling stiffness or tiredness in the body or limbs, feeling hot, pain, numb, aches, etc. Because feeling (*vedanā*) predominates in these cases, it should be noted as "feeling hot", "feeling tired", "feeling painful", etc., as the case may be.

It may also be mentioned that there occur many sensations of touch in the hands, the legs, and so on, on each occasion of bending, stretching, or moving. Because of mentality *wanting* to move, stretch or bend, the material activities of moving, stretching or bending, etc., occur in series. (It may not be possible to notice these incidents at the outset. They can only be noticed after some time, on gaining experience by practice. It is mentioned here for the sake of general information.) All activities in movements and in changing, etc., are done by mentality. When mentality wills to bend, there arises a series of inward movements of the hand or the leg. When mentality wills to stretch or move, there arises a series of outward movements or movements to and fro. They fall away soon after they occur and at the very point of occurrence, as one will notice later.

In every case of bending, stretching, or other activities, there arises first a series of intentions, moments of mentality, inducing or causing in the hands and legs a series of material activities, such as stiffening, bending, stretching, or moving to and fro. These activities come up against other material elements, the bodily sensitivity, and on every occasion of contact between material activities and sensitive qualities, there arises body-consciousness, which feels or knows the sensation of touch. It is therefore clear that material activities are *pre-dominating* factors in these cases. It is necessary to notice the predominating factors. If not, there will surely arise the wrong view which regards these activities as the doings of an "I"—"I am bending", "I am stretching", "my hands", or "my legs". This practice of noting as "bending", "stretching", "moving", is carried out for the purpose of removing such wrong views.

Mind

Depending on the mind-base there arises a series of mental activities, such as thinking, imagining, etc., or generally speaking, a series of mental activities arises depending on the body. In reality, each case is a composition of mentality and materiality, mind-base being materiality, and thinking, imagining, and so forth being mentality. In order to be able to notice materiality and mentality clearly, "thinking", "imagining", and so forth should be noted in each case.

After having carried out the practice in the manner indicated above for some time, there may be an improvement in concentration. One will notice that the mind no longer wanders about but remains fixed on the object to which it is directed. At the same time, the power of noticing has considerably developed. On every occasion of noting, one notices only two processes of materiality and mentality: a dual set of object (materiality) and mental state (mentality), which makes note of the object, arising together.

Again, on proceeding further with the practice of contemplation, after some time one notices that nothing remains permanent, but that everything is in a state of flux. New things arise each time. Each of them is noted as it arises. Whatever arises then passes away immediately and immediately another arises, which is again noted and which then passes away. Thus the process of arising and passing away goes on, which clearly shows that nothing is permanent. One therefore realises that "things are not permanent" because one sees that they arise and pass away immediately. This is insight into impermanence (*aniccānupassanā-ñāṇa*).

Then one also realises that "arising and passing are not desirable". This is insight into suffering (*dukkhanupassanā-ñāṇa*). Besides, one usually experiences many painful sensations in the body, such as tiredness, heat, aching, and at the time of noting these sensations, one generally feels that this body is a collection of sufferings. This is also insight into suffering.

Then at every time of noting it is found that elements of materiality and mentality occur according to their respective nature and conditioning, and not according to one's wishes. One therefore realises that "they are elements; they are not governable; they are not a person or living entity". This is insight into non-self (*anattānupassanā-ñāṇa*).

On having fully acquired these insights into impermanence, suffering, and non-self, the maturity of knowledge of the path (*magga-ñāṇa*) and knowledge of fruition (*phala-ñāṇa*) takes place and realisation of Nibbāna is won. By winning the realisation of Nibbāna in the first stage, one is freed from the round of rebirth in the realms of miserable existence. Everyone should therefore endeavour to reach the first stage, the path and fruit of stream-entry, as a minimum measure of protection against an unfortunate rebirth.

The Beginner's Exercise

It has already been explained that the actual method of practice in *vipassanā* meditation is to note, or to observe, or to contemplate, the successive occurrences of seeing, hearing, and so on, at the six sense doors. However, it will not be possible for a beginner to follow these on all successive incidents as they occur because his mindfulness (*sati*), concentration (*samādhi*), and knowledge (*ñāṇa*) are still very weak. The moments of seeing, hearing, smelling, tasting, touching, and thinking occur very swiftly. It seems that seeing occurs at the same time as hearing, that hearing occurs at the same time as seeing, that seeing and hearing occur simultaneously, that seeing, hearing, thinking, and imagining always occur simultaneously. Because they occur so swiftly, it is not possible to distinguish which occurs first and which second.

In reality, seeing does not occur at the same time as hearing, nor does hearing occur at the same time as seeing. Such incidents can occur only one at a time. A yogi who has just begun the practice and who has not sufficiently developed his mindfulness, concentration, and knowledge will not, however, be in a position to observe all these moments singly as they occur in serial order. A beginner need not, therefore, follow up on many things. He needs to begin with only a few things.

Seeing or hearing occurs only when due attention is given to their objects. If one does not pay heed to any sight or sound, one may pass the time without any moments of seeing or hearing taking place. Smelling rarely occurs. The experience of tasting can only occur while one is eating. In the case of seeing, hearing, smelling, and tasting, the yogi can note them when they occur. Body impressions, however, are ever-present. They usually exist distinctly all the time. During the time that one is sitting, the body impression of stiffness or the sensation of hardness in this position is distinctly felt. Attention should therefore be fixed on the sitting posture and a note made as "sitting, sitting, sitting".

Sitting

Sitting is an erect posture of the body consisting of a series of physical activities, induced by consciousness consisting of a series of mental activities. It is just like the case of an inflated rubber ball which maintains its round shape through the resistance of the air inside it. The posture of sitting is similar in that the body is kept in an erect posture through the continuous process of physical activities. A good deal of energy is required to pull up and keep in an erect position such a heavy load as this body. People generally assume that the body is lifted and kept in an upright position by means of sinews. This assumption is correct in a sense because sinews, blood, flesh, and bones are nothing but materiality. The element of stiffening which keeps the body in an erect posture belongs to the group of materiality and arises in the sinews, flesh, blood, etc., throughout the body, like the air in a rubber ball.

The element of stiffening is the air element, known as *vāyo-dhātu.* The body is kept in an erect position by the air element in the form of stiffening, which is continually coming into existence. At the time of sleepiness or drowsiness, one may drop flat because the supply of new materials in the form of stiffening is cut off. The state of mind in heavy drowsiness or sleep is *bhavaṅga,* the "life-continuum" or passive subconscious flow. During the course of *bhavaṅga,* mental activities are absent, and for this reason, the body lies flat during sleep or heavy drowsiness.

During waking hours, strong and alert mental activities are continually arising, and because of these the air element arises serially in the form of stiffening. In order to know these facts, it is essential to note the bodily posture attentively as "sitting, sitting, sitting". This does not necessarily mean that the body impression of stiffening should particularly be searched for and noted. Attention need only be fixed on the whole form of the sitting posture, that is, the lower portion of the body in a bent circular form and the upper portion held erect.

It may be found that the exercise of observing the mere sitting posture is too easy and does not require much effort. In these circumstances, energy (*viriya*) is less and concentration (*samādhi*) is in excess. One will generally feel lazy and will not want to carry on the noting as "sitting, sitting, sitting" repeatedly for a considerable length of time. Laziness generally occurs when there is an excess of concentration and not enough energy. It is nothing but a state of sloth and torpor (*thīna-middha*).

More energy should be developed, and for this purpose, the number of objects for noting should be increased. After noting as "sitting", the attention should be directed to a spot in the body where the sense of touch is felt and a note made as "touching". Any spot in the leg or hand or hip where a sense of touch is distinctly felt will serve the purpose. For example, after noting the sitting posture of the body as "sitting", the spot where the sense of touch is felt should be noted as "touching". The noting should thus be repeated using these two objects of *the sitting posture* and *the place of touching* alternately, as "sitting, touching, sitting, touching, sitting, touching".

The terms "noting", "observing", and "contemplating" are used here to indicate the fixing of attention on an object. The exercise is simply to note or observe or contemplate as "sitting, touching". Those who already have experience in the practice of meditation may find this exercise easy to begin with, but those without any previous experience may at first find it rather difficult.

Rising-Falling

A simpler and easier form of the exercise for a beginner is this: with every breath there occurs in the abdomen a rising-falling movement. A beginner should start with the exercise of noting this movement. This rising-falling movement is easy to observe because it is coarse and therefore more suitable for the beginner. As in schools where simple lessons are easy to learn, so also is the practice of *vipassanā* meditation. A beginner will find it easier to develop concentration and knowledge with a simple and easy exercise.

Again, the purpose of *vipassanā* meditation is to begin the exercise by contemplating prominent factors in the body. Of the two factors of mentality and materiality, the former is subtle and less prominent, while the latter is coarse and more prominent. At the outset, therefore, the usual procedure for an insight meditator is to begin the exercise by contemplating the material elements.

With regard to materiality, it may be mentioned here that derived materiality (*upādā-rūpa*) is subtle and less prominent, while the four primary physical elements (*mahā-bhūta-rūpa*)—earth, water, fire, and air—are coarse and more prominent. The latter should therefore have priority in the order of objects for contemplation. In the case of rising-falling, the outstanding factor is the air element or *vāyo-dhātu*. The process of stiffening and the movements of the abdomen noticed during the contemplation are nothing but the functions of the air element. Thus it will be seen that the air element is perceptible at the beginning.

According to the instructions of the Satipaṭṭhāna Sutta, one should be mindful of the activities of walking while walking, of those of standing, sitting, and lying down while standing, sitting, and lying down, respectively. One should also be mindful of other bodily activities as each of them occurs. In this connection, it is stated in the commentaries that one should be mindful primarily of the air element in preference to the other three elements. As a matter of fact, all four primary elements are dominant in every action of the body, and it is essential to perceive any one of them. At the time of sitting, either of the two movements of rising and falling occurs conspicuously with every breath, and a beginning should be made by noting these movements.

Some fundamental features in the system of *vipassanā* meditation have been explained for general information. The general outline of basic exercises will now be dealt with.

Outline of Basic Exercises

When contemplating rising and falling, the disciple should keep his mind on the abdomen. He will then come to know the upward movement or expansion of the abdomen on breathing in, and the downward movement or contraction on breathing out. A mental note should be made as "rising" for the upward movement and "falling" for the downward movement. If these movements are not clearly noticed by simply fixing the mind on them, one or both hands should be placed on the abdomen.

The disciple should not try to change the manner of his natural breathing. He should neither attempt slow breathing by the retention of his breath, nor quick breathing or deep breathing. If he does change the natural flow of his breathing, he will soon tire himself. He must therefore keep to the natural rate of his breathing and proceed with the contemplation of rising and falling.

On the occurrence of the upward movement of the abdomen, the mental note of "rising" should be made, and on the downward movement of the abdomen, the mental note of "falling" should be made. The mental notation of these terms should not be vocalised. In *vipassanā* meditation, it is more important to know the object than to know it by term or name. It is therefore necessary for the disciple to make every effort to be mindful of the movement of rising from its beginning to its end and that of falling from its beginning to its end, as if these movements are actually seen with the eyes. As soon as rising occurs, there should be the knowing mind close to the movement, as in the case of a stone hitting a wall. The movement of rising as it occurs and the mind knowing it must come together on every occasion. Similarly, the movement of falling as it occurs and the mind knowing it must come together on every occasion.

When there is no other conspicuous object, the disciple should carry on the exercise of noting these two movements as "rising, falling, rising, falling, rising, falling". While thus being occupied with this exercise, there may be occasions when the mind wanders about. When concentration is weak, it is very difficult to control the mind. Though it is directed to the movements of rising and falling, the mind will not stay with them but will wander to other places. This wandering mind should not be let alone. It should be noted as "wandering, wandering, wandering" as soon as it is noticed that it is wandering. On noting once or twice the mind usually stops wandering, then the exercise of noting "rising, falling" should be continued. When it is again found that the mind has reached a place, it should be noted as "reaching, reaching, reaching". Then the exercise of noting "rising, falling" should be reverted to as soon as these movements are clear.

On meeting with a person in the imagination, it should be noted as "meeting, meeting", after which the usual exercise should be reverted to. Sometimes the fact that it is mere imagination is discovered when one speaks with that imaginary person, and it should then be noted as "speaking, speaking". The real purport is to note every mental activity as it occurs. For instance, it should be noted as "thinking" at the moment of thinking, and as "reflecting", "planning", "knowing", "attending", "rejoicing", "feeling lazy", "feeling happy", "disgusted", etc., as the case may be, on the occurrence of each activity. The contemplation of mental activities and noticing them is called *cittānupassanā*, contemplation of mind.

Because people have no practical knowledge in *vipassanā* meditation, they are generally not in a position to know the real state of the mind. This naturally leads them to the wrong view of holding the mind to be "person", "self", "living entity". They usually believe that "imagination is I", "I am thinking", "I am planning", "I am knowing", and so forth. They hold that there exists a living entity or self which grows up from childhood to adulthood. In reality, such a living entity does not exist, but there does exist a continuous process of elements of mind which occur singly, one at a time, in succession. The practice of contemplation is therefore being carried out with the aim of discovering the true nature of this mind-body complex.

As regards the mind and the manner of its arising, the Buddha stated in the Dhammapada (v. 37):

Dūraṅgaṃ ekacaraṃ
asarīraṃ guhāsayaṃ
ye cittaṃ saññamessanti
mokkhanti mārabandhanā.

Faring far, wandering alone,
Formless and lying in a cave.
Those who do restrain the mind
Are sure released from Māra's bonds.

Faring far. The mind usually wanders far and wide. While the yogi is trying to carry on with the practice of contemplation in his meditation room, he often finds that his mind has wandered to many far-off places, towns, etc. He also finds that his mind can wander to any of the far-off places which he has previously known at the very moment of thinking or imagining. This fact is discovered with the help of contemplation.

Alone. The mind occurs singly, moment to moment in succession. Those who do not perceive the reality of this believe that one mind exists in the course of life or existence. They do not know that new minds are always arising at every moment. They think that the seeing, hearing, smelling, tasting, touching, and thinking of the past and of the present belong to one and the same mind, and that three or four acts of seeing, hearing, touching, knowing usually occur simultaneously.

These are wrong views. In reality, single moments of mind arise and pass away continuously, one after another. This can be perceived on gaining considerable practice. The cases of imagination and planning are clearly perceptible. Imagination passes away as soon as it is noted as "imagining, imagining", and planning also passes away as soon as it is noted as "planning, planning". These instances of arising, noting, and passing away appear like a string of beads. The preceding mind is not the following mind. Each is separate. These characteristics of reality are personally perceptible, and for this purpose one must proceed with the practice of contemplation.

Formless. Mind has no substance, no form. It is not easy to distinguish as is the case with materiality. In the case of materiality, the body, head, hands, and legs are very prominent and are easily noticed. If it is asked what matter is, matter can be handled and shown. Mind, however, is not easy to describe because it has no substance or form. For this reason, it is not possible to carry out analytical laboratory experiments on the mind.

One can, however, fully understand the mind if it is explained as *that which knows an object.* To understand the mind, it is necessary to contemplate the mind at every moment of its occurrence. When contemplation is fairly advanced, the mind's approach to its object is clearly comprehended. It appears as if each moment of mind is making a direct leap towards its object. In order to know the true nature of the mind, contemplation is thus prescribed.

Lying in a cave. Because the mind comes into being depending on the mind-base and the other sense doors situated in the body, it is said that it rests in a cave.

Those who do restrain the mind are sure released from Māra's bonds. It is said that the mind should be contemplated at each moment of its occurrence. The mind can thus be controlled by means of contemplation. On his successful controlling of the mind, the yogi will win freedom from the bondage of Māra, the King of Death. It will now be seen that it is important to note the mind at every moment of its occurrence. As soon as it is noted, the mind passes away. For instance, by noting once or twice as "intending, intending", it is found that intention passes away at once. Then the usual exercise of noting as "rising, falling, rising, falling" should be reverted to.

While one is proceeding with the usual exercise, one may feel that one wants to swallow saliva. It should be noted as "wanting", and on gathering saliva as "gathering", and on swallowing as "swallowing", in the serial order of occurrence. The reason for contemplation in this case is because there may be a persisting personal view as "wanting to swallow is I", "swallowing is also I". In reality, "wanting to swallow" is mentality and not "I", and "swallowing" is materiality and not "I". There exist only mentality and materiality at that moment. By means of contemplating in this manner, one will understand clearly the process of reality. So too, in the case of spitting, it should be noted as "wanting" when one wants to spit, as "bending" on bending the neck (which should be done slowly), as "looking, seeing" on looking, and as "spitting" on spitting. Afterwards, the usual exercise of noting "rising, falling" should be continued.

Because of sitting for a long time, there will arise in the body unpleasant feelings of being stiff, being hot and so forth. These sensations should be noted as they occur. The mind should be fixed on that spot and a note made as "stiff, stiff" on feeling stiff, as "hot, hot" on feeling hot, as "painful, painful" on feeling painful, as "prickly, prickly" on feeling prickly sensations, and as "tired, tired" on feeling tired. These unpleasant feelings are *dukkha-vedanā* and the contemplation of these feelings is *vedanānupassanā*, contemplation of feeling.

Owing to the absence of knowledge in respect of these feelings, there persists the wrong view of holding them as one's own personality or self, that is to say, "I am feeling stiff", "I am feeling painful", "I was feeling well formerly but I now feel uncomfortable", in the manner of a single self. In reality, unpleasant feelings arise owing to disagreeable impressions in the body. Like the light of an electric bulb which can continue to burn on a continuous supply of energy, so it is in the case of feelings, which arise anew on every occasion of coming in contact with disagreeable impressions.

It is essential to understand these feelings clearly. At the beginning of noting as "stiff, stiff", "hot, hot", "painful, painful", one may feel that such disagreeable feelings grow stronger, and then one will notice that a mind wanting to change the posture arises. This mind should be noted as "wanting, wanting". Then a return should be made to the feeling and it should be noted as "stiff, stiff" or "hot, hot", and so forth. If one proceeds in this manner of contemplation with great patience, unpleasant feelings will pass away.

There is a saying that patience leads to Nibbāna. Evidently this saying is more applicable in the case of contemplation than in any other. Plenty of patience is needed in contemplation. If a yogi cannot bear unpleasant feelings with patience, but frequently changes his posture during contemplation, he cannot expect to gain concentration. Without concentration there is no chance of acquiring insight knowledge (*vipassanā-ñāṇa*) and without insight knowledge the attainment of the path, fruition, and Nibbāna cannot be won.

Patience is of great importance in contemplation. Patience is needed mostly to bear unpleasant bodily feelings. There is hardly any case of outside disturbances where it is not necessary to exercise patience. This means the observance of *khantisaṃvara*, restraint by patience. The posture should not be immediately changed when unpleasant sensations arise, but contemplation should be continued by noting them as "stiff, stiff", "hot, hot", and so on. Such painful sensations are normal and will pass away. In the case of strong concentration, it will be found that great pains will pass away when they are noted with patience. On the fading away of suffering or pain, the usual exercise of noting "rising, falling" should be continued.

On the other hand, it may be found that pains or unpleasant feelings do not immediately pass away even when one notes them with great patience. In such a case, one has no alternative but to change posture. One must, of course, submit to superior forces. When concentration is not strong enough, strong pains will not pass away quickly. In these circumstances there will often arise a mind wanting to change posture, and this mind should be noted as "wanting, wanting". After this, one should note "lifting, lifting" on lifting the hand, and "moving, moving" on moving it forward.

These bodily actions should be carried out slowly, and these slow movements should be followed up and noted as "lifting, lifting", "moving, moving", "touching, touching", in the successive order of the process. Again, on moving one should note "moving, moving", and on putting down, note "putting, putting". If, when this process of changing posture has been completed, there is nothing more to be noted, the usual exercise of noting "rising, falling" should be continued.

There should be no stop or break in between. The preceding act of noting and the one which follows should be contiguous. Similarly, the preceding concentration and the one which follows should be contiguous, and the preceding act of knowing and the one which follows should be contiguous. In this way, the gradual development by stages of mindfulness, concentration, and knowledge takes place, and depending on their full development, the final stage of path-knowledge is attained.

In the practice of *vipassanā* meditation, it is important to follow the example of a person who tries to make fire. To make a fire in the days before matches, a person had to constantly rub two sticks together without the slightest break in motion. As the sticks became hotter and hotter, more effort was needed, and the rubbing had to be carried out incessantly. Only when the fire had been produced was the person at liberty to take a rest. Similarly, a yogi should work hard so that there is no break between the preceding noting and the one which follows, and the preceding concentration and the one which follows. He should revert to his usual exercise of noting "rising, falling" after he has noted painful sensations.

While being thus occupied with his usual exercise, he may again feel itching sensations somewhere in the body. He should then fix his mind on the spot and make a note as "itching, itching". Itching is an unpleasant sensation. As soon as it is felt, there arises a mind which wants to rub or scratch. This mind should be noted as "wanting, wanting", after which no rubbing or scratching must be done as yet, but a return should be made to the itching and a note made as "itching, itching". While one is occupied with contemplation in this manner, itching in most cases passes away and the usual exercise of noting "rising, falling" should then be reverted to.

If, on the other hand, it is found that itching does not pass away, but that it is necessary to rub or scratch, the contemplation of the successive stages should be carried out by noting the mind as "wanting, wanting". It should then be continued by noting "raising, raising" on raising the hand, "touching, touching" when the hand touches the spot, "rubbing, rubbing" or "scratching, scratching" when the hand rubs or scratches, "withdrawing, withdrawing" on withdrawing the hand, "touching, touching" when the hand touches the body, and then the usual contemplation of "rising, falling" should be continued. In every case of changing postures, contemplation of the successive stages should be carried out similarly and carefully.

While thus carefully proceeding with the contemplation, one may find that painful feelings or unpleasant sensations arise in the body of their own accord. Ordinarily, people change their posture as soon as they feel even the slightest unpleasant sensation of tiredness or heat without taking heed of these incidents. The change of posture is carried out quite heedlessly just while the seed of pain is beginning to grow. Thus painful feelings fail to take place in a distinctive manner. For this reason it is said that, as a rule, the postures hide painful feelings from view. People generally think that they are feeling well for days and nights on end. They think that painful feelings occur only at the time of an attack of a dangerous disease.

Reality is just the opposite of what people think. Let anyone try to see how long he can keep himself in a sitting posture without moving or changing it. One will find it uncomfortable after a short while, say five or ten minutes, and then one will begin to find it unbearable after fifteen or twenty minutes. One will then be compelled to move or change one's posture by either raising or lowering the head, moving the hands or legs, or by swaying the body either forward or backward. Many movements usually take place during a short time, and the number would be very large if they were to be counted for the length of just one day. However, no one appears to be aware of this fact because no one takes any heed.

Such is the order in every case, while in the case of a yogi who is always mindful of his actions and who is proceeding with contemplation, body impressions in their own respective nature are therefore distinctly noticed. They cannot help but reveal themselves fully in their own nature because he is watching until they come to full view.

Though a painful sensation arises, he keeps on noting it. He does not ordinarily attempt to change his posture or move. Then on the arising of mind wanting to change, he at once makes a note of it as "wanting, wanting", and afterwards he returns again to the painful sensation and continues his noting of it. He changes his posture or moves only when he finds the painful feeling unbearable. In this case he also begins by noting the wanting mind and proceeds with noting carefully each stage in the process of moving. This is why the postures can no longer hide painful sensations. Often a yogi finds painful sensations creeping from here and there or he may feel hot sensations, aching sensations, itching, or the whole body as a mass of painful sensations. That is how painful sensations are found to be predominant because the postures cannot cover them.

If he intends to change his posture from sitting to standing, he should first make a note of the intending mind as "intending, intending", and proceed with the arranging of the hands and legs in the successive stages by noting as "raising", "moving", "stretching", "touching", "pressing", and so forth. When the body sways forward, it should be noted as "swaying, swaying". While in the course of standing up, there occurs in the body a feeling of lightness as well as the act of rising. Attention should be fixed on these factors and a note made as "rising, rising". The act of rising should be carried out slowly.

During the course of practice it is most appropriate if a yogi acts feebly and slowly in all activities just like a weak, sick person. Perhaps the case of a person suffering from lumbago would be a more fitting example here. The patient must always be cautious and move slowly just to avoid pains. In the same manner a yogi should always try to keep to slow movements in all actions. Slow motion is necessary to enable mindfulness, con-centration, and knowledge to catch up. One has lived all the time in a careless manner and one just begins seriously to train oneself in keeping the mind within the body. It is only the beginning, and one's mindfulness, concentration, and knowledge have not yet been properly geared up while the physical and mental processes are moving at top speed. It is thus imperative to bring the top-level speed of these processes to the lowest gear so as to make it possible for mindfulness and knowledge to keep pace with them. It is therefore desirable that slow motion exercises be carried out at all times.

Further, it is advisable for a yogi to behave like a blind person throughout the course of training. A person without any restraint will not look dignified because he usually looks at things and persons wantonly. He also cannot obtain a steady and calm state of mind. The blind person, on the other hand, behaves in a composed manner by sitting sedately with downcast eyes. He never turns in any direction to look at things or persons because he is blind and cannot see them. Even if a person comes near him and speaks to him, he never turns around and looks at that person. This composed manner is worthy of imitation. A yogi should act in the same manner while carrying out the practice of contemplation. He should not look anywhere. His mind should be solely intent on the object of contemplation. While in the sitting posture he must be intently noting "rising, falling". Even if strange things occur nearby, he should not look at them. He must simply make a note as "seeing, seeing", and then continue with the usual exercise of noting "rising, falling". A yogi should have a high regard for this exercise and carry it out with due respect, so much so as to be mistaken for a blind person.

In this respect certain girl-yogis were found to be in perfect form. They carefully carried out the exercise with all due respect in accordance with the instructions. Their manner was very composed and they were always intent on their objects of contemplation. They never looked round. When they walked, they were always intent on the steps. Their steps were light, smooth, and slow. Every yogi should follow their example.

It is necessary for a yogi to behave like a deaf person also. Ordinarily, as soon as a person hears a sound, he turns around and looks in the direction from which the sound came, or he turns towards the person who spoke to him and makes a reply. He does not behave in a sedate manner. A deaf person, on the other hand, behaves in a composed manner. He does not take heed of any sound or talk because he never hears them. Similarly, a yogi should conduct himself in like manner without taking heed of any unimportant talk, nor should he deliberately listen to any talk or speech. If he happens to hear any sound or speech, he should at once make a note as "hearing, hearing", and then return to the usual practice of noting "rising, falling". He should proceed with his contemplation intently, so much so as to be mistaken for a deaf person.

It should be remembered that the *only* concern of a yogi is the carrying out intently of contemplation. Other things seen or heard are not his concern. Even though they may appear to be strange or interesting, he should not take heed of them. When he sees any sights, he must ignore them as if he does not see. So too, he must ignore voices or sounds as if he does not hear. In the case of bodily actions, he must act slowly and feebly as if he were sick and very weak.

Other Exercises

(i) Walking

It is therefore to be emphasised that the act of pulling up the body to the standing posture should be carried out slowly. On coming to an erect position, a note should be made as "standing, standing". If one happens to look around, a note should be made as "looking, seeing", and on walking each step should be noted as "right step, left step" or "walking, walking". At each step, attention should be fixed on the sole of the foot as it moves from the point of lifting the leg to the point of placing it down.

While walking in quick steps or taking a long walk, a note on one section of each step as "right step, left step" or "walking, walking" will do. In the case of walking slowly, each step may be divided into three sections—lifting, moving forward, and placing down. In the beginning of the exercise, a note should be made of the two parts of each step: as "lifting" by fixing the attention on the upward movement of the foot from the beginning to the end, and as "placing" by fixing on the downward movement from the beginning to the end. Thus the exercise which starts with the first step by noting as "lifting, placing" now ends.

Normally, when the foot is put down and is being noted as "placing", the other leg begins lifting to begin the next step. This should not be allowed to happen. The next step should begin only after the first step has been completed, such as "lifting, placing" for the first step and "lifting, placing" for the second step. After two or three days this exercise will be easy, and then the yogi should carry out the exercise of noting each step in three sections as "lifting, moving, placing". For the present a yogi should start the exercise by noting as "right step, left step", or "walking, walking" while walking quickly, and by noting as "lifting, placing" while walking slowly.

(ii) Sitting

While one is walking, one may feel the desire to sit down. One should then make a note as "wanting". If one then happens to look up, note it as "looking, seeing, looking, seeing"; on going to the seat as "lifting, placing"; on stopping as "stopping, stopping"; on turning as "turning, turning". When one feels a desire to sit, note it as "wanting, wanting". In the act of sitting there occur in the body heaviness and also a downward pull. Attention should be fixed on these factors and a note made as "sitting, sitting, sitting". After having sat down there will be movements of bringing the hands and legs into position. They should be noted as "moving", "bending", "stretching", and so forth. If there is nothing to do and if one is sitting quietly, one should then revert to the usual exercise of noting as "rising, falling".

(iii) Lying Down

If in the course of contemplation one feels painful or tired or hot, one should make a note of these and then revert to the usual exercise of noting "rising, falling". If one feels sleepy, one should make a note of it as "sleepy, sleepy"; and proceed with the noting of all acts in preparation to lie down: note the bringing into position of the hands and legs as "raising", "pressing", "moving", "supporting"; when the body sways as "swaying, swaying"; when the legs stretch as "stretching, stretching"; and when the body drops and lies flat as "lying, lying, lying".

These trifling acts in lying down are also important and they should not be neglected. There is every possibility of attaining enlightenment during this short time. On the full development of concentration and knowledge, enlightenment is attainable during the present moment of bending or stretching. In this way the Venerable Ānanda attained Arahatship at the very moment of lying down.

About the beginning of the fourth month after the Buddha's complete passing away, arrangements were made to hold the first council of bhikkhus to collectively classify, examine, confirm, and recite all the teachings of the Buddha. At that time five hundred bhikkhus were chosen for this work. Of these bhikkhus, four hundred and ninety-nine were *Arahats*, while the Venerable Ānanda alone was a *sotāpanna*, a stream-enterer.

In order to attend the council as an *Arahat* on the same level with the others, he made his utmost effort to carry on with his meditation on the day prior to the opening of the council. That was on the fourth of the waning moon of the month of Sāvana (August). He proceeded with mindfulness of the body and continued his walking meditation throughout the night. It might have been in the same manner as noting "right step, left step" or "walking, walking". He was thus occupied with intense contemplation of the processes of mentality and materiality in each step until dawn of the following day, but he still had not yet attained to Arahatship.

Then the Venerable Ānanda thought: "I have done my utmost. Lord Buddha has said, 'Ānanda, you possess full perfections (*pāramīs*). Do proceed with the practice of meditation. You will surely attain Arahatship one day.' I have tried my best, so much so that I can be counted as one of those who have done their best in meditation. What may be the reason for my failure?"

Then he remembered: "Ah! I have been overzealous in keeping solely to the practice of walking throughout the night.

There is an excess of energy and not enough concentration, which indeed is responsible for this state of restlessness. It is now necessary to stop walking practice so as to bring energy in balance with concentration and to proceed with the contemplation in a lying position". The Venerable Ānanda then entered his room, sat down on his bed, and began to lie down. It is said that he attained Arahatship at the very moment of lying down, or rather at the moment of contemplating as "lying, lying".

This manner of attaining Arahatship has been recorded as a strange event in the Commentaries, because it is outside the four regular postures of standing, sitting, lying, and walking. At the moment of his enlightenment, the Venerable Ānanda could not be regarded as strictly in a standing posture because his feet were off the floor, nor could he be regarded as sitting because his body was already at an angle, being quite close to the pillow, nor could he be regarded as lying down since his head had not yet touched the pillow and his body was not yet flat.

The Venerable Ānanda was a stream-enterer and he thus had to develop the three, other higher stages—the path and fruit of once-returning, the path and fruit of non-returning, and the path and fruit of Arahatship in his final attainment. This took only a moment. Extreme care is therefore needed to carry on the practice of contemplation without relaxation or omission.

In the act of lying down, contemplation should therefore be carried out with due care. When a yogi feels sleepy and wants to lie down, a note should be made as "sleepy, sleepy", "wanting, wanting"; on raising the hand as "raising, raising"; on stretching as "stretching, stretching"; on touching as "touching, touching"; on pressing as "pressing, pressing"; after swaying the body and dropping it down as "lying, lying". The act of lying down itself should be carried out very slowly. On touching the pillow it should be noted as "touching, touching". There are many places of touch all over the body but each spot need be noted only one at a time.

In the lying posture there are also many movements of the body in bringing one's arms and legs into position. These actions should be noted carefully as "raising", "stretching", "bending", "moving", and so forth. On turning the body a note should be made as "turning, turning", and when there is nothing in particular to be noted, the yogi should proceed with the usual practice of noting "rising, falling". While one is lying on one's back or side, there is usually nothing in particular to be noted and the usual exercise of "rising, falling" should be carried out.

There may be many times when the mind wanders while one is in the lying posture. This wandering mind should be noted as "going, going" when it goes out, as "arriving, arriving" when it reaches a place, as "planning", "reflecting", and so forth for each state in the same manner as in the contemplation while in the sitting posture. Mental states pass away on being noted once or twice. The usual exercise of noting "rising, falling" should be continued. There may also be instances of swallowing or spitting saliva, painful sensations, hot sensations, itching sensations, etc., or of bodily actions in changing positions or in moving the limbs. They should be contemplated as each occurs. (When sufficient strength in concentration is gained, it will be possible to carry on with the contemplation of each act of opening and closing the eyelids and blinking.) Afterwards, one should then return to the usual exercise when there is nothing else to be noted.

(iv) Sleep

Though it is late at night and time for sleep, it is not advisable to give up the contemplation and go to sleep. Anyone who has a keen interest in contemplation must be prepared to face the risk of spending many nights without sleep.

The scriptures are emphatic on the necessity of developing the qualities of four-factored energy (*caturaṅga-viriya*) in the practice of meditation: "In the hard struggle, one may be reduced to a mere skeleton of skin, bones, and sinews when one's flesh and blood wither and dry up, but one should not give up one's efforts so long as one has not attained whatever is attainable by manly perseverance, energy, and endeavour". These instructions should be followed with a strong determination. It may be possible to keep awake if there is strong enough concentration to beat off sleep, but one will fall asleep if sleep gets the upper hand.

When one feels sleepy, one should make a note of it as "sleepy, sleepy"; when the eyelids are heavy as "heavy, heavy"; when the eyes are felt to be dazzled as "dazzled, dazzled". After contemplating in the manner indicated, one may be able to shake off sleepiness and feel fresh again. This feeling should be noted as "feeling fresh, feeling fresh", after which the usual exercise of noting "rising, falling" should be continued. However, in spite of this determination, one may feel unable to keep awake if one is very sleepy. In a lying posture, it is easier to fall asleep. A beginner should therefore try to keep mostly to the postures of sitting and walking.

When the night is advanced, however, a yogi may be compelled to lie down and proceed with the contemplation of rising and falling. In this position he may perhaps fall asleep. While one is asleep, it is not possible to carry on with the work of contemplation. It is an interval for a yogi to relax. An hour's sleep will give him an hour's relaxation, and if he continues to sleep for two, three or four hours, he will be relaxed for that much longer, but it is not advisable for a yogi to sleep for more than four hours, which is ample enough for a normal sleep.

(v) Waking

A yogi should begin his contemplation from the moment of awakening. To be fully occupied with intense contemplation throughout his waking hours is the routine of a yogi who works hard with true aspiration for the attainment of the path and fruit. If it is not possible to catch the moment of awakening, he should begin with the usual exercise of noting "rising, falling". If he first becomes aware of the fact of reflecting, he should begin his contemplation by noting "reflecting, reflecting", and then revert to the usual exercise of noting "rising, falling". If he first becomes aware of hearing a voice or some other sound, he should begin by noting "hearing, hearing", and then revert to the usual exercise. On awakening there may be bodily movement in turning to this side or that, moving the hands or legs and so forth. These actions should be contemplated in successive order.

If he first becomes aware of the mental states leading to the various actions of body, he should begin his contemplation by noting the mind. If he first becomes aware of painful sensations, he should begin with the noting of these painful sensations and then proceed with the noting of bodily actions. If he remains quiet without moving, the usual exercise of noting "rising, falling" should be continued. If he intends to get up, he should note this as "intending, intending", and then proceed with the noting of all actions in serial order in bringing the hands and legs into position. One should note "raising, raising" on raising the body, "sitting, sitting" when the body is erect and in a sitting posture, and one should also note any other actions of bringing the legs and hands into position. If there is then nothing in particular to be noted, the usual exercise of noting "rising, falling" should be reverted to.

Thus far we have mentioned things relating to the objects of contemplation in connection with the four postures and changing from one posture to another. This is merely a description of the general outline of major objects of contemplation to be carried out in the course of practice. Yet in the beginning of the practice, it is difficult to follow up on all of them in the course of contemplation. Many things will be omitted, but on gaining sufficient strength in concentration, it is easy to follow up in the course of contemplation not only those objects already enumerated, but many, many more. With the gradual development of mindfulness and concentration, the pace of knowledge quickens, and thus many more objects can be perceived. It is necessary to work up to this high level.

(vi) Washing and Eating

Contemplation should be carried out in washing the face in the morning or when taking a bath. As it is necessary to act quickly in such instances due to the nature of the action itself, contemplation should be carried out as far as these circumstances will allow. On stretching the hand to catch hold of the dipper, it should be noted as "stretching, stretching"; on catching hold of the dipper as "holding, holding"; on immersing the dipper as "dipping, dipping"; on bringing the dipper towards the body as "bringing, bringing"; on pouring the water over the body or on the face as "pouring, pouring"; on feeling cold as "cold, cold"; on rubbing as "rubbing, rubbing", and so forth.

There are also many different bodily actions in changing or arranging one's clothing, in arranging the bed or bedsheets, in opening the door, and so on. These actions should be contemplated in detail serially as much as possible.

At the time of taking a meal, contemplation should begin from the moment of looking at the table and noted as "looking, seeing, looking, seeing"; when stretching the hand to the plate as "stretching, stretching"; when the hand touches the food as "touching, hot, hot"; when gathering the food as "gathering, gathering"; when catching hold of the food as "catching, catching"; after lifting when the hand is being brought up as "bringing, bringing"; when the neck is being bent down as "bending, bending"; when the food is being placed in the mouth as "placing, placing"; when withdrawing the hand as "withdrawing, withdrawing"; when the hand touches the plate as "touching, touching"; when the neck is being straightened as "straightening, straightening"; when chewing the food as "chewing, chewing"; while tasting the food as "tasting, tasting", when one likes the taste as "liking, liking"; when one finds it pleasant as "pleasant, pleasant"; when swallowing as "swallowing, swallowing".

This is an illustration of the routine of contemplation on partaking of each morsel of food until the meal is finished. In this case too it is difficult to follow up on all actions at the beginning of the practice. There will be many omissions. Yogis should not hesitate, however, but must try to follow up as much as they can. With the gradual advancement of the practice, it will be easier to note many more objects than are mentioned here.

The instructions for the practical exercise of contemplation are now almost complete. As they have been explained in detail and at some length, it will not be easy to remember all of them. For the sake of easy remembrance, a short summary of the important and essential points will be given.

Summary of Essential Points

In walking, a yogi should contemplate the movements of each step. While one is walking briskly, each step should be noted as "right step, left step" respectively. The mind should be fixed intently on the sole of the foot in the movements of each step. While one is in the course of walking slowly, each step should be noted in two parts as "lifting, placing". While one is in a sitting posture, the usual exercise of contemplation should be carried out by noting the movements of the abdomen as "rising, falling, rising, falling". The same manner of contemplation by noting the movements as "rising, falling, rising, falling" should be carried out while one is also in the lying posture.

If it is found that the mind wanders during the course of noting "rising, falling", it should not be allowed to continue to wander but should be noted immediately. On imagining, it should be noted as "imagining, imagining"; on thinking as "thinking, thinking"; on the mind going out as "going, going"; on the mind arriving at a place as "arriving, arriving", and so forth at every occurrence, and then the usual exercise of noting "rising, falling" should be continued.

When there occur feelings of tiredness in the hands, legs or other limbs, or hot, prickly, aching, or itching sensations, they should be immediately followed up and noted as "tired", "hot", "prickly", "aching", "itching", and so on as the case may be. A return should then be made to the usual exercise of noting "rising, falling".

When there are acts of bending or stretching the hands or legs, or moving the neck or limbs or swaying the body to and fro, they should be followed up and noted in serial order as they occur. The usual exercise of noting as "rising, falling" should then be reverted to.

This is only a summary. Any other objects to be contemplated in the course of training will be mentioned by the meditation teachers when giving instructions during the daily interview with the disciples.

If one proceeds with the practice in the manner indicated, the number of objects will gradually increase in the course of time. At first there will be many omissions because the mind is used to wandering without any restraint whatsoever. However, a yogi should not lose heart on this account. This difficulty is usually encountered in the beginning of practice. After some time, the mind can no longer play truant because it is always found out every time it wanders. It therefore remains fixed on the object to which it is directed.

As rising occurs the mind makes a note of it, and thus the object and the mind coincide. As falling occurs the mind makes a note of it, and thus the object and the mind coincide. There is always a pair, the object and the mind which knows the object, at each time of noting. These two elements of the material object and the knowing mind always arise in pairs, and apart from these two there does not exist any other thing in the form of a person or self. This reality will be personally realised in due course.

The fact that materiality and mentality are two distinct, separate things will be clearly perceived during the time of noting "rising, falling". The two elements of materiality and mentality are linked up in pairs and their arising coincides, that is, the process of materiality in rising arises with the process of mentality which knows it. The process of materiality in falling falls away together with the process of mentality which knows it. It is the same for lifting, moving and placing: these are processes of materiality arising and falling away together with the processes of mentality which know them. This knowledge in respect of matter and mind rising separately is known as *nāma-rūpa-pariccheda-ñāṇa,* the discriminating knowledge of mentality-materiality. It is the preliminary stage in the whole course of insight knowledge. It is important to have this preliminary stage developed in a proper manner.

On continuing the practice of contemplation for some time, there will be considerable progress in mindfulness and concentration. At this high level it will be perceptible that on every occasion of noting, each process arises and passes away at that very moment. But, on the other hand, uninstructed people generally consider that the body and mind remain in a permanent state throughout life, that the same body of childhood has grown up into adulthood, that the same young mind has grown up into maturity, and that both body and mind are one and the same person. In reality, this is not so. Nothing is permanent. Everything comes into existence for a moment and then passes away. Nothing can remain even for the blink of an eye. Changes are taking place very swiftly and they will be perceived in due course.

While carrying on the contemplation by noting "rising, falling", and so forth, one will perceive that these processes arise and pass away one after another in quick succession. On perceiving that everything passes away at the very point of noting, a yogi knows that nothing is permanent. This knowledge regarding the impermanent nature of things is *aniccānupassanā-ñāṇa*, the contemplative knowledge of impermanence.

A yogi then knows that this ever-changing state of things is distressing and is not to be desired. This is *dukkhānupassanā-ñāṇa*, the contemplative knowledge of suffering. On suffering many painful feelings, this body and mind complex is regarded as a mere heap of suffering. This is also contemplative knowledge of suffering.

It is then perceived that the elements of materiality and mentality never follow one's wish, but arise according to their own nature and conditioning. While being engaged in the act of noting these processes, a yogi understands that these processes are not controllable and that they are neither a person nor a living entity nor self. This is *anattānupassanā-ñāṇa*, the contemplative knowledge of non-self.

When a yogi has fully developed the knowledge of impermanence, suffering, and non-self, he will realise Nibbāna. From time immemorial, Buddhas, *Arahats* and *Ariyas* (noble ones) have realised Nibbāna by this method of *vipassanā*. It is the highway leading to Nibbāna. *Vipassanā* consists of the four *satipaṭṭhāna* (applications of mindfulness) and it is *satipaṭṭhāna* which is really the highway to Nibbāna.

Yogis who take up this course of training should bear in mind that they are on the highway which has been taken by Buddhas, *Arahats*, and *Ariyas*. This opportunity is afforded them apparently because of their *pāramī*, that is, their previous endeavours in seeking and wishing for it, and also because of their present mature conditions. They should rejoice at heart for having this opportunity. They should also feel assured that by walking on this highway without wavering they will gain personal experience of highly developed concentration and wisdom, as has already been known by Buddhas, *Arahats*, and *Ariyas*. They will develop such a pure state of concentration as has never been known before in the course of their lives and thus enjoy many innocent pleasures as a result of advanced concentration.

Impermanence, suffering, and non-self will be realised through direct personal experience, and with the full development of these knowledges, Nibbāna will be realised. It will not take long to achieve the objective, possibly one month, or twenty days, or fifteen days, or, on rare occasions, even in seven days for those select few with extraordinary *pāramī*.

Yogis should therefore proceed with the practice of contemplation in great earnestness and with full confidence, trusting that it will surely lead to the development of the noble path and fruit and to the realisation of Nibbāna. They will then be free from the wrong view of self and from spiritual doubt, and they will no longer be subject to the round of rebirths in the miserable realms of the hells, the animal world, and the sphere of *petas.*

May yogis meet with every success in their noble endeavour.

The Message of the Velāma Sutta

by

Susan Elbaum Jootla

WHEEL PUBLICATION NO. 372

The Velāma Sutta

A

1. Once, when the Buddha was dwelling near Sāvatthī at Jeta Grove, in Anāthapiṇḍika's park, the householder Anāthapiṇḍika visited him, and after greeting him politely sat down at one side.

2. The Exalted One addressed Anāthapiṇḍika: "Are alms given in your house, householder?"

B

3. "Yes, Lord, alms are given by my family, but they only consist of broken rice and sour gruel."

4. "Householder, whether one gives coarse or choice alms, if one gives them without respect, without thought, not by one's own hand, gives only leftovers, and without belief in the result of actions, then wherever he is reborn as a result of his having given these alms, his mind will not turn to the enjoyment of fine food and clothing, fine vehicles or the fine objects of the five senses. His children, wife, servants, and labourers will not obey him, and neither listen nor pay attention to him. And why is that so? Because this is the result of actions done without respect.

5. "But whether one gives coarse or choice alms, if one gives them with respect, thoughtfully, by one's own hand, gives things that are not leftovers, and with belief in the result of actions, then wherever he is reborn as a result of his having given these alms, his mind will turn to the enjoyment of fine food, clothes and vehicles, and of the finer objects of the five senses. His children, wife, servants, and labourers will obey him, listen and pay attention to him. And why is this? Because this is the result of actions done with respect.

C

6. "Long ago, householder, there lived a brahman called Velāma. He gave very valuable gifts such as these: He gave eighty-four thousand golden bowls filled with silver; he gave eighty-

four thousand silver bowls filled with gold; he gave eighty-four thousand copper bowls filled with jewels; he gave eighty-four thousand horses with trappings, banners and nets of gold; he gave eighty-four thousand carriages spread with lion skins, tiger skins and leopard skins, with saffron-coloured blankets, with golden trappings, banners and nets; he gave eighty-four thousand milk-giving cows with fine jute ropes and silver milk pails; he gave eighty-four thousand bejewelled maidens; he gave beds with covers of fleece, white blankets, embroidered coverlets, covered with antelope skins, with awnings, and with crimson cushions at the ends; he gave eighty-four thousand lengths of cloth of the best flax, silk, wool, and cotton. And who could describe all the food both hard and soft kinds, sweets and syrups that he gave? They flowed like rivers.

7. "Perhaps, householder, you think that the brahman Velāma who made that very valuable gift was someone else. Do not think that; it was I who was Velāma the brahman who made that very valuable gift.

D

8. "But when those alms were given, householder, there were no recipients worthy of the gift. Although the brahman Velāma gave such a valuable gift, if he had fed one person of right view, the fruit of the latter deed would have been greater.

9. "Though he gave that very rich gift, or though he fed a hundred people of right view, the fruit of feeding a Once-returner would have been greater.

10. "Though he gave that very valuable gift, or though he fed a hundred Once-returners, the fruit of feeding one Non-returner would have been greater.

11. "... though he fed a hundred Non-returners, the fruit of feeding one Arahat would have been greater.

12. "... though he fed a hundred Arahats, the fruit of feeding one Non-Teaching Buddha would have been greater.

13. "... though he fed a hundred Non-Teaching Buddhas, the fruit of feeding one Perfect One, a Teaching Buddha, would have been greater.

14. "... though he fed one Perfect One, a Teaching Buddha, the fruit of feeding the Order of monks (*Saṅgha*) with the Buddha at its head would have been greater.[1]

15. "... though he fed the Order of monks with the Buddha at its head, the fruit of building a monastery for the use of the monks of the Order of the surrounding country would have been greater.

E

16. "... though he built a monastery for the Order, the fruit of sincerely taking refuge in the Buddha, the Dhamma and the Sangha would have been greater.

17. "... though he sincerely took refuge in the Buddha, the Dhamma and the Sangha, the fruit of sincerely undertaking to keep the moral precepts, abstaining from killing, stealing, sexual misconduct, lying, and intoxicants causing sloth, would have been greater.

F

18. "... though he sincerely undertook those precepts, the fruit of developing [concentration on radiating universal] loving-kindness [*mettā*] even just to the extent of a whiff of scent, would have been greater.

G

19. "... though he developed loving-kindness to the extent of a whiff of scent, the fruit of cultivating the thought of impermanence, even for the moment of a finger snap, would have been greater."

---

1. §14 and §16 do not appear in the *Gradual Sayings*, but have been added to complete the sequence. The content of these two paragraphs was dictated by the preceding and succeeding paragraphs.

Introduction

In the Velāma Sutta, the Buddha provides us with a vivid outline of the relative degrees of merit that can be acquired by performing different kinds of good actions (*kusala-kamma*). He does not discuss the specific results produced by meritorious deeds, but only their relative gradation. While his outline is lightly sketched, its implications are extensive and profound.

Good actions are bodily deeds, spoken words, or thoughts, accompanied by wholesome volition (*kusala-cetanā*). Wholesome volition may be rooted in the mental factors of non-greed (or detachment), non-hatred (or goodwill), or non-delusion (wisdom). Sections A, B, C, and D of the Velāma Sutta deal with bodily good deeds: various kinds of charity, generosity or giving, the Triple Refuge, and undertaking the Five Precepts (which are usually all included in the Pali word *dāna*). Section E deals with verbal good deeds: talking done aloud, either alone or by repeating them after a monk or teacher. Sections F and G concern purely mental good deeds, as both deal with aspects of meditation. Mental actions can be very powerful, and the Buddha points out that proper development of concentration (*samādhi*) and wisdom (*paññā*) generate the most potent good results (*vipāka*) of all the many kinds of wholesome kamma. Good kamma brings good future results to the doer in accordance with the natural moral law of cause and effect. Likewise, bad actions yield bad future results in the form of different kinds of suffering. The degree and kind of beneficial result (*vipāka*) or fruit (*phala*) varies widely with the kind and quality of the good kamma or merit (*paññā*) that has been performed. In the Velāma Sutta the Buddha devotes the greater part of his exposition to giving: Sections A, B, C, and D all discuss this most basic kind of wholesome deed. Morality (*sīla*) is dealt with in Section E, concentration (*samādhi*) in Section F, and wisdom or insight (*paññā, vipassanā*) in Section G. These are the four major categories that include all kinds of wholesome kamma. Together they make up the Noble Eightfold Path, which is the Buddha's prescription for putting an end to suffering.[2]

---

2. The eight factors of the noble path are generally divided into a wisdom

Giving

In the Velāma Sutta, the Buddha is speaking to his leading lay disciple, the great donor and rich merchant of Sāvatthī, who was known as Anāthapiṇḍika. He was already renowned as a generous giver of charity to the Buddha and his monks (*bhikkhus*), and also to the poor of the area.

In Section A, the Buddha asks the layman whether dāna, specifically alms-food, is given by his household. Anāthapiṇḍika replies that such charity is given but it consists of only very coarse kinds of food. The commentary explains that he is referring to the alms his family gives to the needy who come to their door, not to the much finer gifts they customarily donate to the Sangha, the Order of Buddhist monks. Another possible explanation for the poor quality of the alms that Anāthapiṇḍika mentions is that this conversation took place at a time when his vast assets had been greatly diminished through a series of misfortunes that drained him of almost all his wealth. At the same time, because of his natural compassion, he was reluctant to press his debtors to repay their debts, and many took advantage of his kindness. Even during this period of stringency for his household, this great benefactor made it a point to give food to the monks daily, but he could only afford plain, simple fare, not the rich curries and sweets he offered to them during more prosperous times.[3]

If this second explanation for the poor alms-food given by Anāthapiṇḍika's family is accepted, then Section B of the discourse may be understood as the Buddha's way of reassuring him that even though at the moment he could not give sumptuous food, he would still continue to earn much merit from his offerings so long as he gave them with the proper mental attitude.

The proper approach to giving and the kammic results it brings form the substance of Section B of the Velāma Sutta. The Buddha explains what kind of giving will bring full benefit

section (right view and right thought); a morality section (right speech, right action and right livelihood; with giving loosely included in right action, and going for refuge in right speech); and a concentration section (right effort, right mindfulness and right concentration).

3. See *Anāthapiṇḍika*, p. 9, referring to Jātaka No. 284.

according to the kammic law, and what kind will not. In all its varieties, dāna is always a meritorious action that leads to pleasant results. Defined very broadly in the Buddhist texts, dāna includes not only the giving of material gifts but also the giving of one's time and energy in voluntary service and the teaching of the Dhamma. It even includes giving other beings freedom from fear by being non-violent oneself.

Whether or not the gift itself is valuable in monetary terms is irrelevant to the Buddha's analysis, as shown by the phrase "whether one gives coarse or choice alms" at the beginning of both paragraphs in Section B. In other sermons the Buddha says that if the value of a gift is proportionate to the donor's financial situation, that is both appropriate and sufficient. A small gift from a poor person can create as much good kamma as a large gift from a wealthy one. A meager gift from a prince would bring a poor acquisition of good kamma, while if a poor man shared the last cup of rice in his house with someone else, this could be extremely beneficial.

In the Velāma Sutta, the Buddha deals first with gifts which will not bring as much merit as they would if offered properly (§ 4). A gift of any quality, fancy or plain, will give only limited future benefits if it is given casually; without respect; thoughtlessly; in an impolite way; by having another person hand it over; if it is left over from one's own meal; or if it is given without considering and understanding the law of kamma and its fruits ("belief in the result of actions" in the words of the sutta). The last is the most important of the five factors.

Even if the result of such a gift puts the donor in a position where, in a subsequent life, he receives fine food, clothes and vehicles, lives in comfortable circumstances and enjoys good health, the Buddha states that he may not be able to enjoy these things. In addition, at this time his children and the people who work for him will not listen to him or pay attention to what he says. The Buddha declares that this happens because such is the natural kammic result of actions performed without respect. In other words, a person who gives in such a haphazard way will not be able to enjoy or appreciate the pleasant results which the act of generosity is bound to bring him.

An example of this is a certain miser discussed in a series of conversations between King Pasenadi of Kosala and the Buddha.[4] The king describes a very wealthy man in Sāvatthī who had recently died without making arrangements for anyone to inherit his property. Under these circumstances, Kosalan law provided that the king was entitled to confiscate the entire fortune; he had just done so when he came to see the Buddha. King Pasenadi mentioned all this to the Buddha because the dead man had been known to be very miserly, even towards himself. He lived as though he were indigent, wearing the roughest kind of clothes, eating stale food and using the cheapest kind of carriage.

In reply the Buddha told King Pasenadi that once, in the distant past, this man had given food to a Non-Teaching Buddha but had regretted his deed immediately afterwards, thinking, "It would have been better if my slaves and workers had eaten it." The offering of this gift to such a wise being had led to his rebirth several times in the celestial planes, and subsequently as an eminently rich man in Sāvatthī. However, the unwholesome kamma generated by his subsequent regret resulted in his miserly temperament and "inclined his heart to denying himself excellent food, clothes, carriages, and enjoyment of sense pleasures."

In § 5 of the Velāma Sutta the Buddha tells Anāthapiṇḍika that if one gives fresh food, considerately, with one's own hands, and after thinking about the deed and with belief in kamma and its fruit, then wherever that almsgiving brings its fruit in future births, the giver's mind will be able to appreciate the sense pleasures available to him, and his children, wife and workers will be obedient and cooperative. This is the opposite of the result of carelessly performed charity. Both are good deeds, but the accompanying states of mind are poles apart, and this influences the result.

It is interesting to note that the Buddha teaches that for ordinary householders, legitimately earned pleasures of the senses (attractive sights, sounds, smells, tastes, or tangibles) need not be avoided when they do not entail breaking the Five Precepts.

Such pleasurable feelings are simply facts of life, the result of our previous good deeds. If they have been earned they might

4. In the Kosala Saṃyutta. *Kindred Sayings*, I pp. 115-17.

as well be enjoyed; there is no "sin" involved as long as the Five Precepts are scrupulously kept.[5] Being miserly creates even worse kamma than spending reasonably on oneself and one's dependents. Sharing one's earned wealth, of course, is good kamma.

The Gifts of Velāma

In Section C the Buddha provides a story from the past to illustrate the practice of generosity. He describes the incredibly lavish gifts he bestowed in one of his previous existences when, as a Bodhisatta developing the perfection of giving (*dāna-pāramī*), he was reborn as the brahman Velāma. His gifts included gold and silver, valuable domestic animals, fancy chariots and luxurious beds. Velāma also gave away food and drink in vast quantities.

The Buddha points out to Anāthapiṇḍika in Section D that even though Velāma's generosity was vast and his gifts were given properly (in accordance with the guidelines in Section B), the results were not as complete as they might have been under different circumstances. In Velāma's time there were no beings available who were, in the most eminent sense, truly worthy to receive his gifts. The proper recipient would have been an Ariya, a Noble One, one who had attained to any of the four stages of holiness by purifying his mind of defilements. The Buddha continues to develop, throughout the rest of this section, this same theme: purity of the recipient is an essential factor that influences the amount of merit earned by an act of generosity.

A series of verses in the Dhammapada make a similar point (vv. 106–108). In these stanzas, it is said that simply paying sincere respect to Ariyas is far more meritorious than making sacrifices, tending ritual fires or giving gifts to non-Ariyas. Respectfully giving a gift to an Ariya must be even more profitable than bowing to one, although such dāna does not figure in these lines.

> "Whatever gifts and oblations one seeking merit might offer in this world for a whole year, all that is not worth one fourth

5. Unwholesome (*akusala*) kamma associated with desire (*taṇhā* or *lobha*) may be generated, however. But for the ordinary householder this kind of relatively weak bad kamma is unavoidable a great deal of the time.

of the merit gained by revering the Upright Ones [*Ariyas*], which is truly excellent."

(Dhp 108)

While the Buddha was alive, and for as long as his teachings are practiced, individuals of great purity arise in the world, and gifts to them bring the greatest merit that can be earned through generosity. Although it may be hard to find Ariyas today, people who keep the moral precepts (*sīla*), practise concentration (*samādhi*), and cultivate wisdom (*paññā*) are certainly available. Such individuals, whether monks or laypeople, share to some extent in the characteristics of Ariyas. For this reason, gifts to them should bear greater fruit than gifts to ordinary folk who make no effort to improve themselves. Wandering ascetics as well as priests may or may not live morally, and they may or may not strive to develop concentration and wisdom. Hence it is uncertain whether such recipients will endow a gift with the maximum of profit for the donor.

From Section D through the rest of the sutta the Buddha describes a scale or hierarchy of meritorious deeds. This scale of merit begins with Velāma's gifts as the broad base, and then ascends by degrees culminating in the wisdom that knows the truth of impermanence (*anicca*).

Above the greatest gift given to non-Ariyas comes feeding different categories of Ariyas. Giving nourishment to beings with such pure minds is a very valuable source of merit. In § 8 the Buddha says that the fruit of feeding a single person of right view would be greater than the fruit of Velāma's vast generosity given to ordinary worldlings. A person of right view is the first kind of Ariya, a Stream-enterer (*sotāpanna*), one assured of liberation in a maximum of seven lifetimes. A Stream-enterer keeps the Five Precepts perfectly; possesses full faith in the Buddha, Dhamma and Sangha; has thoroughly understood that everything comes about as a result of causes and conditions; and has thereby eliminated three defilements from his mental continuum.

These three defilements are the incorrect view that affirms a lasting self or soul, all doubt about the way to liberation, and the belief that rites and rituals can lead to liberation. It is eliminating belief in a self that gives the Stream-enterer the title "one of right view."

The Buddha goes through the remaining three higher kinds of Ariya in order: the Once-returner (*sakadāgāmi*), who has greatly attenuated sense desire and ill will; the Non-returner (*anāgāmi*), who has totally uprooted these two defilements; and the fully liberated Arahat, who has eradicated all traces of greed, hatred and ignorance and all other mental impurities. The Buddha states that feeding one of each higher stage brings greater rewards than feeding a hundred on the stage just below.

The greatest recipients, named next, are Buddhas, who are beings that attain liberation unaided (by discovering the ultimate truths about existence for themselves without the guidance of a teacher). There are two kinds of Buddhas: Non-Teaching Buddhas (*paccekabuddha*) and universal Buddhas who instruct other beings (*sammā-sambuddha*), like Gotama Buddha. Any number of Paccekabuddhas can exist at one time in the world, but they only arise during periods when there is no Samma-sambuddha living, and when the teachings of one are not available, that is, when no Buddha *Sāsana* is extant. However, there can only be one *Sammā-sambuddha* at a time. The Buddha declares that because of his superior stature, feeding a Sammā-sambuddha brings greater results than feeding a hundred Paccekabuddhas. However, the act of dāna that is the most beneficial of all is not a gift of food but constructing a monastery for the use of the Sangha with the Buddha at its head.

During his life, Anāthapiṇḍika performed virtually all the acts of generosity named in the sutta. Shortly after his first encounter with the Buddha he purchased a park known as Jeta Grove (Jetavana) and had a large monastery built there. He then donated the property to the Buddha and the community of monks. Anāthapiṇḍika always gave alms-food, robes and medicine to the monks who came to stay at Jetavana. Among those bhikkhus were the greatest Arahat disciples of the Buddha as well as numerous other Noble Ones.

Morality: The Refuges and Precepts

The hierarchy of merit generated by different forms of good kamma continues beyond generosity and culminates in the final three sections of the Velāma Sutta: E, F and G. Even greater than the fruit of Velāma's gifts, or of feeding any kind and number of Noble Ones, or of building a monastery for the Order, is the merit earned from sincerely going for refuge to the Triple Gem (the first step taken by anyone who considers himself a Buddhist [Section E]).

The value of going for refuge to the Awakened One, to the Truth embodied in his Teaching, and to the community of those who are following his Teaching (the Buddha, the Dhamma and the Sangha) can be vast if it is accompanied by full comprehension:

> "He who has gone for refuge to the Buddha, his Teaching and his Order penetrates with wisdom the Four Noble Truths: suffering, the cause of suffering, the cessation of suffering, and the Noble Eightfold Path leading to the cessation of suffering."
>
> (Dhp 190–91)

This means that going for refuge with understanding can result in penetration of the Four Noble Truths. If one considers the Buddha and Dhamma as one's protection, one will naturally try to follow those teachings, and practice the way to the utter cessation of suffering, which the Buddha devoted his life to explaining. One will try to comprehend the first noble truth, eliminate the second truth by developing the fourth truth (the path) until the third noble truth has been realized.

By taking refuge one enters the way to liberation shown by the Buddha. Giving can be practiced even during the vast periods of cosmic history when no Buddha Sāsana is available, as Velāma's story illustrates. Charity is, after all, central to virtually every religion, to every code of good conduct; it is not exclusively Buddhist. But obviously, one can only take the Triple Refuge while the Buddha-Dhamma is available; at other times the Refuges would be inaccessible.

The Velāma Sutta's elisions in §17 leave some doubt about the exact relationship between going for refuge and keeping the precepts (*sīla*) in the hierarchy of meritorious deeds. Although I have remained close to Hare's translation in my rendering, Hecker says that taking the Triple Refuge "would be perfected if one observed the Five Precepts.[6]" The Venerable Ñāṇamoli's translation combines the two in a slightly different way: "Yet it is still more fruitful to go with a confident heart for refuge to the Buddha, Dhamma and Sangha and undertake the Five Precepts of virtue."[7] The Refuges and the Precepts are closely connected steps of basic Buddhist practice; so regardless of the rendering, we can be confident that the undertaking of the Five Precepts here is additional to, rather than a replacement for, the going for refuge.

The Five Precepts, the minimum moral requirement for a Buddhist layman, consist of abstaining from doing things that would hurt others, from deeds that lead to one's own rebirth in the lower realms where there is unremitting and intense suffering. To undertake the Five Precepts, one declares: "I will refrain from killing, stealing, sexual misconduct, lying and the use of intoxicants," and then observes them to the best of one's ability. Taking the Refuges when one's morality is pure combines two valuable actions which can produce abundant long-term fruits.

Concentration and Loving-kindness

But greater still than mere morality is the merit earned from proper meditation, and it is meditation or "mental development" (*bhāvanā*) that comprises the highest two rungs in the Buddha's ladder of meritorious actions. These rungs are referred to in the concluding sections (F and G) of the Velāma Sutta. Concentration obtained by extending universal loving-kindness (*mettābhāvanā*), even briefly, is of greater benefit than keeping the precepts; but without the base of perfect morality such meditation would be impossible. The sutta indicates the short span of mettā needed to give results greater than those accruing from keeping the precepts with the phrase "a whiff of scent." In the commentary, an analogy is used: for only as long as it takes someone milking

6. *Anāthapiṇḍika*, p. 32.

7. Bhikkhu Ñāṇamoli, "Anicca according to Theravāda," in *Impermanence: Collected Essays* (BPS Wheel No. 186/187), p. 71.

a cow to give one pull on her teat. Both images suggest a brief moment. So valuable is the practice of mettā that even this slight development of it, done properly, brings the practitioner a vast amount of merit.

In a discourse in the Kindred Sayings the Buddha points out, in a similar manner, that such a brief radiation of mettā is kammically far more rewarding than giving a large gift:

> "If anyone, brethren, were to give a morning gift of a hundred coins, and the same at noon and the same in the evening, or if anyone were to practise in the morning, at noon or in the evening a heart of love [mettā], even if it were as slight as one pull at a cow's udder, this practice would be by far the more fruitful of the two."
>
> (Kindred Sayings, II, pp. 176–77)

Concentration practised to the highest level issues in the *jhānas*, the meditative absorptions. Jhāna is one-pointed, alert absorption in the object. All sensory input is cut off and the mind, "secluded from sense pleasures, secluded from unwholesome states," dwells exclusively fixed upon its chosen object, free from extraneous thoughts. But by itself jhāna can lead only to mundane benefits, such as peace and bliss in the present life and an exalted rebirth in the lofty planes of the Brahma-world, where life endures for extremely long periods of time. It does not necessarily lead to liberation.

Concentration on mettā is a highly effective means to attain jhāna, and is also one of the most potent sources of wholesome kamma. In fact, among all purely mundane types of merit, the Buddha praises the meditation on mettā as supreme (in a passage which also underscores its inherent limitations):

> "Bhikkhus, whatever kinds of merit there are, undertaken with a view to rebirth, all of them are not worth one sixteenth part of the heart's release of loving-kindness; in shining and beaming and radiance the heart's release of loving-kindness far excels them.[8]"

8. Itivuttaka, No. 27, *As It Was Said*, p. 13; see too *The Practice of Loving-kindness (Mettā)*, Ñāṇamoli Thera (Wheel No. 7), p. 16.

"Heart's release of loving-kindness" refers to the temporary suppression of mental defilements by concentration on *mettā*. "With a view to rebirth" means aiming at a happy or pleasant rebirth as a result of the merit earned by good kamma.

But all rebirth keeps the round of suffering (*dukkha*) rolling on, and the Buddha's unique teaching aims at permanently eliminating all suffering. Repeated existence is ultimately and inevitably suffering. All beings who are born must grow old, suffer from disease, and eventually die. Even Brahmas, who enjoy exceedingly long and blissful lives as the fruits of cultivating the jhānas, will die and be reborn in other planes of existence, over and over again. Saṃsāra, for all beings, is an ever-repeated process of birth and death, involving suffering, pain, insecurity, and impermanence. Only wisdom can enable us to break out of this vicious cycle. Concentration alone, for all its ability to bring pleasant results, cannot cut the sequence of birth, death and rebirth. Concentration that does not lead to insight in the long run only perpetuates suffering by providing yet more fuel for rebirth. For this reason, the Buddha tells Anāthapiṇḍika (in Section G of the sutta) that the thought of impermanence, which is one aspect of wisdom, creates the greatest good kamma of all meritorious actions.

Wisdom: Insight into Impermanence

If Velāma had been able to meditate directly on impermanence (*anicca*) in his mind or body just for the span of a finger-snap, it would have brought him greater fruit than all the other good deeds mentioned in all the preceding paragraphs of the sutta. But such wisdom was lost to the world in Velāma's time, as he lived during the empty aeons between the arising of two Buddhas. Therefore he had no access to such understanding.

Why is knowing impermanence for oneself of such consummate value? In other discourses that deal specifically with cultivating insight into impermanence the Buddha provides several answers.

First, contemplating impermanence brings the meditator happiness greater than all worldly pleasure because he realizes that with such contemplation he is now moving towards the cessation of all suffering.

"Whenever with insight he sees
the rise and fall of the aggregates,
he experiences joy and happiness.
To the discerning one this reflects the Deathless."

(Dhp 374)

Seeing "the rise and fall of the aggregates" is meditating on the transient (*anicca*) nature of all the components of the personality. Such insight brings detachment from these insubstantial phenomena. Great joy arises in the mind thus freed of desire and aversion. The meditator realizes that when his mind becomes utterly and permanently liberated from these defilements, Nibbāna will be attained.

The second reason for the great value of knowing impermanence is that this insight enables one to develop the Noble Eightfold Path all the way to its ultimate goal: the cessation of suffering. In one discourse in the Gradual Sayings, the Buddha describes six benefits of developing insight into impermanence which convince a monk or meditator that he should cultivate this practice to perfection:

"When a monk sees six rewards it should be enough for him to establish without reserve the thought of impermanence in all phenomena. What six?

"(1) All phenomena will seem to me insubstantial;
(2) my mind will find no relish in all the world;
(3) my mind will emerge from all the world;
(4) my mind will incline towards extinction;
(5) my fetters will come to be abandoned; and
(6) I shall be endowed with the supreme state of a recluse."[9]

The first reward leads the meditator to understand the other two characteristics common to all phenomena: *dukkha* (unsatisfactoriness), and *anattā* (essencelessness). Phenomena are all compounded and conditioned formations (*saṅkhāra*) and the meditator dwelling on impermanence sees that everything within and around him is conditioned by other things, all of which are unstable. As he sees that all the causes are impermanent, he

9. *Gradual Sayings* III, p. 308; see Wheel No. 186/187, p. 71.

comes to realize that the resulting phenomena must likewise be transient and so without lasting substance (insubstantial). That which is impermanent and without substance cannot be said to have a lasting essence, so it is not self (*anattā*). That which is unstable cannot be a source of lasting happiness, so it is unsatisfactory (*dukkha*).

The second reward is the undermining of *taṇhā* (craving), which by relishing and delighting in mundane things of all sorts keeps the mind bound to the round of rebirth in a perpetual search for pleasure and self-perpetuation. Where there is no craving for sense objects, one fears the risk of involvement with them and so develops detachment and disgust towards sensual delights. This leads to the third reward: when the mind seeks an alternative to the misery of impermanent existence, it tends to disengage itself from everything mundane and so to break away from all the world. The fourth reward of knowing impermanence is the converse of the third: the mind with no interest in worldly matters turns towards the supramundane, the unconditioned (Nibbāna).

The fifth reward is the destruction of the fetters which bind beings to the round of rebirth, *saṃsāra*. The ten fetters (*saṃyojanā*) are personality belief, skeptical doubt, clinging to rites and rituals, craving for sense pleasures, ill-will, craving for existence in the fine material planes, craving for existence in the immaterial planes, conceit, restlessness, and ignorance. Knowledge of impermanence can in time eliminate all these mental defilements through the four stages of enlightenment.

The sixth reward refers to Arahatship, the culmination of the other five. This is the state of perfect purity in which no defiling tendencies remain and all possibility of future rebirth has been cut off.

In this way, understanding fully how everything that makes up oneself, and the external world, is utterly unstable, can lift the mind to a level of complete and permanent purity. This is the prime reason why, in the final paragraph of the Velāma Sutta, the Buddha declares that the fruit of even a moment's insight into impermanence brings the greatest of all kammic results. Every moment spent knowing impermanence through insight brings one closer to the goal of total liberation.

In a discourse in the Kindred Sayings, the Buddha explains how consistently and deeply knowing *anicca* in insight meditation (*vipassanā*) can lead all the way to Arahatship.

> "Perceiving impermanence, bhikkhus, developed and frequently practised, removes all sensual desire, removes all desire for material existence, removes all desire for becoming, removes all ignorance, and tears out all conceit of 'I am.'"
>
> (Kindred Sayings, III, p. 132)

Developing the understanding of *anicca* gradually eliminates every trace of craving, desire, aversion, and attachment; for as the meditator comes to realize the transience of all aspects of life, he finds sense objects and all prospects of rebirth profoundly unsatisfactory (*dukkha*). One who has eliminated the craving for sense pleasures is a Non-returner (*anāgāmi*), who will never be reborn in the sensuous realms of existence, among humans or devas, since his mind no longer has the slightest interest in the sense objects which characterize these realms. Non-returners generally take birth in the Pure Abodes, the highest planes of the fine-material world, which are reserved for such great beings. Attaining the stage of Non-returner and rebirth in the Pure Abodes are among the blessings that come from profound insight into impermanence.

Non-returners attain Arahatship by developing further the perception of impermanence in order to remove attraction towards life even in the exalted planes of existence. This corresponds to the other two kinds of desire mentioned in the quotation: desire for material existence and desire for becoming. Simultaneously, every trace of ignorance is eradicated and every remnant of the deluding conceit "I am" is ripped out of the mind. This is the highest good, the ultimate goal of the Buddha's teaching (Arahatship), the living experience of Nibbāna. This total cessation of suffering can come about through perfect understanding of *anicca*.

How can the insight into impermanence eliminate conceit (*māna*)? When the transience of everything we habitually cling to as "I" and "me" is clearly and repeatedly understood, the actual essencelessness (*anattā*) of the supposed "self" becomes perfectly apparent. Thus, fully developed insight into impermanence brings the great benefit of insight into essencelessness, and full comprehension of essencelessness brings liberation.

"For a monk, Meghiya, who thinks on impermanence, the thought of not-self [anattā] endures; thinking on there being no self, he wins to the state wherein the conceit 'I am' has been uprooted, to the cool [Nibbāna], even in this life."

(Gradual Sayings, IV, p. 237)

Without completely and continually understanding that there is no essence, core or self anywhere for anyone, liberation from the round of existence is impossible. As the Buddha told Meghiya, an effective way to come to comprehend the truth of not-self is through knowing the truth of impermanence. This is because it is easier to recognize impermanence on an intellectual level and also easier to experience it for oneself in insight meditation.

This knowing of impermanence is so potent that cultivating it even for a short moment gives the greatest results among all the types of meritorious action. All the other types of good kamma mentioned by the Buddha in the Velāma Sutta may or may not be associated with liberating wisdom. But knowing impermanence is itself an aspect of wisdom or insight, and such wisdom, by its very nature, gradually eliminates ignorance. True insight must tend towards detachment and ultimately towards Nibbāna, the absolute peace that comes with the ending of all the causes of suffering.

Now that we have seen why insight into *anicca* is of such profound value, it will become clear that its results must transcend those of all other kinds of good kamma. Good actions not rooted in wisdom will bear fruit in pleasant existences accompanied by sense pleasures in the human and celestial planes, as the Buddha mentioned in Section B of the Velāma Sutta. Generosity in all its forms, taking the Triple Refuge, keeping the Five Precepts, and even developing the lower levels of concentration may be all done without wisdom. If they are performed in such a way they serve to perpetuate the round of rebirth. If they are accompanied by wisdom consciously aimed at Nibbāna, they will tend towards liberation from the round. The *jhānas* (meditative absorptions) are always associated with a degree of wisdom, but this wisdom does not constitute the kind of insight that leads out of saṃsāra. Only if the meditator, upon emerging from a jhāna, examines that state of mind and sees it as impermanent, unsatisfactory, and essenceless (*anicca, dukkha, anattā*), will the jhāna tend towards release from all suffering.

To illustrate: If gifts are given with the sole aim of obtaining pleasure in the celestial planes, that aim may come to fulfillment, but its fulfillment merely keeps the donor revolving in saṃsāra. Though he may live pleasantly (in relative comfort) as long as his merit bears fruit, when that fruit has been exhausted (as it must sooner or later) he is bound to fall again into the lower realms; he may even be reborn into the hells of the most intense suffering. This is because everyone has a backlog of unwholesome kamma awaiting an opportunity to bear fruit. So many of the volitional actions of body, speech and thought that we perform now are also unwholesome (*akusala*), as they are associated with some degree of greed, hatred or delusion; and unwholesome kamma will cause painful rebirths.

By contrast, cultivating insight into impermanence, suffering and essencelessness leads one out of the round of rebirth towards liberation from all suffering. Deep understanding of the ultimate impermanence of all existence creates a kind of kamma whose tendency is to eliminate all past kamma, good and bad, and so makes liberation possible (as we have already seen). Such insight works towards the state where no more kamma will be created at all:

> "And what Puṇṇa ... is the kamma that conduces to the destruction of kamma? Where, Puṇṇa, there is the volition to get rid of unwholesome kamma, wholesome kamma and mixed kamma ... this Puṇṇa is called ... the kamma that conduces to the destruction of kamma."
>
> (Middle Length Sayings, II, p. 58)

The Arahat makes no new kamma: his mind is free of the ignorance that underlies the unenlightened mind, so his thoughts and intentions are merely functional and do not bring any kammic results.

Giving, taking the Triple Refuge, keeping the Five Precepts, and practising concentration, all have essential roles to play in maturing one's spiritual faculties so that one can cultivate the understanding of the true nature of existence: the marks of impermanence, suffering, and non-self. The earlier stages cannot be dispensed with: the Buddha taught that morality is to be constantly observed and concentration to be continually strengthened. Otherwise any apparent "insight" that arises will not be pure and deep enough to bring about the cessation of craving. Only when insight has a solid base of merit will it be powerful enough to penetrate the thick murk of ignorance that keeps us thinking "I am permanent" or "I am real."

Conclusion

As a devoted lay Buddhist, Anāthapiṇḍika was well known for his generosity; the name by which he is known to us is actually an epithet meaning "one who gives alms to the unprotected," to the poor. He gave open-handedly to all beings and especially to the Buddha and his monks. Anāthapiṇḍika had firm confidence in the enlightenment of the Buddha, in the truth of the Dhamma he taught, and in the purity of the Sangha. Thus he sincerely took refuge in the Triple Gem. He also kept the Five Precepts at all times, so his morality was excellent.

In the Velāma Sutta the Buddha may be indirectly telling Anāthapiṇḍika that he should not lose sight of the ultimate goal through his devotion to the endless possibilities of mundane good deeds, since these can only bring mundane, temporary results. He is reminding the lay follower that the meditation on loving-kindness for cultivating concentration, and the meditation on impermanence for cultivating insight, are by far the greatest sources of profound merit. By showing Anāthapiṇḍika this ladder of good deeds, the Teacher may have been urging the layman at this stage of his life to devote more effort to mental purification.

Giving gifts, taking the Refuges, and keeping the Precepts are essential to build the foundation of good kamma. But the way out of the misery of the round of repeated births is to develop a mind sufficiently concentrated to penetrate the ultimate truth. It is by fully comprehending the impermanent, unsatisfactory and essenceless nature of all things in all the planes of conditioned existence that the final goal, the Deathless, is to be won.

> "Better a single day of life perceiving how things rise and fall than to live a century without ever perceiving their rise and fall."
>
> (Dhp 113)

Appendix

Perception of Impermanence

At Sāvatthī the Blessed One said:

"Bhikkhus, when the perception of impermanence is developed and cultivated, it eliminates all sensual lust, it eliminates all attachment to material form, it eliminates all ignorance, it uproots all conceit of 'I am'.

"Just as, bhikkhus, in the autumn a ploughman ploughing with a great ploughshare cuts through all the network of roots as he ploughs, so too when the perception of impermanence is developed and cultivated, it eliminates all sensual lust ... it uproots all conceit of 'I am'.

"Just as a cutter of reeds would cut down a reed, grab it by its top, and shake it down, and shake it out, and thump it about, so too when the perception of impermanence is developed and cultivated, it eliminates all sensual lust ... it uproots all conceit of 'I am'.

"Just as, when the stalk of a bunch of mangoes has been cut, all the mangoes attached to the stalk follow along with it, so too when the perception of impermanence is developed and cultivated, it eliminates all sensual lust ... it uproots all conceit of 'I am'.

"Just as all the rafters of a peaked house lead to the roof peak, slope towards the roof peak and converge upon the roof peak, and the roof peak is declared to be their chief, so too when the perception of impermanence is developed and cultivated, it eliminates all sensual lust ... it uproots all conceit of 'I am'.

"Just as, of all fragrant roots, black fragrant anusari is declared to be their chief, so too when the perception of impermanence is developed and cultivated, it eliminates all sensual lust ... it uproots all conceit of 'I am'.

"Just as, of all fragrant heartwoods, red sandalwood is declared to be their chief, so too when the perception of impermanence is developed and cultivated, it eliminates all sensual lust ... it uproots all conceit of 'I am'.

"Just as, of all fragrant flowers, the jasmine is declared to be their chief, so too when the perception of impermanence is developed and cultivated, it eliminates all sensual lust ... it uproots all conceit of 'I am'.

"Just as all petty princes are the vassals of a Wheel-turning Monarch and the Wheel-turning Monarch is declared to be their chief, so too when the perception of impermanence is developed and cultivated, it eliminates all sensual lust ... it uproots all conceit of 'I am'.

"Just as the radiance of all the stars does not amount to a sixteenth part of the radiance of the moon, and the radiance of the moon is declared to be their chief, so too when the perception of impermanence is developed and cultivated, it eliminates all sensual lust ... it uproots all conceit of 'I am'.

"Just as, in the autumn, when the sky is clear and cloudless, the sun rises above the earth dispelling all darkness from space as it shines and beams and radiates, so too when the perception of impermanence is developed and cultivated, it eliminates all sensual lust, it eliminates all attachment to material form, it eliminates all attachment to being, it eliminates all ignorance, it uproots all conceit of 'I am'.

"And how, bhikkhus, is the perception of impermanence developed and cultivated so that it eliminates all sensual lust ... and uproots all conceit of 'I am'?

"'Such is material form, such its origin, such its passing away; such is feeling, such its origin, such its passing away; such is perception, such its origin, such its passing away; such are mental formations, such their origin, such their passing away; such is consciousness, such its origin, such its passing away'—that is how the perception of impermanence is developed and cultivated so that it eliminates all sensual lust, eliminates all attachment to material form, eliminates all attachment to being, eliminates all ignorance, and uproots all conceit of 'I am'."

(Saṃyutta Nikāya, 22:102)

Looking Inward

Observations on the Art of Meditation

by

Tan Acharn Kor
Khao-suan-luang

WHEEL PUBLICATION NO. 373/374

The Practice in Brief

March 17, 1954

Those who practice the Dhamma should train themselves to understand in the following stages:

The training that is easy to learn, gives immediate results, and is suitable for every time, every place, for people of every age and either sex, is to study in the school of this body—a fathom long, a cubit wide, and a span thick—with its perceiving mind in charge. This body has many things, ranging from the crude to the subtle, that are well worth knowing.

The steps of the training:

1. To begin with, know that the body is composed of various physical properties, the major ones being the properties of earth, water, fire, and wind; the minor ones being the aspects that adhere to the major ones: things like colour, smell, shape, etc.

These properties are unstable (inconstant), stressful, and unclean. If you look into them deeply, you will see that there's no substance to them at all. They are simply impersonal conditions, with nothing worth calling "me" or "mine." When you can clearly perceive the body in these terms, you will be able to let go of any clinging or attachment to it as an entity, your self, someone else, this or that.

2. The second step is to deal with mental phenomena (feelings, perceptions, thought-formations, and consciousness). Focus on keeping track of the truth that these are characterised by arising, persisting, and then disbanding. In other words, their nature is to arise and disband, arise and disband, repeatedly. When you investigate to see this truth, you will be able to let go of your attachments to mental phenomena as entities, as your self, someone else, this or that.

3. Training on the level of practice doesn't simply mean studying, listening, or reading. You have to practise so as to see clearly with your own mind in the following steps:

Start out by brushing aside all external concerns and turn to look inside at your own mind until you can know in what ways it is clear or murky, calm or unsettled. The way to do this is to have mindfulness and self-awareness in charge as you keep aware of the body and mind until you've trained the mind to stay firmly in a state of normalcy, i.e. neutrality.

Once the mind can stay in a state of normalcy, you will see mental formations or preoccupations in their natural state of arising and disbanding. The mind will be empty, neutral, and still—neither pleased nor displeased—and will see physical and mental phenomena as they arise and disband naturally, of their own accord.

When the knowledge that there is no self to any of these things becomes thoroughly clear, you will meet with something that lies further inside, beyond all suffering and stress, free from the cycles of change—deathless—free from birth as well as death, since all things that take birth must by nature age, grow ill, and die.

When you see this truth clearly, the mind will be empty, not holding onto anything. It won't even assume itself to be a mind or anything at all. In other words, it won't latch onto itself as being anything of any sort. All that remains is a pure condition of Dhamma.

Those who see this pure condition of Dhamma in full clarity are bound to grow disenchanted with the repeated sufferings of life. When they know the truth of the world and the Dhamma throughout, they will see the results clearly, right in the present, *that there exists that which lies beyond all suffering.* They will know this without having to ask or take it on faith from anyone, for the Dhamma is *paccattaṃ*, i.e. something really to be known for oneself. Those who have seen this truth within themselves will attest to it always.

An Hour's Meditation

March 3, 1977

For those of you who have never sat in meditation, here is how it's done: Fold your legs, one on top of the other, but don't cut off the nerves or the blood flow, or else the breath energy in your legs will stagnate and cause you pain. Sit straight and place your hands, one on top of the other, on your lap. Hold your head up straight and keep your back straight, too—as if you had a yardstick sticking down your spine. You have to work at keeping it straight, you know. Don't spend the time slouching down and then stretching up again, or else the mind won't be able to settle down and be still ...

Keep the body straight and your mindfulness firm—firmly with the breath. However coarse or refined your breath may be, simply breathe in naturally. You don't have to force the breath or tense your body. Simply breathe in and out in a relaxed way. Only then will the mind begin to settle down. As soon as the breath grows normally refined and the mind has begun to settle down, focus your attention on the mind itself. If it slips off elsewhere, or any thoughts come in to intrude, simply know right there at the mind. Know the mind right at the mind with every in-and-out breath for the entire hour ...

When you focus on the breath, using the breath as a leash to tie the mind in place so that it doesn't go wandering off, you have to use your endurance. That is, you have to endure pain. For example, when you sit for a long time there's going to be pain, because you've never sat for so long before. So first make sure that you keep the mind normal and neutral. When pain arises, don't focus on the pain. Let go of it as much as you can. Let go of it and focus on your mind ... For those of you who've never done this before, it may take a while. Whenever any pain or anything arises, if the mind is affected by craving or defilement, it'll struggle because it doesn't want the pain. All it wants is pleasure.

This is where you have to be patient and endure the pain, *because pain is something that has to occur.* If there's pleasure, don't get enthralled with it. If there's pain, don't push it away. Start out by keeping the mind neutral as your basic stance. Then whenever pleasure or pain arises, don't get pleased or upset. Keep the mind continuously neutral and figure out how to let go. If there's a lot of pain, you first have to endure it and then relax your attachments. Don't think of the pain as being *your* pain. Let it be the pain of the body, the pain of nature.

If the mind latches tightly onto anything, it really suffers. It struggles. So here we patiently endure and let go. You have to practise so that you're really good at handling pain. If you can let go of physical pain, you'll be able to let go of all sorts of other sufferings and pains as well ... Keep watching the pain, knowing the pain, letting it go. Once you can let it go, you don't have to use a lot of endurance. It takes a lot of endurance only at the beginning. Once the pain arises, separate the mind from it. Let it be the pain of the body. Don't let the mind be pained, too ...

This is something that requires equanimity. If you can maintain equanimity in the face of pleasure or pain, it can make the mind peaceful—peaceful even though the pain is still pain. The mind keeps knowing, enduring the pain so as to let it go.

After you've worked at this a good while, you'll come to see how important the ways of the mind are. The mind may be hard to train, but if you keep training it—if you have the time, you can practise at home, at night or early in the morning, keeping watch on your mind—you'll gain the understanding that comes from mindfulness and discernment. Those who don't train the mind like this go through life—birth, ageing, illness, and death—not knowing a thing about the mind at all.

When you know your own mind, then when any really heavy illness comes along, the fact that you know your mind will make the pain less and less. But this is something you have to work at doing correctly. It's not easy, yet once the mind is well trained there's no match for it. It can do away with pain and suffering, and doesn't get restless and agitated. It grows still and cool—refreshed and blooming right there within itself. So try to experience this still, quiet mind ...

This is a really important skill to develop, because it will make craving, defilement, and attachment grow weaker and weaker. We all have defilements, you know. Greed, anger, and delusion cloud all of our hearts. If we haven't trained ourselves in meditation, our hearts are constantly burning with suffering and stress. Even the pleasure we feel over external things is pleasure only in half-measures, because there's suffering and stress in the delusion that thinks it's pleasure. As for the pleasure that comes from the practice, it's a cool pleasure that lets go of everything, really free from any sense of "me" or "mine." I ask that you reach the Dhamma that's the real meat inside this thing undisturbed by defilement, undisturbed by pain or anything else.

Even though there's pain in the body, you have to figure out how to let it go. The body is simply the four elements—earth, water, wind, and fire. It has to keep showing its inconstancy and stressfulness, so keep your mindfulness neutral, at equanimity. Let the mind be above its feelings—above pleasure, above pain, above everything ...

All it really takes is endurance—endurance and relinquishment, letting things go, seeing that they're not us, not ours. This is a point you have to hammer at, over and over again. When we say you have to endure, you *really* have to endure. Don't be willing to surrender. Craving is going to keep coming up and whispering—telling you to change things, to try for this or that kind of pleasure—but don't you listen to it. You have to listen to the Buddha—the Buddha who tells you to let go of craving. Otherwise, craving will plaster and paint things over; the mind will struggle and won't be able to settle down. So you have to give it your all. Look at this hour as a special hour—special in that you're using special endurance *to keep watch on your own heart and mind.*

A Basic Order in Life

January 29, 1964

The most important thing in the daily life of a person who practises the Dhamma is to keep to the precepts and to care for them more than you care for your life—to maintain them in a way that the Noble Ones would praise. If you don't have this sort of regard for the precepts, then the vices that run counter to them will become your everyday habits ...

Meditators who see that the breaking of a precept is something trifling and insignificant spoil their entire practice. If you can't practise even these basic, beginning levels of the Dhamma, you will ruin all the qualities you'll be trying to develop in the later stages of the practice. This is why you have to stick to the precepts as your basic foundation and to keep a lookout for anything in your behaviour that falls short of them. Only then will you be able to benefit from your practice for the sake of eliminating your sufferings with greater and greater precision.

If you simply act in line with the cravings and desires swelling out of the sense of self that has no fear of the fires of defilement, you'll have to suffer both in this life and in lives to come. If you don't have a sense of conscience—a sense of shame at the thought of doing shoddy actions, and a fear of their consequences—your practice can only deteriorate day by day ...

When people live without any order to their lives—without even the basic order that comes with the precepts—there's no way they can attain purity. We have to examine ourselves: In what ways at present are we breaking our precepts in thought, word, or deed? If we simply let things pass and aren't intent on examining ourselves to see the harm that comes from breaking the precepts and following the defilements, our practice can only sink lower and lower. Instead of extinguishing defilements and suffering, it will simply succumb to the power of craving. If this is the case, what damage is done? How much freedom does the mind lose? These are things we have to learn for ourselves. When we do, our practice of self-inspection in higher matters will get solid results and won't go straying off into nonsense. For this reason, whenever craving or defilement shows itself in any way in any of our actions, we have to catch hold of it and examine what's going on inside the mind.

Once we're aware with real mindfulness and discernment, we'll see the poison and power of the defilements. We'll feel disgust for them and want to extinguish them as much as we can. But if we use our defilements to examine things, they'll say everything is fine. The same as when we're predisposed to liking a certain person: Even if he acts badly, we say he's good. If he acts wrongly, we say he's right. This is the way the defilements are. They say that everything we do is right and throw all the blame on other people, other things. So we can't trust it—this sense of "self" in which craving and defilement lord it over the heart. We can't trust it at all ...

The violence of defilement, or this sense of self, is like that of a fire burning a forest or burning a house. It won't listen to anyone, but simply keeps burning away, burning away inside of you. And that's not all. It's always out to set fire to other people, too.

The fires of suffering, the fires of defilement consume all those who don't contemplate themselves or who don't have any means of practice for putting them out. People of this sort can't withstand the power of the defilements, can't help but follow along wherever their cravings lead them. The moment they're provoked, they follow in line with these things. This is why the sensations in the mind when provoked by defilement are very important, for they can lead you to do things with no sense of shame, no fear for the consequences of doing evil at all—which means that you're sure to break your precepts.

Once you've followed the defilements, they feel really satisfied—like arsonists who feel gleeful when they've set other people's places on fire. As soon as you've called somebody something vile or spread some malicious gossip, the defilements really like it. Your sense of self really likes it, because acting in line with defilements like that gives it real satisfaction. As a consequence, it keeps filling itself with the vices that run counter to the precepts, falling into hell in this very lifetime without realising it. So take a good look at the violence the defilements do to you, to see whether you should keep socialising with them, to see whether you should regard them as your friends or your enemies ...

As soon as any wrong views or ideas come out of the mind, we have to analyse them and turn around so as to catch sight of the facts within us. No matter what issues the defilements raise, focusing on the faults of others, we have to turn around and look within. *When we realise our own faults and can come to our senses:* That's where our study of the Dhamma, our practice of the Dhamma, shows its real rewards.

Continuous Practice

January 14, 1964

The passage for reflection on the four requisites (clothing, food, shelter, and medicine) is a fine pattern for contemplation, but we never actually get down to putting it to use. We're taught to memorise it in the beginning not simply to pass the time of day or so that we can talk about it every now and then, but so that we can use it to contemplate the requisites until we really know them with our own mindfulness and discernment. If we actually get down to contemplating in line with the established pattern, our minds will become much less influenced by unwise thoughts. But it's the rare person who genuinely makes this a continuous practice ... For the most part we're not interested. We don't feel like contemplating this sort of thing. We'd much rather contemplate whether this or that food will taste good or not, and if it doesn't taste good, how to fix it so that it will. That's the sort of thing we like to contemplate.

Try to see the filthiness of food and of the physical properties in general, to see their emptiness of any real entity or self. There's nothing of any substance to the physical properties of the body, which are all rotten and decomposing. The body is like a restroom over a cesspool. We can decorate it on the outside to make it pretty and attractive, but on the inside it's full of the most horrible, filthy things. Whenever we excrete anything, we ourselves are repelled by it; yet even though we're repelled by it, it's there inside us, in our intestines—decomposing, full of worms, awful smelling. There's just the flimsiest membrane covering it up, yet we fall for it and hold tight to it. We don't see the constant decomposition of this body, in spite of the filth and smells it sends out ...

The reason we're taught to memorise the passage for reflecting on the requisites, and to use it to contemplate, is so that we'll see the inconstancy of the body, to see that there's no "self" to any of it or to any of the mental phenomena we sense with every moment.

We contemplate mental phenomena to see clearly that they're not-self, to see this with every moment. The moments of the mind—the arising, persisting, and disbanding of mental sensations—are very subtle and fast. To see them, the mind has to be quiet. If the mind is involved in distractions, thoughts, and imaginings, we won't be able to penetrate in to see its characteristics as it deals with its objects, to see what the arising and disbanding within it is like.

This is why we have to practise concentration: to make the mind quiet, to provide a foundation for our contemplation. For instance, you can focus on the breath, or be aware of the mind as it focuses on the breath. Actually, when you focus on the breath, you're also aware of the mind. And again, the mind is what knows the breath. So you focus exclusively on the breath together with the mind. Don't think of anything else, and the mind will settle down and grow still. Once it attains stillness on this level, you've got your chance to contemplate.

Making the mind still so that you can contemplate it, is something you have to keep working at in the beginning. The same holds true with training yourself to be mindful and fully aware in all your activities. This is something you really have to work at continuously in this stage, something you have to do all the time. At the same time, you have to arrange the external conditions of your life so that you won't have any concerns to distract you ...

Now, of course, the practice is something you can do in any set of circumstances—for example, when you come home from work you can sit and meditate for a while—but when you're trying seriously to make it continuous, to make it habitual, it's much more difficult than that. "Making it habitual" means being fully mindful and aware with each in-and-out breath, wherever you go, whatever you do, whether you're healthy, sick, or whatever, and regardless of what happens inside or out. *The mind has to be in a state of all-encompassing awareness while keeping track of the arising and disbanding of mental phenomena at all times*—to the point where you can stop the mind from forming thoughts under the power of craving and defilement the way it used to before you began the practice.

Every In-and-out Breath

January 29, 1964

Try keeping your awareness with the breath to see what the still mind is like. It's very simple, all the rules have been laid out, but when you actually try to do it, something resists. It's hard. But when you let your mind think 108 or 1009 things, no matter what, it's all easy. It's not hard at all. *Try and see if you can engage your mind with the breath in the same way it's been engaged with the defilements.* Try engaging it with the breath and see what happens. See if you can disperse the defilements with every in-and-out breath. Why is it that the mind can stay engaged with the defilements all day long and yet go for entire days without knowing how heavy or subtle the breath is at all?

So try and be observant. The bright, clear awareness that stems from staying focused on the mind at all times: Sometimes a strong sensory contact comes and can make it blur and fade away with no trouble at all. But if you can keep hold of the breath as a reference point, that state of mind can be more stable and sure, more insured. It has two fences around it. If there's only one fence, it can easily break.

Taking a Stance

January 14, 1964

Normally the mind isn't willing to stop and look, to stop and know itself, which is why we have to keep training it continually so that it will settle down from its restlessness and grow still. Let your desires and thought-processes settle down. Let the mind take its stance in a state of normalcy, not liking or disliking anything. To reach a basic level of emptiness and freedom, you first have to take a stance. If you don't have a stance against which to measure things, progress will be very difficult. If your practice is hit-or-miss—a bit of that, a little of this—you won't get any results. So the mind first has to take a stance.

When you take a stance that the mind can maintain in a state of normalcy, don't go slipping off into the future. Have the mind know itself in the stance of the present: "Right now it's in a state of normalcy. No likes or dislikes have arisen yet. It hasn't created any issues. It's not being disturbed by a desire for this or that."

Then look on in to the basic level of the mind to see if it's as normal and empty as it should be. If you're really looking inside, really aware inside, then *that which is looking and knowing is mindfulness and discernment in and of itself.* You don't need to search for anything anywhere else to come and do your looking for you. As soon as you stop to look, stop to know whether or not the mind is in a state of normalcy, then if it's normal you'll know immediately that it's normal. If it's not, you'll know immediately that it's not.

Take care to keep this awareness going. If you can keep knowing like this continuously, the mind will be able to keep its stance continuously as well. As soon as the thought occurs to you to check things out, you'll immediately stop to look, stop to know, without any need to go searching for knowledge from anywhere else. You look, you know, right there at the mind and can tell whether or not it's empty and still. Once you see that it is, then you investigate to see *how* it's empty, *how* it's still. It's not the case that once it's empty, that's the end of the matter; once it's still, that's the end of the matter. *That's not the case at all.* You have to keep watch of things, you have to investigate at all times. Only then will you see the changing—the arising and disbanding—occurring in that emptiness, that stillness, that state of normalcy.

The Details of Pain

December 28, 1972

To lead your daily life by keeping constant supervision over the mind is a way of learning what life is for. It's a way of learning how we can act so as to rid ourselves more and more of suffering and stress—because the suffering and stress caused by defilement, attachment, and craving are sure to take all sorts of forms. Only by being aware with true mindfulness and discernment can we comprehend them for what they are. Otherwise, we'll simply live obliviously, going wherever events will lead us. This is why mindfulness and discernment are tools for reading yourself, for testing yourself within so that you won't be careless or complacent, oblivious to the fact that suffering is basically what life is all about.

This point is something we really have to comprehend so that we can live without being oblivious. The pains and discontent that fill our bodies and minds all show us the truths of inconstancy, stress, and not-selfness within us. If you contemplate what's going on inside until you can get down to the details, you'll see the truths that appear within and without, all of which come down to inconstancy, stress, and not-selfness. But the delusion basic to our nature will see everything wrongly—as constant, easeful, and self—and so make us live obliviously, even though there is nothing to guarantee how long our lives will last.

Our dreams and delusions make us forget that we live in the midst of a mass of pain and stress—the stress of defilements, the pain of birth. Birth, ageing, illness, and death: All these are painful and stressful, in the midst of instability and change. They're things we have no control over, for they must circle around in line with the laws of *kamma* and the defilements we've been amassing all along. Life that floats along in the round of rebirth is thus nothing but stress and pain.

If we can find a way to develop our mindfulness and discernment, they'll be able to cut the round of rebirth so that we won't have to keep wandering on. They'll help us know that birth is painful, ageing is painful, illness is painful, death is painful, and that these are all things that defilement, attachment, and craving keep driving through the cycles of change.

So as long as we have the opportunity, we should study the truths appearing throughout our body and mind, and we'll come to know that the elimination of stress and pain, the elimination of defilement, is a function of our practice of the Dhamma. If we don't practise the Dhamma, we'll keep floating along in the round of rebirth that is so drearily repetitious—repetitious in its birth, ageing, illness, and death, driven on by defilement, attachment, and craving, causing us repeated stress, repeated pain. Living beings for the most part don't know where these stresses and pains come from or what they come from, because they've never studied them, never contemplated them, so they stay stupid and deluded, wandering on and on without end ...

If we can stop and be still, the mind will have a chance to be free, to contemplate its sufferings, and to let them go. This will give it a measure of peace, because it will no longer want anything out of the round of rebirth—for it sees that there's nothing lasting to it, that it's simply stress over and over again. Whatever you grab hold of is stress. This is why you need mindfulness and discernment to know and see things for yourself, so that you can supervise the mind and keep it calm, without letting it fall victim to temptation.

This practice is something of the highest importance. People who don't study or practise the Dhamma have wasted their birth as human beings, because they're born deluded and simply stay deluded. But if we study the Dhamma, we'll become wise to suffering and know the path of practice for freeing ourselves from it ...

Once we follow the right path, the defilements won't be able to drag us around, won't be able to burn us, because *we're* the ones burning *them* away. We'll come to realise that the more we can burn them away, the more strength of mind we'll gain. If we let the defilements burn us, the mind will be sapped of its strength, which is why this is something you have to be very careful about. Keep trying to burn away the defilements in your every activity, and you'll be storing up strength for your mindfulness and discernment so that they'll be brave in dealing with all sorts of suffering and pain.

You must come to see the world as nothing but stress. There's no real ease to it at all. The awareness we gain from mindfulness and discernment will make us disenchanted with life in the world because it will see things for what they are in every way, both within us and without.

The entire world is nothing but an affair of delusion, an affair of suffering. People who don't know the Dhamma, who don't practise the Dhamma—no matter what their status or position in life—lead deluded, oblivious lives. When they fall ill or are about to die, they're bound to suffer enormously because they haven't taken the time to understand the defilements that burn their hearts and minds in everyday life. Yet if we make a constant practice of studying and contemplating ourselves as our everyday activity, it will help free us from all sorts of suffering and distress. And when this is the case, how can we *not* want to practise?

Only intelligent people, though, will be able to stick with the practice. Foolish people won't want to bother. They'd much rather follow the defilements than burn them away. To practise the Dhamma you need a certain basic level of intelligence—enough to have seen at least *something* of the stresses and sufferings that come from defilement. Only then can your practice progress. And no matter how difficult it gets, you'll have to keep practising on to the end.

This practice isn't something you do from time to time, you know. You have to keep at it continuously throughout life. Even if it involves so much physical pain or mental anguish that tears are bathing your cheeks, you have to keep with the chaste life because you're playing for real. If you don't follow the chaste life, you'll get mired in heaps of suffering and flame. So you have to learn your lessons from pain. Try to contemplate it until you can understand it and let it go, and you'll gain one of life's greatest rewards.

Don't think that you were born to gain this or that level of comfort. You were born to study pain and the causes of pain, and to follow the practice that frees you from pain. This is the most important thing there is. Everything else is trivial and unimportant. What's important all lies with the practice.

Don't think that the defilements will go away easily. When they don't come in blatant forms, they come in subtle ones—and the dangers of the subtle ones are hard to see. Your contemplation will have to be subtle, too, if you want to get rid of them. You'll come to realise that this practice of the Dhamma, in which we contemplate to get to the details inside us, is like sharpening our tools so that, when stress and suffering arise, we can weaken them and cut them away. If your mindfulness and discernment are brave, the defilements will have to lose out to them. But if you don't train your mindfulness and discernment to be brave, the defilements will crush you to pieces.

We were born to do battle with the defilements and to strengthen our mindfulness and discernment. We'll find that the worth of our practice will grow higher and higher because in our everyday life we've done continuous battle with the stresses and pains caused by defilement, craving, and temptation all along—so that the defilements will grow thin and our mindfulness and discernment stronger. We'll sense within ourselves that the mind isn't as troubled and restless as it used to be. It's grown peaceful and calm. The stresses and sufferings of defilement, attachment, and craving have grown weaker. Even though we haven't yet wiped them out completely, they've grown continually weaker—because we don't feed them. We don't give them shelter. We do what we can to weaken them so that they grow thinner and thinner each time.

And we have to be brave in contemplating stress and pain, because when we don't feel any great suffering we tend to get complacent. But when the pains and sufferings in our body and mind grow sharp and biting, we have to use our mindfulness and discernment to be strong. *Don't let your spirits be weak.* Only then will you be able to do away with your sufferings and pains.

We have to learn our lessons from pain so that ultimately the mind can gain its freedom from it, instead of being weak and losing out to it all of the time. We have to be brave in doing battle with it to the ultimate extreme—until we reach the point where we can let it go. Pain is something always present in this conglomerate of body and mind. It's here for us to see with every moment. If we contemplate it till we know all its details, we can then make it our sport: seeing that the pain is the pain of natural conditions and not *our* pain. This is something we have to research so as to get to the details: *that it's not our pain,* it's the pain of the aggregates [form, feeling, perception, thought-formations, and consciousness]. Knowing in this way means that we can separate out the properties—the properties of matter and those of the mind—to see how they interact with one another, how they change. It's something really fascinating ... Watching pain is a way of building up lots of mindfulness and discernment.

But if you focus on pleasure and ease, you'll simply stay deluded like people in general. They get carried away with the pleasure that comes from watching or listening to the things they like—but then when pain comes to their bodies and minds to the point where tears are bathing their cheeks, think of how much they suffer! And then they have to be parted from their loved ones, which makes it even worse. But those of us who practise the Dhamma don't need to be deluded like that, because we know and see with every moment that only stress arises, only stress persists, only stress passes away. Aside from stress, nothing arises; aside from stress, nothing passes away. This is there for us to perceive with every moment. If we contemplate it, we'll see it.

So we can't let ourselves be oblivious. This is what the truth is, and we have to study it so as to know it—especially in our life of the practice. We have to contemplate stress all the time to see its every manifestation. The arahats live without being oblivious because they know the truth at all times, and their hearts are clean and pure. As for us with our defilements, we have to keep trying, because if we continually supervise the mind with mindfulness and discernment, we'll be able to keep the defilements from making it dirty and obscured. Even if it does become obscured in any way, we'll be able to remove that obscurity and make the mind empty and free.

This is the practice that weakens all the defilements, attachments, and cravings within us. It's because of this practice of the Dhamma that our lives will become free. So I ask you to keep working at the practice without being complacent, because if in whatever span of life is left to you, you keep trying to the full extent of your abilities, you'll gain the mindfulness and discernment to see the facts within yourself, and be able to let go—free from any sense of self, free from any sense of self—continuously.

Aware Right at Awareness

November 3, 1975

The mind, if mindfulness and awareness are watching over it, won't meet with any suffering as the result of its actions. If suffering *does* arise, we'll be immediately aware of it and able to put it out. This is one point of the practice we can work at constantly. And we can test ourselves by seeing how refined and subtle our all-around awareness is inside the mind. Whenever the mind slips away and goes out to receive external sensory contact: Can it maintain its basic stance of mindfulness or internal awareness? The practice we need to work at in our everyday life is to have constant mindfulness, constant all-around present awareness like this. This is something we work at in every posture: sitting, standing, walking, and lying down. Make sure that your mindfulness stays continuous.

Living in this world—the mental and physical phenomena of these five aggregates—gives us plenty to contemplate. We must try to watch them, to contemplate them, so that we can understand them—because the truths we must learn how to read in this body and mind are here to be read with every moment. We don't have to get wrapped up with any other extraneous themes, because all the themes we need are right here in the body and mind. As long as we can keep the mind constantly aware all around, we can contemplate them.

If you contemplate mental and physical events to see how they arise and disband right in the here and now, and don't get involved with external things—like sights making contact with the eyes, or sounds with the ears—then there really aren't a lot of issues. The mind can be at normalcy, at equilibrium—calm and undisturbed by defilement or the stresses that come from sensory contact. It can look after itself and maintain its balance. You'll come to sense that if you're aware right at awareness in and of itself, without going out to get involved in external things like the mental labels and thoughts that will tend to arise, the mind will see their constant arising and disbanding—and won't be embroiled in anything. This way it can be disengaged, empty, and free. But if it goes out to label things as good or evil, as "me" or "mine," or gets attached to anything, it'll become unsettled and disturbed.

You have to know that if the mind can be still, totally and presently aware, and capable of contemplating with every activity, then blatant forms of suffering and stress will dissolve away. Even if they start to form, you can be alert to them and disperse them immediately. Once you see this actually happening—even in only the beginning stages—it can disperse a lot of the confusion and turmoil in your heart. In other words, don't let yourself dwell on the past or latch onto thoughts of the future. As for the events arising and passing away in the present, you have to leave them alone. Whatever your duties, simply do them as you have to—and the mind won't get worked up about anything. It will be able, to at least some extent, to be empty and still.

This one thing is something you have to be very careful about. You have to see this for yourself: *that if your mindfulness and discernment are constantly in charge, the truths of the arising and disbanding of mental and physical phenomena are always there for you to see,* always there for you to know. If you look at the body, you'll have to see it simply as physical properties. If you look at feelings, you'll have to see them as changing and inconstant: pleasure, pain, neither pleasure nor pain. To see these things is to see the truth within yourself. Don't let yourself get caught up with your external duties. Simply keep watch in this way inside. If your awareness is the sort that lets you read yourself correctly, the mind will be able to stay at normalcy, at equilibrium, at stillness, without any resistance.

If the mind can stay with itself and not go out looking for things to criticise or latch onto, it can maintain a natural form of stillness. So this is something we have to try for in our every activity. Keep your conversations to a minimum, and there won't be a whole lot of issues. Keep watch right at the mind. When you keep watch at the mind and your mindfulness is continuous, your senses can stay restrained.

Being mindful to keep watch in this way is something you have to work at. Try it and see: Can you keep this sort of awareness continuous? What sort of things can still get the mind engaged? What sorts of thoughts and labels of good and bad, me and mine, does it think up? Then look to see if these things arise and disband.

The sensations that arise from external contact and internal contact all have the same sorts of characteristics. You have to look till you can see this. If you know how to look, you'll see it—and the mind will grow calm.

So the point we have to practise in this latter stage doesn't have a whole lot of issues. There's nothing you have to do, nothing you have to label, nothing you have to think a whole lot about. Simply look carefully and contemplate, and in this very lifetime you'll have a chance to be calm and at peace, to know yourself more profoundly within. You'll come to see that the Dhamma is amazing *right here in your own heart.* Don't go searching for the Dhamma outside, for it lies within. Peace lies within, but we have to contemplate so that we're aware all around—subtly, deep down. If you look just on the surface, you won't understand anything. Even if the mind is at normalcy on the ordinary, everyday level, you won't understand much of anything at all.

You have to contemplate so that you're aware all around in a skilful way. The word "skilful" is something you can't explain with words, but you can know for yourself when you see the way in which awareness within the heart becomes special, when you see what this special awareness is about. This is something you can know for yourself.

And there's not really much to it: simply arising, persisting, disbanding. Look until this becomes plain—really, really plain—and everything disappears. All suppositions, all conventional formulations, all those aggregates and properties get swept away, leaving nothing but awareness pure and simple, not involved with anything at all—and there's nothing you have to do to it. Simply stay still and watch, be aware, letting go with every moment.

Simply watching this one thing is enough to do away with all sorts of defilements, all sorts of suffering and stress. If you don't know how to watch it, the mind is sure to get disturbed. It's sure to label things and concoct thoughts. As soon as there's contact at the senses, it'll go looking for things to latch onto, liking and disliking the objects it meets in the present and then getting involved with the past and future, spinning a web to entangle itself.

If you truly look at each moment in the present, there's really nothing at all. You'll see with every mental moment that things disband, disband, disband—really nothing at all. The important point is that you don't go forming issues out of nothing. The physical elements perform their duties in line with their elementary physical nature. The mental elements keep sensing in line with their own affairs. But our stupidity is what goes looking for issues to cook up, to label, to think about. It goes looking for things to latch onto and then gets the mind into a turmoil. This point is all we really have to see for ourselves. This is the problem we have to solve for ourselves. If things are left to their nature, pure and simple, there's no "us," no "them." This is a singular truth that will arise for us to know and see. There's nothing else we can know or see that can match it in any way. Once you know and see this one thing, it extinguishes all suffering and stress. The mind will be empty and free, with no meanings, no attachments, for anything at all.

This is why looking inward is so special in so many ways. Whatever arises, simply stop still to look at it. Don't get excited by it. If you become excited when any special intuitions arise when the mind is still, you'll get the mind worked up into a turmoil. If you become afraid that this or that will happen, that too will get you in a turmoil. So you have to stop and look, stop and know. The first thing is simply to look. The first thing is simply to know. And don't latch onto what you know—because whatever it is, it's simply a phenomenon that arises and disbands, arises and disbands, changing as part of its nature.

So your awareness has to take a firm stance right at the mind in and of itself. In the beginning stages, you have to know that when mindfulness is standing firm, the mind won't be affected by the objects of sensory contact. Keep working at maintaining this stance, holding firm to this stance. If you gain a sense of this for yourself, really knowing and seeing for yourself, your mindfulness will become even more firm. If anything arises in any way at all, you'll be able to let it go—and all the many troubles and turmoils of the mind will dissolve away.

If mindfulness slips and the mind goes out giving meanings to anything, latching onto anything, troubles will arise, so you have to keep checking on this with every moment. There's nothing else that's so worth checking on. You have to keep check on the mind in and of itself, contemplating the mind in and of itself. Or else you can contemplate the body in and of itself, feelings in and of themselves, or the phenomenon of arising and disbanding—i.e., the Dhamma—in and of itself. All of these things are themes you can keep track of entirely within yourself. You don't have to keep track of a lot of themes, because having a lot of themes is what will make you restless and distracted. First you'll practise this theme, then you'll practise that, then you'll make comparisons, all of which will keep the mind from growing still.

If you can take your stance at awareness, if you're skilled at looking, the mind can be at peace. You'll know how things arise and disband. First practise keeping awareness right within yourself so that your mindfulness can be firm, without being affected by the objects of sensory contact, so that it won't label things as good or bad, pleasing or displeasing. You have to keep checking to see that when the mind can be at normalcy, centred and neutral as its primary stance, then—whatever it knows or sees—it will be able to contemplate and let go.

The sensations in the mind that we explain at such length are still on the level of labels. Only when there can be *awareness right at awareness* will you really be able to know that the mind that is aware of awareness in this way doesn't send its knowing outside of this awareness. There are no issues. Nothing can be concocted in the mind when it knows in this way. In other words:

An inward-staying
unentangled knowing,
All outward-going knowing
cast aside.

The only thing you have to work at maintaining is the state of mind at normalcy—knowing, seeing, and still in the present. If you don't maintain it, if you don't keep looking after it, then when sensory contact comes it will have an effect. The mind will go out with labels of good and bad, liking and disliking. So make sure you maintain the basic awareness that's aware right at yourself. And don't let there be any labelling. No matter what sort of sensory contact comes, you have to make sure that this awareness comes first.

If you train yourself correctly in this way, everything will stop. You won't go straying out through your senses of sight, hearing, etc. The mind will stop and look, stop and be aware right at awareness, so as to know the truth that all things arise and disband. There's no real truth to anything. Only our stupidity is what latches onto things, giving them meanings and then suffering for it—suffering because of its ignorance, suffering because of its unacquaintance with the five aggregates—form, feelings, perceptions, thought-formations, and consciousness—all of which are inconstant, stressful, and not-self.

Use mindfulness to gather your awareness together, and the mind will stop getting unsettled, stop running after things. It will be able to stop and be still. Then make it know in this way, see in this way *constantly*—at every moment, with every activity. Work at watching and knowing the mind in and of itself: That will be enough to cut away all sorts of issues. You won't have to concern yourself with them.

If the body is in pain, simply keep watch of it. You can simply keep watch of feelings in the body because the mind that's aware of itself in this way can keep watch of anything within or without.

Or it can simply be aware of itself to the point where it lets go of things outside, lets go of sensory contact, and keeps constant watch on the mind in and of itself. That's when you'll know that this is what the mind is like when it's at peace: It doesn't give meanings to anything. It's the emptiness of the mind unattached, uninvolved, unconcerned with anything at all.

These words—unattached, uninvolved, and unconcerned—are things you have to consider carefully, because what they refer to is subtle and deep. "Uninvolved" means uninvolved with sensory contact, undisturbed by the body or feelings. "Unconcerned" means not worried about past, future, or present. You have to contemplate these things until you know them skilfully. Even though they're subtle, you have to contemplate them until you know them thoroughly. And don't go concerning yourself with external things, because they'll keep you unsettled, keep you running, keep you distracted with labels and thoughts of good and bad and all that sort of thing. You have to put a stop to these things. If you don't, your practice won't accomplish anything, because these things keep playing up to you and deceiving you—i.e., once you see anything, it will fool you into seeing it as right, wrong, good, bad, and so forth.

Eventually you have to come down to the awareness that everything simply arises, persists, and then disbands. *Make sure you stay focused on the disbanding.* If you watch just the arising, you may get carried off on a tangent, but if you focus on the disbanding you'll see emptiness: Everything is disbanding every instant. No matter what you look at, no matter what you see, it's there for just an instant and then disbands. Then it arises again. Then it disbands. There's simply arising, knowing, disbanding.

So let's watch what happens of its own accord—because the arising and disbanding that occurs by way of the senses is something that happens of its own accord. You can't prevent it. You can't force it. If you look and know it without attachment, there will be none of the harm that comes from joy or sorrow. The mind will stay in relative normalcy and neutrality. But if you're forgetful and start latching on, labelling things in pairs in any way at all—good and bad, happy and sad, pleasing and displeasing—the mind will become unsettled: no longer empty, no longer still. When this happens, you have to probe on in to know why.

All the worthless issues that arise in the mind have to be cut away. Then you'll find that you have less and less to say, less and less to talk about, less and less to think about. These things grow less and less on their own. They stop on their own. But if you get involved in a lot of issues, the mind won't be able to stay still. *So we have to keep watching things that are completely worthless and without substance,* to see that they're not-self. Keep watching them repeatedly, because your awareness, coupled with the mindfulness and discernment that will know the truth, has to see that, "This isn't my self. There's no substance or worth to it at all. It simply arises and disbands right here. It's here for just an instant and then it disbands."

All we have to do is stop and look, stop and know clearly in this way, and we'll be able to do away with many, many kinds of suffering and stress. The normal stress of the aggregates will still occur—we can't prevent it—but we'll know that it's the stress of nature and won't latch onto it as ours.

So we keep watch of things that happen on their own. If we know how to watch, we keep watching things that happen on their own. Don't latch onto them as being you or yours. Keep this awareness firmly established in itself, as much as you can, and there won't be much else you'll have to remember or think about.

When you keep looking, keep knowing like this at all times, you'll come to see that there are no big issues going on. There's just the issue of arising, persisting, and disbanding. You don't have to label anything as good or bad. If you simply look in this way, it's no great weight on the heart. But if you go dragging in issues of good and bad, self and all that, then suffering starts in a big way. The defilements start in a big way and weigh on the heart, making it troubled and upset. So you have to stop and look, stop and investigate really deep down inside. It's like water covered with duckweed: Only when we take our hand to part the duckweed and take a look will we see that the water beneath it is crystal clear.

As you look into the mind, you have to part it, you have to stop: stop thinking, stop labelling things as good or bad, stop everything. You can't go branding anything. Simply keep looking, keep knowing. When the mind is quiet, you'll see that there's nothing there. Everything is all still. Everything has all stopped inside. But as soon as there's labelling, even in the stillness, the stopping, the quiet, it will set things in motion. And as soon as things get set into motion, and you don't know how to let go right from the start, issues will arise, waves will arise. Once there are issues and waves, they strike the mind and it goes splashing all out of control. This splashing of the mind includes craving and defilement as well, because *avijjā*—ignorance—lies at its root ...

Our major obstacle is this aggregate of perceptions, of labels. If we aren't aware of the arising and disbanding of perceptions, these labels will take hold. Perceptions are the chief instigators that label things within and without, so we have to be aware of their arising and disbanding. Once we're aware in this way, perceptions will no longer function as a cause of suffering. In other words, they won't give rise to any further thought-formations. The mind will be aware in itself and able to extinguish these things in itself.

So we have to stop things at the level of perception. If we don't, thought-formations will fashion things into issues and then cause consciousness to wobble and waver in all sorts of ways. But these are things we can stop and look at, things we can know with every mental moment ... If we aren't yet really acquainted with the arising and disbanding in the mind, we won't be able to let go. We can talk about letting go, but we can't do it because we don't yet know. As soon as anything arises we grab hold of it—even when actually it's already disbanded, but since we don't really see, we don't know ...

So I ask that you understand this basic principle. Don't go grasping after this thing or that, or else you'll get yourself all unsettled. The basic theme is within: Look on in, keep knowing on in until you penetrate everything. The mind will then be free from turmoil. Empty. Quiet. Aware. So keep continuous watch of the mind in and of itself, and you'll come to the point where you simply run out of things to say. Everything will stop on its own, grow still on its own, *because the underlying condition that has stopped and is still is already there*, simply that we aren't aware of it yet.

The Pure Present

June 3, 1964

We have to catch sight of the sensation of knowing when the mind gains knowledge of anything and yet isn't aware of itself, to see how it latches onto things: physical form, feeling, perceptions, thought-formations, and consciousness. We have to probe on in and look on our own. We can't use the teachings we've memorised to catch sight of these things. That won't get us anywhere at all. We may remember, "The body is inconstant," but even though we can say it, we can't see it.

We have to focus on in to see exactly *how* the body is inconstant, to see how it changes. And we have to focus on feelings—pleasant, painful, and neutral—to see how they change. The same holds true with perceptions, thought-formations, and so forth. We have to focus on them, investigate them, contemplate them to see their characteristics *as they actually are.* Even if you can see these things for only a moment, it'll do you a world of good. You'll be able to catch yourself: The things you thought you knew, you didn't really know at all ... This is why the knowledge we gain in the practice has to keep changing through many, many levels. It doesn't stay on just one level.

So even when you're able to know arising and disbanding with every moment right in the present: If your contemplation isn't continuous, it won't be very clear. You have to know how to contemplate the bare sensation of arising and disbanding, simply arising and disbanding, without any labels of "good" or "bad." Just keep with the pure sensation of arising and disbanding. When you do this, other things will come to intrude—but no matter how they intrude, it's still a matter of arising and disbanding, so you can keep your stance with arising and disbanding in this way.

If you start labelling things, they get confusing. All you need to do is keep looking at the right spot: the bare sensation of arising and disbanding. Simply make sure that you really keep watch of it. Whether there's awareness of sights, sounds, smells, tastes, or tactile sensations, just stay with the sensation of arising and disbanding. Don't go labelling the sight, sound, smell, taste, or tactile sensation. If you can keep watch in this way, you're with the pure present—and there won't be any issues.

When you keep watch in this way, you're keeping watch on inconstancy, on change, as it actually occurs—because even the arising and disbanding changes. It's not the same thing arising and disbanding all the time. First this sort of sensation arises and disbands, then that sort arises and disbands. If you keep watch on bare arising and disbanding like this, you're sure to arrive at insight. But if you keep watch with labels—"That's the sound of a cow," "That's the bark of a dog"—you won't be watching the bare sensation of sound, the bare sensation of arising and disbanding. As soon as there's labelling, thought-formations come along with it. Your senses of touch, sight, hearing, and so forth will continue their bare arising and disbanding, but you won't know it. Instead, you'll label everything—sights, sounds, etc.—and then there will be attachments, feelings of pleasure and displeasure, and you won't know the truth.

The truth keeps going along on its own. Sensations keep arising and then disbanding. If we focus right here—at the consciousness of the bare sensation of sights, sounds, smells, tastes, and tactile sensations, then we'll be able to gain insight quickly ...

If we know how to observe things in this way, we'll be able to see easily when the mind is provoked by passion or greed, and even more easily when it's provoked by anger. As for delusion, that's something more subtle ... something you have to take a great interest in and investigate carefully. You'll come to see all sorts of hidden things—how the mind is covered with many, many layers of film. It's really fascinating. But then that's what insight meditation is for—to open your eyes so that you can know and see, so that you can destroy your delusion and ignorance.

The Deceits of Knowing

January 29, 1964

You have to find approaches for contemplating and probing at all times so as to catch sight of the flickerings of awareness, to see in what ways it streams out to know things. Be careful to catch sight of it both when its knowing is right and when it's wrong. Don't mix things up, taking wrong knowledge for right, or right knowledge for wrong. This is something extremely important for the practice, this question of right and wrong knowing, for these things can play tricks on you.

When you gain any new insights, don't go getting excited. You can't let yourself get excited by them at all, because it doesn't take long for your insight to change—to change right now, before your very eyes. It's not going to change at some other time or place. It's changing right now. You have to know how to observe, how to acquaint yourself with the deceits of knowledge. *Even when it's correct knowledge, you can't latch onto it.*

Even though we may have standards for judging what sort of knowledge is correct in the course of our practice, don't go latching onto correct knowledge—because correct knowledge is inconstant. It changes. It can turn into false knowledge, or into knowledge that is even more correct. You have to contemplate things very carefully—very, very carefully—so that you won't fall for your knowledge, thinking, "I've gained right insight; I know better than other people," so that you won't start assuming yourself to be special. The moment you assume yourself, your knowledge immediately turns wrong. Even if you don't let things show outwardly, the mere mental event in which the mind labels itself is a form of wrong knowing that obscures the mind from itself in an insidious way.

This is why meditators who neglect to contemplate things, who don't catch sight of the deceits of every form of knowledge—right and wrong, good and bad—tend to get bogged down in their knowledge. The knowledge that deceives them into thinking, "What I know is right," gives rise to strong pride and conceit within them, without their even realising it.

This is because the defilements are always getting into the act without our realising it. They're insidious, and in their insidious way they keep getting into the act as a matter of course, for the defilements and mental effluents are still there in our character. Our practice is basically a probing deep inside, from the outer levels of the mind to the inner ones. This is an approach that requires a great deal of subtlety and precision ... The mind has to use its own mindfulness and discernment to dig everything out of itself, leaving just the mind in and of itself, the body in and of itself, and then keep watch over them.

The basic challenge in the practice is this one point and nothing else: *this problem of how to look inward so that you see clear through.* If the mind hasn't been trained to look inward, it tends to look outward, simply waiting to receive its objects from outside—and all it gets is the confusion of its sensations going in and out, in and out. And even though this confusion is one aspect of change and inconstancy, we don't see it that way. Instead, we see it as issues, good and bad, pertaining to the self. When this is the case, we're back right where we started, not knowing what's what. This is why the mind's sensations, when it isn't acquainted with itself, are so secretive and hard to perceive. If you want to find out about them by reading a lot of books, you end up piling more defilements onto the mind, making it even more thickly covered than before.

So when you turn to look inward, you shouldn't use concepts and labels to do your looking for you. If you use concepts and labels to do your looking, there will be nothing but concepts arising, changing, and disbanding. Everything will get all concocted into thoughts—and then how will you be able to watch in utter silence? The more you take what you've learned from books to look inside yourself, the less you'll see.

So whatever you've learned, when you come to the practice you have to put all the labels and concepts you've gained from your learning to one side. You have to make yourself an innocent beginner once more. Only then will you be able to penetrate in to read the truths within you. If you carry all the paraphernalia of the concepts and standards you've gained from your learning to gauge things inside you, you can search to your dying day and yet won't meet with any real truths at all. This is why you have to hold to only one theme in your practice. If the mind has lots of themes to concern itself with, it's still just wandering around—wandering around to know this and that, going out of bounds without realising it and not really wanting to know itself. This is why those with a lot of learning like to teach others, to show off their level of understanding. And this is precisely how the desire to stand out keeps the mind obscured.

Of all the various kinds of deception, *there's none as bad as deceiving yourself.* When you haven't yet really seen the truth, what business do you have making assumptions about yourself, that you've attained this or that sort of knowledge, or that you know enough to teach others correctly? The Buddha is quite critical of teachers of this sort. He calls them "people in vain." Even if you can teach large numbers of people to become arahats, while you yourself haven't tasted the flavour of the Dhamma, the Buddha says that you're a person in vain. So you have to keep examining yourself. If you haven't yet really trained yourself in the things you teach to others, how will you be able to extinguish your own suffering?

Think about this for a moment. Extinguishing suffering, gaining release from suffering: Aren't these subtle matters? Aren't they completely personal within us? If you question yourself in this way, you'll be on the right track. But even then you have to be careful. If you start taking sides with yourself, the mind will cover itself up with wrong insights and wrong opinions. If you don't observe really carefully, you can get carried off on a tangent—because the awareness with which the mind reads itself and actually sees through itself is something really extraordinary, really worth developing—and it really eliminates suffering and defilement. This is the real, honest truth, not a lot of propaganda or lies. It's something you really have to practise, and then you'll really have to see clearly in this way. When this is the case, how can you *not* want to practise?

If you examine yourself correctly in this way, you'll be able to know what's real. But you have to be careful to examine yourself correctly. If you start latching onto any sense of self, thinking that you're better than other people, then you've failed the examination. No matter how correct your knowledge, you have to keep humble and respectful above all else. You can't let there be any pride or conceit at all, or it will destroy everything.

This is why the awareness that eliminates the sense of self depends more than anything else on your powers of observation—to check and see if there's still anything in your knowledge or opinions that comes from the force of pride in any sense of self ... You have to use the full power of your mindfulness and discernment to cut these things away. It's nothing you can play around at. If you gain a few insights or let go of things a bit, don't go thinking you're anything special. The defilements don't hold a truce with anyone. They keep coming right out as they like. So you have to be circumspect and examine things on all sides. Only then will you be able to benefit in ways that make your defilements and sufferings lighter and lighter.

When we probe in to find the instigator—the mind, or this property of consciousness—that's when we're on the right track, and our probing will keep getting results, will keep weakening the germs of craving and wiping them out. In whatever way craving streams out, for "being" or "having" in any way at all, we'll be able to catch sight of it every time. To catch hold and examine this "being" and "having" in this way, though, requires a lot of subtlety. If you aren't really mindful and discerning, you won't be able to catch sight of these things at all, because the mind is continually wanting to be and to have. The germs of defilement lie hidden deep in the seed of the mind, in this property of consciousness. Simply to be aware of them skilfully is no mean feat—so we shouldn't even *think* of trying to wipe them out with our mere opinions. We have to keep contemplating, probing on in, until things come together just right, in a single moment, and then it's like reaching the basic level of knowing that exists on its own, with no willing or intention at all.

This is something that requires careful observation: the difference between willed and unwilled knowing. Sometimes there's the intention to look and be aware within, but there come times when there's no intention to look within, and yet knowledge arises on its own. If you don't yet know, look at the intention to look inward: What is it like? What is it looking for? What does it see? This is a basic approach you have to hold to. This is a level you have to work at, and one in which you have to make use of intention—the intention to look inward in this way ... But once you reach the basic level of knowing, then as soon as you happen to focus down and look within, the knowledge will occur on its own.

Sabbe Dhammā Anattā

July 9, 1971

One night I was sitting in meditation outside in the open air—my back straight as an arrow—firmly determined to make the mind quiet, but even after a long time it wouldn't settle down. So I thought, "I've been working at this for many days now, and yet my mind won't settle down at all. It's time to stop being so determined and to simply be aware of the mind." I started to take my hands and feet out of the meditation posture, but at the moment I had unfolded one leg but had yet to unfold the other, I could see that my mind was like a pendulum swinging more and more slowly, more and more slowly—until it stopped.

Then there arose an awareness that was sustained by itself. Slowly I put my legs and hands back into position. At the same time, the mind was in a state of awareness absolutely and solidly still, seeing clearly into the elementary phenomena of existence as they arose and disbanded, changing in line with their nature—and also seeing a separate condition inside, with no arising, disbanding, or changing, a condition beyond birth and death: something very difficult to put clearly into words, because it was a realisation of the elementary phenomena of nature, completely internal and individual.

After a while I slowly got up and lay down to rest. This state of mind remained there as a stillness that sustained itself deep down inside. Eventually the mind came out of this state and gradually returned to normal.

From this I was able to observe how practice consisting of nothing but fierce desire simply upsets the mind and keeps it from being still. But when one's awareness of the mind is just right, an inner awareness will arise naturally of its own accord. Because of this clear inner awareness, I was able to continue knowing the facts of what's true and false, right and wrong, from that point on, and it enabled me to know that the moment when the mind let go of everything was a clear awareness of the elementary phenomena of nature, because it was an awareness that knew within and saw within of its own accord—not something you can know or see by wanting.

For this reason the Buddha's teaching, "*Sabbe dhammā anattā*—All phenomena are not-self," tells us not to latch onto *any* of the phenomena of nature, whether conditioned or unconditioned. From that point on I was able to understand things and let go of attachments step by step.

Going Out Cold

May 26, 1964

It's important to realise how to focus on events in order to get special benefits from your practice. You have to focus so as to observe and contemplate, not simply to make the mind still. Focus on how things arise, how they disband. Make your focus subtle and deep.

When you're aware of the characteristics of your sensations, then—if it's a physical sensation—contemplate that physical sensation. There will have to be a feeling of stress. Once there's a feeling of stress, how will you be aware of it simply as a feeling so that it won't lead to anything further? Once you can be aware of it simply as a feeling, it stops right there without producing any taste in terms of a desire for anything. The mind will disengage right there—right there at the feeling. If you don't focus on it in this way, craving will arise on top of the feeling—craving to attain ease and be rid of the stress and pain. If you don't focus on the feeling in the proper way right from the start, craving will arise before you're aware of it, and if you then try to let go of it, it'll be very tiring ...

The way in which preoccupations take shape, the sensations of the mind as it's aware of things coming with every moment, the way these things change and disband: These are all things you have to focus on to see clearly. This is why we make the mind disengaged. We don't disengage it so that it doesn't know or amount to anything. That's not the kind of disengagement we want. The more the mind is truly disengaged, the more it sees clearly into the characteristics of the arising and disbanding within itself. All I ask is that you observe things carefully, that your awareness be all-around at all times. Work at this as much as you can. If you can keep this sort of awareness going, you'll find that the mind or consciousness under the supervision of mindfulness and discernment in this way is different from—the direct opposite of—unsupervised consciousness. It will be the opposite sort of thing continually.

If you keep the mind well supervised so that it's sensitive in the proper way, it will yield enormous benefits, not just small ones. If you don't make it properly sensitive and aware, what can you expect to gain from it?

When we say that we gain from the practice, we're not talking about anything else: We're talking about gaining disengagement. Freedom. Emptiness. Before, the mind was embroiled. Defilement and craving attacked and robbed it, leaving it completely entangled. Now it's disengaged, freed from the defilements that used to gang up to burn it. Its desires for this or that thing, its concocting of this or that thought, have all fallen away. So now it's empty and disengaged. It can be empty in this way right before your very eyes. Try to see it right now, before your eyes, right now as I'm speaking and you're listening. Probe on in so as to know.

If you can be constantly aware in this way, you're following in the footsteps or taking within you the quality called "*buddho*," which means one who knows, who is awake, who has blossomed in the Dhamma. Even if you haven't fully blossomed—if you've blossomed only to the extent of disengaging from the blatant levels of craving and defilement—you still benefit a great deal, for when the mind really knows the defilements and can let them go, it feels cool and refreshed in and of itself. This is the exact opposite of the defilements that, as soon as they arise, make us burn and smoulder inside. If we don't have the mindfulness and discernment to help us know, the defilements will burn us. But as soon as mindfulness and discernment know, the fires go out—and they go out cold.

Observe how the defilements arise and take shape—they also disband in quick succession, but when they disband on their own in this way, go out on their own in this way, they go out hot. If we have mindfulness and discernment watching over them, they go out cold. Look so that you can see what the true knowledge of mindfulness and discernment is like: It goes out; it goes out cold. As for the defilements, even when they arise and disband in line with their nature, they go out hot—hot because we latch onto them, hot because of attachment. When they go out cold, look again—it's because there's no attachment. They've been let go, put out.

This is something really worth looking into: the fact that there's something very special like this in the mind—special in that when it really knows the truth, it isn't attached. It's unentangled, empty, and free. This is how it's special. It can grow empty of greed, anger, and delusion, step after step. It can be empty of desire, empty of mental processes. The important thing is that you really see for yourself that the true nature of the mind is that it can be empty ... This is why I said this morning that *nibbāna* doesn't lie anywhere else. It lies right here, right where things go out and are cool, go out and are cool. It's staring us right in the face.

Reading the Heart

March 15, 1974

The Buddha taught that we are to know with our own hearts and minds. Even though there are many, many words and phrases coined to explain the Dhamma, we need focus only on the things we can know and see, extinguish and let go of, right in each moment of the immediate present—better than taking on a load of other things. Once we can read and comprehend our inner awareness, we'll be struck deep within us that the Buddha awakened to the truth right here in the heart. His truth is truly the language of the heart.

When they translate the Dhamma in all sorts of ways, it becomes something ordinary. But if you keep close and careful watch right at the heart and mind, you'll be able to see clearly, to let go, to put down your burdens. If you don't know right here, your knowledge will send out all sorts of branches, turning into thought-formations with all sorts of meanings in line with conventional labels—and all of them way off the mark.

If you know right at your inner awareness and make it your constant stance, there's nothing at all: no need to take hold of anything, no need to label anything, no need to give anything names. Right where craving arises, right where it disbands: That's where you'll know what *nibbāna* is like ... "*Nibbāna* is simply this disbanding of craving." That's what the Buddha stressed over and over again.

The Essential Practice, Part I

Dhamma Discourses of
Venerable Webu Sayadaw

Translated from the Burmese by

Roger Bischoff

WHEEL PUBLICATION NO. 375/376

What Really Matters

Sayadaw: You have taken up moral conduct (*sīla*). Now that you have undertaken to perfect yourselves in the perfection of morality (*sīla-pāramī*), fulfil it to the utmost. Only if you fulfil *sīla* to the utmost will all your aspirations be met. You will be happy now and in the future.

Only the teachings of the Buddha can give you real happiness—in the present and in the remainder of *saṃsāra*.[1] The teachings of the Buddha are enshrined in the Three Collections, or the canonical Tipiṭaka.[2] The Tipiṭaka is very extensive. If we take the essence out of the Tipiṭaka we shall find the thirty-seven Factors of Awakening (*bodhipakkhiyādhammā*).[3] The essence of the thirty-seven Factors of Awakening is the eight constituents of the Noble Eightfold Path (*maggaṅgas*). The essence of the Noble Eightfold Path is the threefold training (*sikkhā*): higher morality, higher mindfulness, and higher wisdom (*adhisīla, adhicitta, adhipaññā*). The essence of the threefold training is the unique Universal Law (*eko dhammo*).[4]

If your body and mind are under control, as they are now, there can be no roughness of physical or verbal action. This is *adhisīla* or perfect morality.

---

1. The cycle of birth and death that is without discernible beginning, but which ends with the attainment of Nibbāna.
2. The Three Collections are the Vinaya-piṭaka or monastic discipline; the Sutta-piṭaka or book of discourses; and the Abhidhamma-piṭaka or philosophical treatises.
3. *Bodhipakkhiya dhamma.* These are thirty-seven aspects of practice taught by the Buddha. They include the four foundations of mindfulness, the four great efforts, the four bases of accomplishment, the five spiritual faculties, the five powers, the seven factors of awakening, and the eight constituents of the Noble Eightfold Path.
4. Discourses about the Dhamma or the "Universal Law" as explained by the Buddha are given by monks to lay disciples on request. Monks normally give a Dhamma lecture after a meal offered to them, but there are also Dhamma lectures organized for big gatherings and given by famous monks.

If *adhisīla* becomes strong, the mind will become peaceful and tranquil and lose its harshness. This is called *adhicitta*.[5]

If *adhicitta* (*samādhi*) becomes strong and the mind stays one-pointed for a long period, then you will realise that in a split second matter arises and dissolves billions and billions of times. If mind (*nāma*) knows matter (*rūpa*), it knows that matter becomes and disintegrates billions and billions of times in the wink of an eye.[6] This knowledge of arising and disintegration is called *adhipaññā*.

Whenever we breathe in or out, the in-coming and the out-going air touches somewhere in or near the nostrils. The sensitive matter (*kāya-pasāda*) registers the touch of air.[7] In this process, the entities touching are matter, and the entity knowing the touch is mind. So do not go around asking others about mind and matter, observe your breathing and you will find out about them for yourselves.

When the air comes in, it will touch. When the air goes out, it will touch. If you know this touch continuously, then wanting (*lobha*), dislike (*dosa*), and delusion (*moha*) do not have the opportunity to arise, and the fires of greed, anger, and delusion will subside.

You cannot know the touch of air before it actually occurs. After it has gone, you cannot know it any more. Only while the air moves in or out can you feel the sensation of touch. This we call the present moment.

While we feel the touch of air, we know that there are only mind and matter. We know for ourselves that there is no "I," no other person, no man and woman, and we realise for ourselves that what the Buddha said is indeed true. We needn't ask others. While we know in-breath and out-breath, there is no I or *attā*.[8]

---

5. *Citta* in Pali means mind and mental functions. *Adhicitta* here means "concentrated mind," i.e., *samādhi*.

6. Matter, according to Buddhism, consists of subatomic particles (*kalapas*) arising and disintegrating billions and billions of times in the wink of an eye.

7. *Kāya-pasāda* is the sensitive matter contained in the five physical sense organs that registers light (sight), sound waves, smells, tastes, and tactile sensations.

8. *Attā*, Pali for "I," "soul," "personality," or any other type of permanent personal entity. Buddhism holds that such an entity does not exist and that the erroneous belief in a self is due to wishful thinking and wrong view of reality. See Saṃyutta Nikāya, III 78, 196.

When we know this, our view is pure; it is right view. We know in that moment that there is nothing but *nāma* and *rūpa*, mind and matter. We also know that mind and matter are two different entities. If we thus know how to distinguish between *nāma* and *rūpa*, we have attained the ability to distinguish between mind and matter (*nāma-rūpa-pariccheda-ñāṇa*).

If we know the touch of air as and when it occurs, our mind is pure and we get the benefits thereof. Do not think that the benefits you get thus, even in a split second, are few. Do not think that those who meditate do not get any advantages from their practice. Now that you are born in a happy plane and encounter the teachings of a Buddha, you can obtain great benefits. Do not worry about eating and drinking, but make all the effort you can.

Sayadaw: Is this present time not auspicious?

Disciple: Yes sir, it is.

Sayadaw: Yes, indeed! Can't those good people attain their aspiration to Nibbāna who, with an open mind, receive and practise the teachings of the Buddha, just like the noble people of the past who received the instructions from the Buddha himself?

Disciple: Yes sir, they can.

Sayadaw: So, how long does the Buddha's Sāsana (teaching) last?[9]

Disciple: For five thousand years, sir.

Sayadaw: And now tell me, how many of these five thousand years have passed?

Disciple: Sir, about half this time span has gone.

Sayadaw: So, how much remains still?

Disciple: About two thousand five hundred years, sir.

Sayadaw: What is the life span of a human being now?[10]

Disciple: About one hundred years, sir.

---

9. There is a belief in Buddhist countries that the Buddha's Teaching (*sāsana*) lasts five thousand years on the human plane and then is lost.

10. The life span of human beings is believed to change according to the level of morality observed on the human plane. It ranges from an incalculable (*asaṅkheyya*) down to ten years. See: Dīgha Nikāya, III 81ff., and Ledi Sayadaw, *Manuals of Buddhism*, pp. 112 f., 116 f.

Sayadaw: How old are you?

Disciple: I am thirty-seven years old, sir.

Sayadaw: So, how much longer do you have to live?

Disciple: Sixty-three years, sir.

Sayadaw: But can you be sure that you will live that long?

Disciple: That I don't know, sir.

Sayadaw: You don't know yourself how long you are going to live?

Disciple: No, sir, it isn't possible to know this for sure.

Sayadaw: But even as we are born we can be sure to have to suffer old age, disease, and death.

Disciple: Yes, sir.

Sayadaw: Can we request old age, pain, and death to desist for some time, to go away for some time?

Disciple: No, sir.

Sayadaw: No, they never rest. Can we ask them to stop their work?

Disciple: No, sir, we cannot.

Sayadaw: In that case we can be certain that we have to die?

Disciple: Yes, sir, it is certain that we all have to die.

Sayadaw: It is certain that all have to die. What about living?

Disciple: We can't be sure how long we have left to live, sir.

Sayadaw: Someone whose life span is thirty years dies when the thirty years are up. If your life span is forty or fifty years, you will die when you are forty or fifty years old. Once someone is dead, can we get him back?

Disciple: No, sir, we can't.

Sayadaw: However many years of your life have passed, they have passed. What is it that you have not accomplished yet?

Disciple: The happiness of the Paths and Fruition States, Nibbāna.

Sayadaw: Yes, inasmuch as you haven't attained the Paths and Fruition States yet, you have been defeated. Have you used the years that have passed well or have you wasted your time?

Disciple: I have wasted my time, sir.

Sayadaw: Then do not waste the time that you have got left. This time is there for you to strive steadfastly with energy. You can be sure that you will die, but you can't be sure how much longer you have got to live. Some live very long. Venerable Mahā-Kassapa and Venerable Mahā-Kaccāyana lived to over one hundred years of age. Some live for eighty years. To be able to live that long we have to be full of respect for those who deserve respect, and we have to be very humble. Do you pay respects to your father and mother?

Disciple: We do, sir.

Sayadaw: Do you pay respects to people who are older than you or of a higher standing than you?

Disciple: We do pay respects to people who are older than us or are holding a higher position than we do. Even if someone is just one day older or even just half a day older, we pay respects, sir.

Sayadaw: When do you pay respects to them?

Disciple: At night, before we go to bed, we pay respects to the Buddha, and at that time we also pay respects to our seniors.

Sayadaw: What about other times?

Disciple: At other times we do not pay respects, sir.

Sayadaw: You say that you pay respects to your seniors after you have paid respects to the Buddha. But do you show respect to those who live with you and to those who are of the same age? If I were to put parcels of money worth $1000 each along the road for anyone to take, would you fellows take one?

Disciple: Of course we would, sir.

Sayadaw: And if you found a second one, would you take that too?

Disciple: Of course we would, sir.

Sayadaw: And if you found a third bundle of bank notes, would you take that as well?

Disciple: We would take it, of course, sir.

Sayadaw: After having got one, wouldn't you want someone else to have one?

Disciple: We wouldn't think that way, sir.

Sayadaw: If you happened to be with a friend, would you let him find one bundle of notes thinking, "I shall pretend not to see that one. After all, I have one already"? Would you let him have one or would you grab them all and run for it?

Disciple: I would grab all I could get and run for it, sir.

Sayadaw: Yes, yes, you fellows are not very pleasant. When it comes to money, you are unable to give to anyone. But then you say that you are respectful and humble just because you pay respects to the Buddha in the evenings. If you cherish thoughts such as, "Why is he better off than I am? Is his understanding greater than mine?", then your mind is still full of pride. If you pay respects to your parents and teachers, to those older, wiser, or of higher standing, without pride, then you will live to more than one hundred years. If you show respect to such people, will you get only $1000? Will you get only money?

Disciple: It will be more than just money.

Sayadaw: Yes, indeed! And though you know what really matters, you wouldn't even give $1000 to someone else, but would rather run and get it for yourselves. When the Buddha, out of compassion, taught the Dhamma, did everybody understand it?

Disciple: No, sir, not everyone understood it.

Sayadaw: Why is this so?

Disciple: Some didn't listen to the Buddha, sir.

Sayadaw: Only if you take the teachings of the Buddha for yourselves can you attain *sammā-sam-bodhi* (Buddhahood), *pacceka-bodhi* (Pacceka-Buddhahood), *agga-sāvaka-bodhi* (chief-discipleship), *mahā-sāvaka-bodhi* (leading-discipleship), *pakati-sāvaka-bodhi* (Arahatship). If you want to attain one of these forms of awakening, you can. Through the teachings of the Buddha you can attain happiness now, a happiness that will stay with you also in the future.

How long does it take for a paddy seed to sprout?

Disciple: Only overnight, sir.

Sayadaw: It takes only a day for it to sprout. Now, if you keep the seed, a good quality seed of course, after sprouting and do not plant it, will it grow?

Disciple: No, sir, it won't.

Sayadaw: Even though you have a good quality seed, if you do not plant it, it will not grow. It is just the same with the teachings of the Buddha; only if you accept them will you understand them. If you learn how to live with the awareness of mind and matter arising, what do you achieve?

Disciple: This awareness is called *vijjā* sir.

Sayadaw: If one lives without the teachings of the Buddha, what do you call that?

Disciple: That is *avijjā*, sir, ignorance.

Sayadaw: If you live all your life with *vijjā*, understanding of the Buddha-Dhamma, then where will you go after death?

Disciple: To some good existence, sir.

Sayadaw: What will happen after a life full of ignorance?

Disciple: One will go to the lower realms, sir.

Sayadaw: Now, say an old man about seventy years old is paying respects to the Buddha. While doing so, he cannot keep his mind focused on the Dhamma, but he allows it to wander here and there. If this old man dies at that moment, where will he be reborn?

Disciple: He will go to the lower worlds, sir.

Sayadaw: Really? Think carefully before you answer. He is paying respects to the Buddha, and he is meditating. So, where will he go if he dies at that moment?

Disciple: He will go to the lower worlds, sir.

Sayadaw: But why?

Disciple: Because his mind is wandering all over, sir.

Sayadaw: Yes. What are the qualities arising in the mind of a person living in ignorance?

Disciple: They are greed (*lobha*), aversion (*dosa*), and delusion (*moha*).[11]

Sayadaw: What is *lobha*?

Disciple: *Lobha* is to want something, sir.

Sayadaw: *Lobha* includes any liking, being attracted by something, wanting. One who dies with any liking or wanting in his mind is said to be reborn as a ghost.

But what is *dosa*?

Disciple: *Dosa* is enmity, sir.

Sayadaw: Yes, *dosa* is the cause for your fighting. *Dosa* arises because you do not get what you want and what you get you don't want. Dislike is *dosa*. If you die with dislike in your mind, you are reborn in hell. *Moha* is ignorance about benefits derived from being charitable, being moral and practising meditation. If you die with delusion in your mind, you will be reborn as an animal. Nobody, no god, no *deva* or *brahmā* has created body and mind. They are subject to the law of nature, to arising and dissolution, just as the Buddha taught. If a person dies concentrating on the awareness of mind and matter and knowing about arising and dissolution of these, then, according to the teaching of the Buddha, he will be reborn as a man, *deva*, or *brahmā*. If someone is going where he wants to go, does he need to ask others for the way?

Disciple: No, sir.

Sayadaw: Does one have to ask others, "Do I live with knowledge or in ignorance?"

Disciple: No, sir.

Sayadaw: No. Indeed not. Therefore, work hard to bring the perfections (*pāramī*) you have accumulated in the whole of *saṃsāra* to fruition. Be steadfast in your effort.

---

11. Greed (*lobha*), aversion (*dosa*), and delusion or illusion (*moha*) are the three root causes of all suffering. *Lobha* includes all degrees of wanting, looking forward to, desiring, lust, etc. *Dosa* includes all degrees of aversion from slight aversion to intense hatred. Fear is also part of *dosa* as it contains aversion against the thing feared. *Moha* means delusion about the nature of physical and mental states. When a person does away with *moha*, he recognizes that all states of body and mind are unsatisfactory, impermanent, and devoid of a self or soul.

Act as the wise people of the past did after receiving the teachings directly from the Buddha; they worked for Nibbāna. Knowing that you too have been born in a favourable plane of existence, nothing can stop you from working up to the attainment of the eight stages of Nibbāna.

Practise with strong effort and with steadfastness, and make sure that not even a little time is wasted. Advise and urge others to practise too. Strive with happiness in your heart and when you are successful, be truly happy.

A Roof That Does Not Leak

Sayadaw: The contents of the Tipiṭaka taught by the Buddha are so vast that it is impossible to know all they contain. Only if you are intelligent will you be able to understand clearly what the monks have been teaching you out of great compassion. You have to pay attention only to this.

Disciple: Sir, we don't quite understand what you mean by: "You have to pay attention only to this."

Sayadaw: Let me try to explain in this way. If you build a house, you put a roof on it, don't you?

Disciple: Yes, sir, we cover our houses with roofs.

Sayadaw: When you put the roof on you make sure that it is watertight, don't you? If you cover your house well and it rains a little, will the roof leak?

Disciple: No, sir, it won't.

Sayadaw: And if it rains very hard, will the roof leak?

Disciple: No, sir.

Sayadaw: And when the sun burns down, will it still give you good shelter?

Disciple: It will, sir.

Sayadaw: Why is this so? Because your roof is well built. Will you be able to know whether your roof is leaking or not after it rains?

Disciple: Yes, sir, when it rains it is easy to find out.

Sayadaw: You see, you think that the teachings of the Buddha are vast and varied, but really they are just one single way of escape from suffering. Only if you take up one object of meditation given by the Buddha and pursue it with steadfast effort to the end can you justly claim that your roof is not leaking any more. If your roof is not rain-proof yet, you have to be aware of this. There must be many houses in your neighbourhood and they all have roofs. What are the materials used for roofing?

Disciple: There are corrugated iron roofs, there are tiled roofs, there are houses roofed with palm leaves or bamboo.

Sayadaw: Yes, of course. Now, if a palm-leaf roof is well built, is it reliable?

Disciple: Oh yes, sir, it won't leak.

Sayadaw: If a tin roof is well assembled, is it rain proof?

Disciple: Yes, sir, it is.

Sayadaw: What about a well-made tile roof?

Disciple: No rain will come through, sir.

Sayadaw: What about bamboo roofs or roofs made out of planks?

Disciple: If they are well done, they are watertight, sir.

Sayadaw: So, if you take the roofing material you like best and build a good roof, will it give you shelter when it rains and when the sun shines?

Disciple: If we build it well, it will not leak, sir.

Sayadaw: We are building roofs because we don't want to get wet when it rains, and we want to avoid the scorching sun. The teachings of the Buddha are available now. Take up one of the techniques the Buddha taught, establish steadfast effort and practise. Only if you are steadfast does your practice resemble a roof, and greed, anger, and ignorance cannot leak through. Only if the roof is not leaking can we say that we are sheltered. If the roof is still leaking rain, is this because it is good or is not so good?

Disciple: Because it is not so good, sir.

Sayadaw: Is it leaking because the palm leaves are not a good roofing material?

Disciple: No, sir, palm leaves are a good roofing material.

Sayadaw: Or is it because corrugated iron, or tiles, or bamboo, or planks are not suitable as roofing materials?

Disciple: No, sir, all these are quite okay.

Sayadaw: Then why is the roof leaking?

Disciple: Because it isn't well built, sir.

Sayadaw: But, of course, the mistake is made now. Is it difficult to repair it?

Disciple: If one is skilful, it is quite easy, sir.

Sayadaw: Tell me then, if it leaks in a certain place, what do you have to do?

Disciple: We have to patch up the leak, sir.

Sayadaw: It is just the same in meditation. Now that you exert effort, there is no leak; you are safe. If greed, anger, and ignorance still drip in, in spite of your practising the teachings of the Buddha, you have to be aware of the fact that your roof is not yet rain-proof. You have to know whether the roof you built for your own house is keeping the rain out or not.

Disciple: Sir, we have all the roofing materials, but the roof is still leaking. We would like to know the technique of building a good roof.

Sayadaw: Don't build a thin, shaky roof; build a thick, strong roof.

Disciple: How are we to build a strong roof, sir? While we are sitting here like this, we still have to endure being drenched by the rain.

Sayadaw: The wise people of old practised the teachings without allowing their efforts to diminish in any of the four postures,[12] and they kept up such a perfect continuity of awareness that there never was any gap. You too have to practise in this way. The disciples of the Buddha established awareness on the spot and then did not allow their minds to shift to another object. Now, can the rains of greed, anger, and ignorance still affect those who are steadfast?

Disciple: No, sir, they can't.

Sayadaw: If you establish the same quality of awareness whether sitting, standing, or walking, will the rain still be able to penetrate your protecting roof?

Disciple: Sir, please teach us the technique which will give us shelter.

Sayadaw: Tell me, all of you are breathing, aren't you?

Disciple: Oh yes, sir, all are breathing.

Sayadaw: When do you first start breathing?

Disciple: Why, when we are born of course, sir.

Sayadaw: Are you breathing when you are sitting?

12. The four postures are sitting, standing, lying down, and walking.

Disciple: Yes, sir.

Sayadaw: Are you breathing while you are standing, walking, and working?

Disciple: Of course, sir.

Sayadaw: When you are very busy and have a lot to do, do you stop breathing, saying, "Sorry, no time to breathe now, too much work!"

Disciple: No, sir, we don't.

Sayadaw: Are you breathing while asleep?

Disciple: Yes, sir, we are.

Sayadaw: Then, do you still have to search for this breath?

Disciple: No, sir, it's there all the time.

Sayadaw: There is no one, big or small, who doesn't know how to breathe. Now, where does this breath touch when you breathe out?

Disciple: Somewhere below the nose or above the upper lip, sir.

Sayadaw: And when you breathe in?

Disciple: At the same spot, sir.

Sayadaw: If you pay attention to this small spot and the touch of air as you breathe in and out, can't you be aware of it?

Disciple: It is possible, sir.

Sayadaw: When you are thus aware, is there still wanting, aversion, ignorance, worry, and anxiety?

Disciple: No, sir.

Sayadaw: You see, you can come out of suffering immediately. If you follow the teachings of the Buddha, you instantly become happy. If you practise and revere the Dhamma, you remove the suffering of the present moment and also the suffering of the future. If you have confidence in the monks and teachers, this confidence will result in the removal of present and future suffering.

The only way out of suffering is to follow the teachings of the Buddha, and at this moment you are revering the teachings by establishing awareness. Do you still have to go and ask others how the Dhamma, if practised, brings immediate relief from suffering?

Disciple: We have experienced it ourselves, so we don't have to go and ask others any more.

Sayadaw: If you know for yourselves, is there still doubt and uncertainty?

Disciple: No, sir, there isn't.

Sayadaw: By keeping your attention at the spot for a short time only, you have understood this much. What will happen if you keep your mind focused for a long time?

Disciple: Understanding will become deeper, sir.

Sayadaw: If your time were up and you were to die while your attention is focused on the spot, would there be cause for worry?

Disciple: There is no need to worry about one's destiny if one dies while the mind is under control.

Sayadaw: This frees us from suffering in the round of rebirths, and having discovered this for ourselves, we need not ask others about it. If we establish strong and steadfast effort in accordance with our aspiration for awakening, is there still cause for doubt: "Shall I get it or shall I not?"

Disciple: No, sir, we have gone beyond doubt.

Sayadaw: So, then you have full confidence in what you are doing and due to your effort the *viriya-iddhipāda* factor arises. Suppose people come and say to you, "You haven't got the right thing yet; how could you ever succeed?" Will doubt arise in you?

Disciple: No, sir.

Sayadaw: You know that though you are certain that you will be able to reach the goal with your practice, other people might tell you that you will not.

Disciple: Sir, knowing for oneself, one will not have doubts, whatever people may say.

Sayadaw: What if not just a hundred people or a thousand people come to tell you that what you are doing is no good, but say the whole town?

Disciple: Even if the whole town comes, no doubt will arise, sir.

Sayadaw: Suppose the whole country came to contradict you?

Disciple: Even so, sir, there will be no space for doubt to arise, because we realised this happiness for ourselves.

Sayadaw: Yes, you know how much effort you have established. But don't think that your effort is perfect yet. You are only at the beginning. There is still much room for improvement. While you sit, walk, stand, and work it is always possible to be aware of the in-breath and the out-breath, isn't it?

Disciple: Yes, sir.

Sayadaw: If you focus your attention on the spot, are you unhappy?

Disciple: No, sir.

Sayadaw: Does it cost you anything?

Disciple: No, sir.

Sayadaw: The people, *devas* and *brahmās* who received the teachings after the Buddha's awakening practised continuously, and therefore their respective aspirations for awakening were fulfilled.

What the Buddha taught is enshrined in the Tipiṭaka. If you keep your attention focused on the spot and on the in-breath and the out-breath, the whole of the Tipiṭaka is there.

Disciple: We don't quite understand this, sir.

Sayadaw: Oh dear. Why shouldn't you understand this? Of course, you understand.

Disciple: But we would like to be certain that we understand this in detail, sir.

Sayadaw: You have understood already. Have you checked whether all of the Buddha's teaching is contained in this awareness?

Disciple: But, sir, our awareness is not deep enough to check this.

Sayadaw: But you can talk about the Buddha's discourses, the monks' rules, and Abhidhamma philosophy.

Disciple: When we discuss these, we just talk without really knowing.

Sayadaw: Talking into the blue. Now, if you keep your attention at this spot, can you tell me whether the whole of the teaching is present there?

Disciple: We don't know, sir.

Sayadaw: Are you not telling me because you are tired?

Disciple: No, sir, we aren't tired. We would like to answer.

Sayadaw: If we want to make an end to suffering we have to observe the behaviour of mind and matter. Everyone says this. Matter is composed of eight basic elements. There are fifty-three mental concomitants. All of you can tell me this off the top of your head.

You are intelligent. When others discuss the teachings you correct them and tell them where they went wrong and where they left something out. You refute them and criticise them. You are debating like this, aren't you?

We said just now that the thing that doesn't know is matter and the entity that knows is mind. These two entities must be evident to you. Under which of the two comes the spot below the nose; is it mind or matter?

Disciple: I think that the spot is matter, sir. The *kāya-pasāda* (sensitive matter) through which we feel touch sensation is *rūpa.* But those who study Abhidhamma philosophy tell us that we are just concepts (*paññatti*) and that the spot too is but a concept, sir ... When we have debates with people who are proficient in the Abhidhammattha-saṅgaha we become angry and agitated and get little merit.

Sayadaw: If you can't keep your attention on the spot, you will of course get involved in discussions.

Disciple: But, sir, if we don't answer, we have to admit defeat.

Sayadaw: Tell me, what do you have to do when you are hungry?

Disciple: We have to eat rice, sir.

Sayadaw: What about monks, what do you have to give them to still their hunger?

Disciple: We have to give them oblation rice, sir.

Sayadaw: Are the oblation rice they eat and the rice you eat two completely different things?

Disciple: They aren't different, sir. In order to show respect to the monks we call their rice "oblation rice," but it is the same as we eat.

Sayadaw: So, whether we call it "rice" or "oblation rice," it will satisfy our hunger.

Disciple: Yes, sir, both fill the stomach.

Sayadaw: Now what about the nose, the spot? You can call it by its conventional name, or you can talk about sensitive matter. It's just the same as with rice and oblation rice. Is it worth arguing about?

Disciple: No, sir, there is no need for long discussions.

Sayadaw: Having understood this, will you stop arguing, or will you carry on with your debates?

Disciple: No, sir, we shall not debate, but those Abhidhamma students will.

Sayadaw: In that case you just don't take part in the discussion of such issues. You have known all along that rice and oblation rice are the same, but we have to talk about it so that you understand. Now, what do we call the entity that is aware?

Disciple: It is called mind, sir.

Sayadaw: Only if you have gained such control over your mind that it doesn't jump from one object to another are you able to distinguish clearly between mind (*nāma*) and matter (*rūpa*).

Disciple: Yes, sir, now we are able to distinguish between mind and matter.

Sayadaw: Is this knowledge of mind and matter you have gained called understanding (*vijjā*) or ignorance (*avijjā*)?

Disciple: It is understanding, sir.

Sayadaw: Is there still ignorance present when you are able to distinguish clearly between mind and matter?

Disciple: No, sir, ignorance has run away.

Sayadaw: When you concentrate at the spot there is understanding, and ignorance has been banned. Now, if we continue to concentrate on the spot, will ignorance spring back up again?

Disciple: No, sir, it won't.

Sayadaw: Yes, you see, you have to establish understanding in this way. You have found it now; don't allow it to escape again. Can you again suddenly be overpowered by delusion if your understanding keeps growing moment by moment? Do good people still have to moan and complain, saying that it is difficult to get rid of ignorance once they have been given the teachings of the Buddha, which are the tools to overcome and defeat ignorance?

Disciple: No, sir, they shouldn't complain. All they need to do is to put forth effort.

Sayadaw: So, you realise that all the Buddha taught is contained in this meditation. If you put forth effort, establish yourselves in perfect effort, then you will reach full understanding. You told me that many types of material are suitable to build a good roof. Not only a tin roof or a palm leaf roof are safe; you can choose from many different materials. I think you have collected quite a variety of good roofing materials. Now you have to build a roof that really protects you against rain. Once you have built a good shelter, you won't get wet, and you won't have to suffer the heat of the sun anymore. If you build your shelter in the jungle, will it be good?

Disciple: Yes, sir, it will.

Sayadaw: If you build your roof in a city?

Disciple: It will be safe, sir.

Sayadaw: Does it make any difference whether you build your shelter in this country or in any other country?

Disciple: Sir, it will give shelter here and there.

Sayadaw: Are you happy if you're drenched by rain or if you have to live under the scorching sun?

Disciple: No, sir, I would be unhappy.

Sayadaw: In that case, put forth full effort so that you won't have to suffer sun and rain ever again.

The Flight of an Arrow

Sayadaw: You have taken *sīla*. Having taken *sīla*, practise it. Only if you fulfil the perfection of morality completely can you be successful in attaining all the various aspirations for awakening without exception.

Now that you have understood that you have been born at an auspicious time and into a good existence, take up the practice of the teachings of the Buddha with all your strength and establish yourselves in them. The noble disciples of the Teacher practised without slackening in their effort and were mindful in all the four postures of the body, without ever resting. They worked with steadfastness, and they all attained the goal they desired. You too should take up this practice with this strong will to reach your goal.

What is this practice without break or rest to be compared to? It is like the flight of an arrow. If we shoot an arrow with a bow, we take aim according to our desire. Now tell me, does the arrow at times slow down and then speed up again after we shoot it? Does it at times take rest and then again proceed toward the target?

Disciple: Sir, it flies fast and at a steady speed.

Sayadaw: And when does it stop?

Disciple: It stops only when it hits the target, sir.

Sayadaw: Yes, only when it hits its aim, its target, does it stop. In just the same way did the direct disciples of the Buddha strive to attain the goal they had taken as their target. Moving at a steady pace without a break, without interruption, they finally attained that type of awakening (*bodhi*) they desired in their hearts.

Of course, there are various types of awakening. All of them can be attained if you work without resting. If you work for *sammā-sam-bodhi* (Buddhahood), you have to work continuously. If you work for *pacceka-bodhi* (Non-teaching Buddhahood), you have to keep up the continuity of practice. If you aim for *sāvaka-bodhi* (Arahatship), you have to practise steadily, just as an arrow flies steadily. If you practise with steadfastness you will be able to attain your goal.

Though you practise without interruption, you will not get tired or exhausted. As you take up the teachings of the Buddha, incomparable happiness will come to you.

Some people think that the Buddha taught many different things. You all remember some parts of the holy scriptures as the monks out of great compassion taught them to you. At times you may think, "The teachings of the Buddha are so vast and manifold. I can't follow and understand all this and therefore I can't attain my goal." Or some people say, "What is true for oneself one can only know oneself." Or others, "I can't work because I can't feel the breath yet." Now tell me what is your excuse?

Disciple: Saying that we have to make a living to maintain our body, we postpone meditation from the morning to the evening and from the evening to the morning. In this way we keep delaying the work of putting forth effort.

Sayadaw: And what else do people tend to say?

Disciple: Some say they can't meditate because of old age and some are afraid that it will make them ill.

Sayadaw: What do those say who are still young?

Disciple: That they can't meditate because they have to study. While they are young and healthy they want to enjoy themselves.

Sayadaw: And if you are unwell and ill?

Disciple: Then, sir, we worry. We call the doctor and think about medicine, but we still don't practise.

Sayadaw: And when you have recovered?

Disciple: We somehow manage to postpone meditation day by day and let time pass.

Sayadaw: But you do actually want to attain happiness, don't you?

Disciple: Yes, sir.

Sayadaw: So, if you really want it, why then postpone striving for it?

Disciple: I don't want it really, sir.

Sayadaw: Does this apply to you only or to all of you here?

Disciple: There must be some in this audience who really aspire to attain happiness and others like me who are not so serious about it.

Sayadaw: If you put forth effort as you are doing now, you will of course get it. But thoughts and doubts may come up in your minds, "Will I have to suffer? Will this practice be trying?" You have already acquired some knowledge of the Buddha's teachings according to your individual capabilities. Thinking about these, however, will slow down your progress. So listen well to the teachings now and practise. If you practise, you will arrive at your goal, and the reality of it may or may not correspond with your thoughts about it.

Only when you know for yourselves will you also know that your thoughts and speculations about the goal were not correct. All of you know from Dhamma lectures that if you follow the teachings of the Buddha, you will get great happiness in the present and in the future. In fact, you are all preachers of the Dhamma yourselves. Don't you think that thinking and speculating will slow your progress down? If you think and analyse, will every thought be correct?

Disciple: No, sir.

Sayadaw: If you establish your goal as I told you and keep thinking about wanting to attain it, will this help?

Disciple: No, sir.

Sayadaw: So, will you continue to think and ponder?

Disciple: If we analyse and think all the time we shall go the wrong way, sir.

Sayadaw: Once we start thinking there will be very many thoughts. Will much of what we think be of use to us?

Disciple: It is difficult to think useful thoughts. Thoughts often become quite useless and misleading.

Sayadaw: The community of noble monks has expounded the teachings which are real and true to you and still your thoughts are apt to mislead you. How is this possible?

But tell me, where are you from? ... You are from Kemmendine. Your house must have a garden and a fence around it.

Disciple: Yes, sir, this is correct.

Sayadaw: On which side of the compound is the gate?

Disciple: I have one gate opening to the south and one opening to the north, sir.

Sayadaw: How many storeys does your house have?

Disciple: It is a single storey house, sir.

Sayadaw: On which side do you have your door?

Disciple: There are two doors, sir, one in the west wall and one in the south wall.

Sayadaw: So, now we know that you live in Kemmendine, that you have a fence around your garden with gates to the north and south. Your house is a one storey building and has two doors facing south and west respectively. You see, because you told me, I know everything about your place. Now my knowledge and your knowledge about your house are about the same, aren't they?

Disciple: They cannot be, sir.

Sayadaw: But why? You know your village, your garden, and your house; you told me that you live in Kemmendine; and you described your garden and your house to me as you know them. Therefore I know your village, your garden, and your house. I know the reality about it, as you do.

Disciple: You don't know it in the same way I know it, sir.

Sayadaw: My dear friend, why should what I know be different from what you know? Just ask me where you live and I shall reply that you live in Kemmendine. Furthermore, I know about your garden and house just as you do. What is there that you can tell me that I don't know already?

Disciple: Even if I told you the house number and the street, you wouldn't be able to find the house, sir.

Sayadaw: Tell me then what you know more about this matter than I do.

Disciple: I can't tell you more about it, sir, but I know more because I have actually been there.

Sayadaw: In that case I shall think about it and figure out where Kemmendine is.

Disciple: You can't find out by thinking about it, sir.

Sayadaw: I shall think a lot and for a long time. Some of it is bound to be right. I will think about a house in Kemmendine with two gates, two doors, one storey. Will some of my findings about your house be correct?

Disciple: I don't think so, sir.

Sayadaw: Is it that difficult then? Well, I'll think in many different ways; some of it will turn out right. I shall ponder over this problem for about one year. Will I find the answer then?

Disciple: If you just think about it, sir, you won't find it. But if you come and look, you will really know for yourself.

Sayadaw: Now, what if I were to think about it really deeply for about forty or fifty years? Or ... better, if I don't just think but also talk about it. Will I come to know it then?

Disciple: Even if you think and talk about it, sir, you will never get there.

Sayadaw: Then please tell me where Kemmendine is.

Disciple: From here you would have to walk towards the south-west.

Sayadaw: So, if I walk in a southwesterly direction, will I get there?

Disciple: Yes, sir, you will, but you will still not find my house.

Sayadaw: Well I'll begin now. I'll think very deeply and at the same time I'll recite (your instructions and descriptions). In this way I'll come to know.

Disciple: No, sir, I don't think so.

Sayadaw: You tell me that you know all this about your house, but if I repeat what I know from you, then you tell me that I am talking into the blue. I cannot bear this.

Disciple: Sir, you simply repeat what you heard, but you don't actually know.

Sayadaw: So, all I say about this house is correct, but he claims that I still don't know it the way he does. I don't know whether this is true ... But now if I were to think about it deeply and recite my thoughts, would there still be a difference in understanding? Or if I were to recite all you said day and night, would it still not be possible for me to really know?

Disciple: Sir, you would still not know it in the same way you would if you went there yourself.

Sayadaw: Before you told me about your house I didn't know anything about it, but now I know something.

Disciple: Yes, sir, this is true, but if you came to see it you would know everything about it.

Sayadaw: Tell me, if I were to walk according to your directions, would I arrive at your house?

Disciple: Yes, sir.

Sayadaw: And if I didn't know the house number?

Disciple: You would wander aimlessly, sir.

Sayadaw: And if you go there?

Disciple: I head straight for my house, sir.

Sayadaw: Will you worry about how to get there and whether you are on the right road?

Disciple: If you come with me, sir, you can't get lost, because I have been there before.

Sayadaw: The Buddha taught what he had realised for himself. Now, all of you are able to accept good advice. The Buddha's teachings are vast. There is the Suttanta, the Vinaya, and the Abhidhamma. You need not study all these. Choose one object of meditation, one technique that suits you, and then work with firm determination. Once you have established yourselves in this way and arrive at the goal, you will understand deeply and completely.

But even now, before I finish speaking, you do get some understanding. This immediate understanding is called *akāliko*, immediate understanding.

Our teachers and parents, who instruct us out of great compassion and love, tell us: "Learn this and that ...," and when we go to bed at night they call us and say: "Why didn't you pay respects to the Buddha before going to bed? Come, pay respects." If we don't follow their instructions, they may even have to beat us. They have to do this even though they don't wish to do it. Through their help these resistances in us are overcome. But, of course, we get immediate knowledge of the Buddha-Dhamma only if we are interested in it ourselves. When does it actually become *akāliko*, immediate?

Disciple: Only when we really find the Dhamma, sir.

Sayadaw: And when will we really find the Dhamma?

Disciple: After having worked for it, sir.

Sayadaw: At what particular time do we have to practise in order to be successful?

Disciple: The hour of the day or night is of no importance. If we practise and then reach the goal we shall gain immediate knowledge, sir.

Sayadaw: It is very easy. You have received the teachings of the Buddha. All you have to do is to make efforts in the same way that the disciples of the Buddha did. It is easy. This is not my own knowledge. I too have learned the teachings of the Buddha and I am passing them on to you. All of you are very intelligent and bright. What I am telling you, you know already. Why do you think the Buddha taught the Dhamma?

Disciple: He taught people to be continuously aware of mind and matter.

Sayadaw: He taught so that people who desire to attain the goal may be able to do so. He taught because he wished them to be able to travel on the path. But some of you may say that this is not a good time to practise. The mind is not settled with all this coming and going of people. "We shall meditate when the mind is tranquil," you may decide. And if the mind becomes tranquil after some time, what will happen?

Disciple: When the mind is calm, we will go to sleep, sir.

Sayadaw: Oh really, and this you call meditation?

Disciple: Sir, we are only perfect in talking about meditation.

Sayadaw: And then, when you have a bad conscience about not having practised and decide to go to a meditation centre, what do you take along?

Disciple: We take food with us, sir.

Sayadaw: Tell me, after having taken the precepts, do you stuff yourselves?

Disciple: Yes, sir. The ladies offer food, and we just eat. We start early, and then we continue eating right up until twelve noon.[13]

Sayadaw: Do you eat more than on ordinary days?

Disciple: Oh yes, sir, much more.

---

13. The sixth precept forbids the consumption of solid food including milk after twelve noon.

Sayadaw: Tell me now, do you stop eating at noon?

Disciple: Well, you see, sir, some say that even then it is all right to continue eating. Once one stops, then one can't start again after twelve noon, but if I started before noon I can continue eating even after midday. So I've heard.

Sayadaw: What about you? Do you carry on eating?

Disciple: I continue eating even while we are talking like this, sir.

Sayadaw: And what do you do after you have finished eating?

Disciple: Then my stomach is full, sir, so I lie down flat on my back.

Sayadaw: And then?

Disciple: Then I sleep, sir.

Sayadaw: And when do you wake up again?

Disciple: At about 3.00 or 4.00 p.m., sir.

Sayadaw: Do you meditate then, being fully awake and alert?

Disciple: No, sir, then I ask for some juice and lemonade.

Sayadaw: Do you drink a lot or just a little?

Disciple: I drink to the full, sir.

Sayadaw: Even if you drink a lot, some will be left over. Do you share that with others?

Disciple: No, sir, I drink it all myself because I like to keep it for myself.

Sayadaw: But do you feel good if you drink too much?

Disciple: No, sir, not very good.

Sayadaw: Tell me, do you meditate then?

Disciple: Well, sir, as I don't feel very well I have to lie down.

Sayadaw: And then what happens?

Disciple: I sleep again, sir.

Sayadaw: And when do you get up?

Disciple: The following morning, sir, when the sun rises. I say to myself, "Well, look, the sun has risen," and I get up and have breakfast.

Sayadaw: Now tell me, if you don't attain Nibbāna, do you think that it is because there is no such person as a fully awakened Buddha and that Nibbāna doesn't exist?

Disciple: No, sir, it's because I eat too much.

Sayadaw: Well, you do make some efforts, but this greed is still a little strong, I think. Tell me, when you start to meditate and someone whispers near your ear, do you hear it or not?

Disciple: If the concentration is not so good, we prick up our ears and listen to what is being whispered, sir.

Sayadaw: When you hear this whispering, do you accept it and respect the people who are whispering?

Disciple: Sir, when the determination to meditate is strong, then I do get angry at the people who are whispering.

Sayadaw: Meditators get angry?

Disciple: If people come and whisper in the place where I'm meditating, of course I will get angry, sir.

Sayadaw: Is it skilful to get angry and think, "Do they have to whisper here? Where is this chap from anyway? Who is he?" Will a meditator who reacts in this way attain his goal quicker? If he becomes angry and then dies, where will he be reborn?

Disciple: He will be reborn in the lower worlds, sir.

Sayadaw: Even if he is observing the eight Uposatha precepts?

Disciple: If he becomes angry, he will go to the lower worlds even then, sir.

Sayadaw: How should we approach the problem of being disturbed by whispers while we are meditating? We should reflect in the following way: "I have come here to meditate. My fellow meditators are whispering and I hear them. If the others find out that I pay attention to whispers, I will feel ashamed because all will know then that I don't make sufficient effort. I shall make more effort." We should be grateful to the people who show us through their whispering that our effort isn't sufficient. If your effort is good, your concentration will be good, and you won't hear anything. Being grateful, you should hope that these people continue talking, and you should continue to meditate. There is no need to go up to them and actually say, "Thank you." Simply continue to meditate, and as your awareness of the object of meditation becomes continuous, you don't hear disturbances any more. Would you hear people if they spoke quite loudly?

Disciple: If they spoke loudly, I think I would hear them, sir.

Sayadaw: Again we have to be grateful. "They are telling me to improve my efforts." Being grateful to those people, I steady my mind and focus on the spot again. To meditate means to be so closely aware of the object that it never escapes our attention.

Disciple: Please, sir, explain to us how to be so closely aware of the object.

Sayadaw: You just have to keep your attention fully collected, concentrated on the spot. All of you have been breathing ever since the moment you were born. Can you feel where the air touches as you breathe in and out?

Disciple: Sir, for me the touch sensation is most evident under the right nostril.

Sayadaw: Not in two places?

Disciple: No, sir, only in one place.

Sayadaw: Yes, it touches at this small spot when you breathe in and when you breathe out. Tell me, does it enter with intervals or is it a continuous flow?

Disciple: There are intervals, sir.

Sayadaw: Is it the stream of air that is interrupted or the awareness of it? Is the touch of air continuous while you breathe in and out?

Disciple: It is uninterrupted, sir.

Sayadaw: Then you have to know this flow of air without interruption. Don't look elsewhere. Just know this touch of the breath. If you can't feel it, then try touching the spot of contact with your finger. When you know the sensation of touch, then take your finger away and stay with the awareness of touch-feeling at the spot. You have to become aware of the touch of air which is continuous as being continuous. If you are aware of this spot without a gap in the continuity of awareness, will you still hear whispers?

Disciple: No, sir, I don't think so.

Sayadaw: If the attention is firmly and steadfastly anchored at this spot, will you hear loud voices?

Disciple: No, sir.

Sayadaw: You know this spot below the nose above the upper lip so exclusively that you don't hear sounds any more. Is this spot matter (*rūpa*) or mind (*nāma*)?

Disciple: It is matter, sir.

Sayadaw: And the entity that knows it, that which is aware, what is it?

Disciple: That is mind, sir.

Sayadaw: So, if you are aware of the spot without interruption, you are continuously aware of mind and matter, are you not?

Disciple: Yes, sir, this is true, sir.

Sayadaw: If you are aware of mind and matter in this way, you know that there is no self, there is no man, there is no woman, there are no human beings or *devas* or *brahmās*? This is what the Buddha taught. If we are aware of mind and matter, do we still think in terms of human beings, *devas*, and *brahmās*?

Disciple: No, sir, we don't.

Sayadaw: Is it easy to be thus aware?

Disciple: Yes, sir, it is easy.

Sayadaw: This is knowing things as they are. Mind and matter arise without interruption. They arise and then disintegrate. How many times do they disintegrate in a flash of lightning?

Disciple: I have heard that they disintegrate one hundred billion times in the wink of an eye, sir.

Sayadaw: Tell me then, how can you count to one hundred billion in the wink of an eye?

Disciple: I can't, sir.

Sayadaw: Suppose you were given one hundred billion gold coins and would have to count them, how long would it take you?

Disciple: I think it would take about a month, sir. Even if I were to count greedily day and night, it would take about that long.

Sayadaw: The peerless Buddha penetrated all this with his own super-knowledge and then was able to teach it. But what can we know for ourselves? We can know mind and matter simultaneously. And what will we get from this awareness? We will be able to understand the characteristic of their behaviour. You needn't do anything special. Just practise as you are practising now. Keep your attention focused on the spot and as you gain the ability to keep your attention with the awareness of breathing and the spot, mind and matter will talk to you.

Disciple: Do we have to think of *anicca* (impermanence) when one in-breath comes to an end, sir?

Sayadaw: It is good if you think of *anicca* as a breath comes to an end. If you know *anicca* in this way, will you be able to attain Nibbāna?

Disciple: Not yet, sir.

Sayadaw: So if you can't get Nibbāna yet, keep concentrating on the spot and you will come to know.

Disciple: What do we have to know as being impermanent, sir?

Sayadaw: You say that sugar is sweet, don't you? But if I have never before tasted sugar, how are you going to explain sweetness to me?

Disciple: It is much better than even palm sugar, sir, but we can't explain it so that you will really know.

Sayadaw: But you have tasted it, so why can't you tell me about it?

Disciple: Well, sir, sugar looks like salt, but ants don't go for salt while they do like sugar. But this won't help you very much, sir. You have to taste it, sir.

Sayadaw: So salt and sugar look similar. Now, if I eat some salt, calling it sugar, will I taste sugar?

Disciple: No, sir, salt will remain salty.

Sayadaw: In that case I'll think that sugar is salty.

Disciple: This is just the same as us not knowing how to recognise impermanence, sir.

Sayadaw: When we talk about the outer appearance of sugar, there are many possibilities of mistaking something else for sugar. Only if you explain the taste of sugar properly can I understand.

Disciple: We would like to advise you to eat some sugar, sir.

Sayadaw: Will you have to sit next to me while I'm eating it and say, "It is sweet, it is sweet ..."?

Disciple: If I recited this, it would just bother you, and it isn't necessary to do this for sugar to be sweet. As soon as you put sugar into your mouth, you will be able to taste its sweetness, sir.

Sayadaw: But let's say there is a jungle bhikkhu who wants to taste sugar. Will the sugar think: "This is a jungle bhikkhu. I won't be fully sweet for him. I shall be only half as sweet for him as I am for people in towns"?

Disciple: Sugar isn't partial, sir; it is as sweet for one as for the other.

Sayadaw: It is just the same with the awareness of mind and matter. If you keep up this awareness you will taste the Dhamma immediately, just as you taste sweetness when you eat sugar. Is it possible that you still mistake salt for sugar? You go to the market so many times, and you can easily distinguish between salt and sugar. You are not going to buy salt for sugar. The peerless Buddha penetrated the truth and really knew it. He can distinguish between what is liberation and what is suffering, and therefore he gave this liberation to human beings, *devas*, and *brahmās* alike. He just asked them to "eat." Just eat, it's real. Will you remain here without eating, afraid that it could turn out not to be true liberation?

Disciple: We haven't reached that point yet, sir. We are just listening to your words.

Sayadaw: Eat as I told you. You will not go wrong. And why can't you go wrong? Because mind and matter are actually arising and disintegrating continuously.

Why should you concentrate on the spot, though you don't know liberation yet? If you don't eat something, will you ever know what it tastes like? You know a lot about the Dhamma. You know about *nāma* and *rūpa*; you know what the Suttas are and you know about the Vinaya and the Abhidhamma. You know this is *samatha*, this is *vipassanā*.

Disciple: But, sir, all this is mixed up in our head like a giant hodgepodge.

Sayadaw: Let it be a mix up. Pay attention to this spot only, as I taught you. Later this mix up will be disentangled, everything will fall into place. If we go east we will get to a place in the east; if we go west we will arrive at a place in the west. The spot is like a vehicle. If you want to go to Mandalay, you have to board a train to Mandalay and stay on it. The spot is like the train; don't leave it. Keep your attention focused on it very closely. This is all I have to say. There is nothing to be said apart from this.

Do you know the eight constituents of the Noble Eightfold Path? How do you think they apply to this practice of concentrating on the spot?

Disciple: If one concentrates on the spot with right concentration then one attains the knowledge of right view, sir.

Sayadaw: Are the other elements of the Noble Eightfold Path pertinent to this practice?

Disciple: Sir, the eight constituents of the Noble Eightfold Path are: (1) right view, (2) right thought, (3) right speech, (4) right action, (5) right livelihood, (6) right effort, (7) right mindfulness, (8) right concentration. When our mind is fixed on the spot, we don't think unskilful thoughts in any way. Therefore right thought is there, sir. As we are not talking at all, we don't speak lies and therefore there is right speech. As awareness of breathing is a good action, right action is included in this practice. There is right livelihood too, as we are not trying to make a living by deceiving others, sir. We are putting our entire effort into keeping our attention on the spot, so there is right effort. Because we focus our attention on the breath without letting go, we have right mindfulness, and as the attention remains at the spot without wandering here and there, we have attained right concentration.

Sayadaw: So, do you think this is like a boat or a train?

Disciple: Yes, sir, it is like a boat, a train, or a cart or car that takes a person to his goal.

Sayadaw: Do not leave this vehicle, do you understand? Keep your attention firmly focused here, on the spot, and never leave this spot. In this way you will reach your goal.

Sometimes you may become impatient travelling on the train to Mandalay and think, "I want to go to Mandalay, but is this train really going there or is it going to Rangoon?" If this happens, will you get off? Don't! Continue on your journey and you will see that you will eventually arrive in Mandalay.

If you get fed up and bored, don't leave the train. When you are enjoying yourselves, don't get down. When you are ill, stay on the train, and stay also when you are strong and healthy. When you have plenty of company, stay. When you are all alone, don't leave. When people say unpleasant things to you, persist, and when they speak to you respectfully, don't get off your train. What would you do if people were to hit you because they don't like you?

Disciple: Sir, I think I would run away.

Sayadaw: Just keep your attention on the spot. Even if robbers hit you, they can't strike down this awareness.

Disciple: True, sir, but I think this awareness would go if they struck me.

Sayadaw: Not necessarily. Our Bodhisatta, in one of his lives, became the king of monkeys. One day he found a brahman who had fallen down a precipice in the jungle and was helpless and certainly going to die down there. This brahman was lamenting his fate and crying, "Oh poor me, I have fallen into a chasm a hundred yards deep. I shall certainly die down here. Oh poor me, oh, oh, oh ... My relatives and friends, my wife and children, don't know about my misfortune. Nobody is here to help me. Oh, oh ...," and he cried.

Now, noble beings are always concerned with the welfare of all beings, without exception. And as the Bodhisatta was such a noble being, he who was then the monkey king felt pity for the brahman in the same way he would have felt pity for his own children. And so he climbed down the precipice and went up to the brahman. "Do not fear, do not despair, I won't let you die. I shall take you back to the place you want to go," he said to the brahman to reassure him and to cheer him up. And he meant it too. But he wasn't ready yet to put him on his shoulders and carry him up the rocks, because he was afraid that he might fall and that the brahman might be hurt. He took a big rock of about the same weight as the brahman, put it on one shoulder and tried to carry it up the precipice, jumping from rock to rock. Only after having passed this test did he carefully take the brahman on his shoulders and climbed back up jumping from one boulder to the next.

After this great effort, the monkey king was exhausted. He was happy while performing this good action, but he was still happier when he had accomplished it and had saved a life. He was confident that the brahman he had saved from certain death was trustworthy, and said, "After carrying you up, I am a little tired. Please keep watch for a while so that I can rest." Then he placed his head in the brahman's lap thinking himself well protected from all the dangers of the jungle. But while the king of the monkeys slept, the brahman thought, "I shall go back home soon, but I have nothing to give to my wife and children. I shall kill this big monkey and give his flesh to them as a gift." He took the rock the Bodhisatta had carried up for the test-run and dealt the Bodhisatta's head a deadly blow. He didn't do this hesitatingly, feeling sorry for his saviour, but he hit him hard, so as to kill him with the first blow.

When the Bodhisatta felt the pain of the blow, he quickly climbed the next tree, and he asked himself who or what had attacked him. He then saw that there was no enemy around, but that the brahman himself had tried to kill him. He thought to himself: "Yes, there are people like this in the world too." As the Bodhisatta was thinking this, the brahman started lamenting again, exclaiming that he was lost in this big jungle and that he would perish after all. But the monkey king said to him, speaking from the tree, "Don't worry; don't be afraid. I have promised to take you back to your home and I shall not break this promise. I shall take you home. I can't carry you on my shoulder any more, but as you opened my skull, there is blood dripping to the ground continuously. Just follow the track of blood I shall make for you from up in the trees."

This is how the Bodhisatta acted. He took all this on himself because his goal was Omniscience, Buddhahood. He worked on all the ten *pāramīs*.

Did the Bodhisatta turn away from accomplishing the good deed he had undertaken to complete because he was afraid that the man who had attempted to take his life might again try to kill him? Did he abandon him in the jungle?

Disciple: No, sir, the Bodhisatta led the brahman home with great loving kindness, in order to perfect his *pāramīs*.

Sayadaw: You see, if one aspires to omniscient Buddhahood, one has to fulfil the perfections, the ten *pāramīs* in this way, without ever taking a break, without ever resting. Otherwise one can't attain Buddhahood. Do you understand? One never rests, one never becomes lax, but works on the ten perfections all the time.

You told me only a moment ago that you couldn't keep up your awareness if robbers attacked you and tried to kill you?

Disciple: I couldn't keep it up as yet, sir.

Sayadaw: But you are aspiring to awakening, aren't you?

Disciple: Yes, sir, I am.

Sayadaw: If you want it you can achieve it. If you keep your attention focused as I taught you, you will get much out of it, even if people should hit you, pound you, and destroy you. Have you heard the story of Tissa Thera?

Disciple: No, sir, I haven't.

Sayadaw: Tissa Thera received the teachings of the Buddha and appreciating their value he thought: "Now I can't continue living in this grand style." So he gave all his possessions to his younger brother. He became a monk and went to live and meditate in the jungle with his begging bowl and his set of three robes.

Now his brother's wife thought: "It is very enjoyable to possess all the riches of my husband's older brother. If he remains a monk we shall have these riches for the rest of our life. But maybe he will not attain awakening, and then he may possibly return to lay life. So, I had best have him killed." And she gave money to some robbers and said to them, "Go and kill Tissa Thera. I shall give you more money after you have completed the job."

So, the robbers went to the forest where Tissa Thera lived and grabbed him. He said, "I don't possess anything, but if you want to take my bowl and my robes, please do so."

"We only want to kill you," the robbers replied. "Your brother's wife gave us money to kill you, and she will give us more still after we have completed the job. That is why we have to kill you."

Tissa Thera thought, "I am not emancipated from suffering yet," and he felt ashamed of himself. He said to the robbers, "Yes, yes, you have to kill me, but please give me until dawn and then only make an end to my life."

The bandits replied, "Everyone is afraid of death, and if this monk escapes, we shall not get our money."

"You don't trust me?" Tissa Thera asked. "Well, I shall make you trust me." And he took a rock and smashed both his legs. Then he said, "Now I can't run away any more, so please don't kill me until dawn."

Though the robbers were very rough people, due to the loving kindness of Tissa Thera they felt compassion and decided to let him live until daybreak.

Tissa Thera admonished himself: "Venerable Tissa, there is not much time left, dawn is close. Put forth effort!" He put forth strong effort in the practice of the Buddha's teachings, and as he worked with a steady mind, dawn arrived. As the sun rose, he fulfilled his aspiration and attained happiness. "I have attained release from the cycle of birth and death!" he rejoiced. He then woke the robbers and said, "The day has dawned, rise and come!" And he was full of joy. Now, was Tissa Thera a real disciple of the Buddha, an Arahat?

Disciple: Yes, sir, he was.

Sayadaw: Who has faster development do you think, someone who meditates with both legs broken, or someone who meditates as you do?

Disciple: Sir, I would prefer to meditate without first breaking my legs.

Sayadaw: Tissa Thera got it before dawn even with both his legs broken. Will you get it before the day breaks?

Disciple: I don't think that I could get it, sir. It will take me longer than that. We take it easy, sir. If one doesn't have to break one's legs, effort is less, and progress therefore slower.

Sayadaw: In that case, you are not so eager to attain your goal quickly?

Disciple: Sir, we like to go slowly, slowly.

Sayadaw: Well, then maybe you should break your legs and then meditate.

Disciple: I don't have the courage to do that, sir. I say that I aspire to Nibbāna, but in my mind I am still fearful. I don't have the strength to accept being killed after breaking my own legs.

Sayadaw: In that case, work just the same, but without breaking your legs.

Disciple: We shall work hard in the way you taught us, sir. We are emulating Visākha and Anāthapiṇḍika, sir. It says in the scriptures that they are enjoying a good life in the *deva* planes now and we would like to have that same type of enjoyment also, sir.

Sayadaw: They are enjoying a good life after having attained a lot. But you have not attained to the same stage yet, have you? Are you really doing as they did? Anāthapiṇḍika went to Rājagaha as a banker on business. Only when he reached there did he come to know that a Buddha had arisen in the world. He didn't go to Rājagaha to meditate or to pay respects to the Buddha. But when he was told about the Buddha, he went to him immediately, in the middle of the night. He had to leave the city walls to go to the place where the Buddha resided. When he stood before the Buddha, he attained what he had aspired for. If someone drops everything and hurries to the Buddha in the middle of the night, is the effort of that person great or small? Do you think he ever let go of the Buddha as the object of his mind while on the way to him?

Disciple: No, sir, he didn't.

Sayadaw: Now, tell me about yourselves.

Disciple: We lose the awareness of the object while we walk, or while we think and so on, sir.

Sayadaw: If you want to become like Anāthapiṇḍika, you have to strive as he strove.

Disciple: Anāthapiṇḍika had to go through a cemetery on his way to the Buddha, sir. That much we can do too, sir.

Sayadaw: It is said that Anāthapiṇḍika began his meditation in the first watch of the night and attained stream-entry (*sotāpatti-magga-phala*) when the day broke. But if you can't get it by daybreak, never mind. It is good enough if you can get it by the time the sun has risen and it is light. Tell me, will you work so that you can attain the goal by tomorrow?

Disciple: Sir, we too shall go through a cemetery to come to your monastery and in this way we shall emulate Anāthapiṇḍika.

Sayadaw: Did he allow the continuity of awareness to be interrupted?

Disciple: He didn't, sir, but we are doing the same as he did only as far as the way is concerned.

Sayadaw: If you really want to become like Anāthapiṇḍika, you have to work. If you work, you can fulfil your aspiration. If you don't work, you won't achieve anything. Is it not possible for you to concentrate on the spot where the air touches?

Disciple: It is possible, sir.

Sayadaw: To become like Anāthapiṇḍika you have to practise as I taught you. Will you tell me tomorrow that you attained your goal?

Disciple: I shall tell you that I haven't attained it yet, sir.

Sayadaw: Do you know how much Anāthapiṇḍika did after he had attained the first stage of awakening? He thought, "This is incomparable! My king, my people, my relatives, my sons and daughters, the city dwellers and country folk, all of them have not yet heard that a Buddha has arisen. I want them to experience the same bliss I have experienced. Now, how can I accomplish this? I have to invite the Buddha and make him stay for some time in my city, Sāvatthī, and all can go and meet him. The Buddha, out of great compassion, will teach them, and at the end of the teaching human beings and gods alike will attain the bliss I have attained."

Anāthapiṇḍika understood the ultimate truth, and he knew the reason he understood it. He invited the Buddha in order to help others to understand too. He had rest houses built every ten miles along the road from Rājagaha to his native city. In Sāvatthī he built the Jetavana monastery for the Buddha, and he arranged everything in such a way that there was a place for everyone. He provided everything, giving to all, from beggar to the king. Thanks to Anāthapiṇḍika's arrangements, the people who met the Buddha on his journey to Sāvatthī gained benefits also. During the Buddha's journey, many people, *devas*, and *brahmās* attained what they had aspired to. How many do you think were those who benefited?

Disciple: We don't know, sir.

Sayadaw: How many human beings, how many celestial beings attained Nibbāna then?

Disciple: A great many, sir.

Sayadaw: How many beings fulfilled their aspiration in the wink of an eye? It was 180 millions of *brahmās* and one *asaṅkheyyā* of *devas*. How many beings attained awakening as time went by?

Disciple: They must be innumerable, sir.

Sayadaw: Anāthapiṇḍika continued to support the teaching of the Buddha and due to his effort many attained the Deathless. Understanding this, you have to make a lot of effort to attain your goal by tomorrow. Will you do this?

Disciple: Do not think too highly of me, sir. I don't think I am able to get it by tomorrow.

Sayadaw: You are hungry and your wife offers you food, but still you don't eat?

Disciple: When it comes to food, I will even force my way to the table, sir.

Sayadaw: Do you eat even though you don't want to eat or because you want to eat?

Disciple: Because I want to eat, sir.

Sayadaw: For how long is your hunger appeased if you eat once?

Disciple: For about half a day, sir.

Sayadaw: For how long will your hunger be stilled if you eat the way Anāthapiṇḍika ate?

Disciple: For the remainder of the cycle of birth and death, sir.

Sayadaw: Tell me, what is the best for you? The food your wife offers you and that keeps you satisfied for half a day, or what the Buddha offers you that keeps you satisfied for the remainder of the cycle of birth and death?

Disciple: I have to answer that what the Buddha offers is best for me, sir.

Sayadaw: You eat what your wife offers you. What then do you do with the food the Buddha offers?

Disciple: I'm hesitant about that, sir. That's why I don't approve of myself, sir.

Sayadaw: Good, good. Work hard. You put so much effort into doing all these other things because you don't view mind and matter properly. But you do feel respect for the Buddha. Having decided to meditate, meditate. As you meditate you may find that your limbs ache and become stiff. Now, don't think: "Why do I get this pain? Is it dangerous?" But make a resolve: "Let it be dangerous! If I have to die, so be it. I have died in the past too." How many times have you died, do you think?

Disciple: Innumerable times, sir.

Sayadaw: Tell me, have you ever died while you were meditating?

Disciple: No, sir, I have died while being unskilful only. That is why I am still so agitated.

Sayadaw: So, if we have to die, how should we look at it? "I have never died so far while meditating. I shall not wait until dawn. Let me even die right now, so that I can get the experience of dying while meditating." You should think in this way. If you die while meditating, will you become miserable?

Disciple: No, sir.

Sayadaw: If you live a life of laziness and sloth, will you become happy?

Disciple: No, sir. I shall continue going round in the cycle of birth and death, *saṃsāra*, sir.

Sayadaw: "I have never, in the whole of *saṃsāra*, had stiff and aching limbs because of meditation. It is good if I experience these troubles now." Thus should you look at your pains. Even though your limbs ache, do not give up. Know that wise people of the past have walked on the same path. You have to work. If you only talk about putting forth effort, you will not attain anything. Only if you meditate can you come to understand. Now you are probably thinking: "We want to meditate, but this venerable monk is talking for a long time." So, focus your mind now as the Buddha taught you to, and meditate with firm effort and perseverance.

ABOUT PARIYATTI

Pariyatti is dedicated to providing affordable access to authentic teachings of the Buddha about the Dhamma theory (*pariyatti*) and practice (*paṭipatti*) of Vipassana meditation. A 501(c)(3) nonprofit charitable organization since 2002, Pariyatti is sustained by contributions from individuals who appreciate and want to share the incalculable value of the Dhamma teachings. We invite you to visit www.pariyatti.org to learn about our programs, services, and ways to support publishing and other undertakings.

Pariyatti Publishing Imprints

Vipassana Research Publications (focus on Vipassana as taught by S.N. Goenka in the tradition of Sayagyi U Ba Khin)

BPS Pariyatti Editions (selected titles from the Buddhist Publication Society, copublished by Pariyatti)

MPA Pariyatti Editions (selected titles from the Myanmar Pitaka Association, copublished by Pariyatti)

Pariyatti Digital Editions (audio and video titles, including discourses)

Pariyatti Press (classic titles returned to print and inspirational writing by contemporary authors)

Pariyatti enriches the world by

- disseminating the words of the Buddha,
- providing sustenance for the seeker's journey,
- illuminating the meditator's path.

www.ingramcontent.com/pod-product-compliance
Lightning Source LLC
Chambersburg PA
CBHW020350170426
43200CB00005B/125

* 9 7 8 1 6 8 1 7 2 2 1 6 0 *